ROUTLEDGE LIBRARY EDITIONS: FOLKLORE

Volume 6

EWE COMIC HEROES

EWE COMIC HEROES
Trickster Tales in Togo

ZINTA KONRAD

LONDON AND NEW YORK

First published in 1994

This edition first published in 2015
by Routledge
2 Park Square, Milton Park, Abingdon, Oxon, OX14 4RN

and by Routledge
711 Third Avenue, New York, NY 10017

Routledge is an imprint of the Taylor & Francis Group, an informa business

© 1994 Zinta Konrad

All rights reserved. No part of this book may be reprinted or reproduced or utilised in any form or by any electronic, mechanical, or other means, now known or hereafter invented, including photocopying and recording, or in any information storage or retrieval system, without permission in writing from the publishers.

Trademark notice: Product or corporate names may be trademarks or registered trademarks, and are used only for identification and explanation without intent to infringe.

British Library Cataloguing in Publication Data
A catalogue record for this book is available from the British Library

ISBN: 978-1-138-84217-5 (Set)
eISBN: 978-1-315-72831-5 (Set)
ISBN: 978-1-138-84270-0 (Volume 6)
eISBN: 978-1-315-73135-3 (Volume 6)

Publisher's Note
The publisher has gone to great lengths to ensure the quality of this reprint but points out that some imperfections in the original copies may be apparent.

Disclaimer
The publisher has made every effort to trace copyright holders and would welcome correspondence from those they have been unable to trace.

EWE COMIC HEROES

Trickster Tales in Togo

Zinta Konrad

GARLAND PUBLISHING, INC.
NEW YORK & LONDON / 1994

© 1994 Zinta Konrad
All rights reserved

Library of Congress Cataloging-in-Publication Data

Konrad, Zinta.
    Ewe comic heroes : trickster tales in Togo / Zinta Konrad.
      p. cm. — (The Albert Bates Lord studies in oral tradition :
vol. 9) (Garland reference library of the humanities ; vol. 1020)
    Includes bibliographical references.
    ISBN 0-8240-7639-7 (alk. paper)
    1. Ewe (African people)—Folklore. 2. Trickster—Togo. 3. Oral
tradition—Togo. 4. Tales—Togo. I. Title. II. Series.
III. Series: Garland reference library of the humanities ; vol.
1020.
GR351.52.E83K65   1993
398.21'089'963374—dc20   93-34584

Printed on acid-free, 250-year-life paper
Manufactured in the United States of America

Maniem mīļiem vecākeim—
bez kuru atbalstu šis darbs nebūtu iespējams.

Contents

Series Preface		ix
Preface		xi
Introduction		xv
Chapter One:	The Collection	3
Chapter Two:	Origins of Trickster	17
Chapter Three:	Methodology	27
Chapter Four:	Formal Features of Trickster Narratives	41
Chapter Five:	Metaphor and Meaning in Trickster Narratives	69
Chapter Six:	Style in Performance	93
Chapter Seven:	Why Trickster?	131
Appendix		145
Bibliography		287

Series Preface

The purpose of the Albert Bates Lord Studies in Oral Tradition, in conjunction with the journal *Oral Tradition*, is to bring before an interdisciplinary constituency essays, monographs, and collections that, in focusing on one or more oral or oral-derived traditions, offer insights that can be useful for investigators in many of the more than one hundred language areas now influenced by this field. Thus earlier volumes have treated orality and the Hebrew *Mishnah* (Jacob Neusner), *Beowulf* and shamanism (Stephen Glosecki), Hispanic balladry (Ruth Webber, editor), the *Count Claros* ballad tradition (Judith Seeger), the Middle English romances (Murray McGillivray), Marcel Jousse's *The Oral Style* (Edgard Sienaert and Richard Whitaker, translators), Turkic oral epic (Karl Reichl), and *Beowulf and the Bear's Son* (J. Michael Stitt). Future volumes in this series will include studies of identification in Homeric epic (Carolyn Higbie) and of the Brother Peter folktale tradition in Guatemala (Jane Frances Morrissey and Christina Canales), as well as collections of essays on oral traditions in ancient and medieval contexts. The overall aim is to initiate and to sustain conversations among scholars who, because of the categories according to which we are segregated in modern academia, seldom if ever have a chance to talk to one another. With this goal in mind, we extend a warm invitation to new voices to join the conversation—both as readers of these and other volumes and, hopefully, as authors with contributions to the ongoing discourse.

This ninth volume in the series, *Ewe Comic Heroes* by Zinta Konrad, is an especially distinguished piece of work. True to the scholarly imperative that informed Albert Lord's own career, this research begins in personal experience of an oral tradition and proceeds through an exceptionally well-documented and thorough analysis toward an in-depth portrayal of that tradition. In Konrad's case, the body of performance consists of trickster tales principally from southern Togo, with a small sampling from the contiguous Ewe population in Ghana. As she explains in the introduction and her opening chapter on the collection, she gathered some 400 of these tales in 1979–80, eventually selecting 30 of them for the exposition offered below.

These stories are of unusual significance for at least three reasons. First, they provide a window into the totality of oral expressive forms among the Ewe, constituting as they do a species of *gliwo*, which Konrad translates as "oral expressive narratives." Second, they serve the overall purpose of the Lord series by providing another perspective on the infinitely various phenomenon we inadequately call "oral tradition," helping to pluralize our notions at the same time as they provide an analogy for expressive forms from other cultures. Third, the Togo tales make an important contribution to the international scholarship on the trickster figure—that ubiquitous hero, coward, mediator, and thief whose contradictory exploits range far and wide throughout the world's traditions, and whom Konrad tellingly designates "a metaphor for pure possibility" (p. 143). In support of this third dimension, the book contains a seventh chapter that considers some of the aspects of and explanations for the popularity of this fascinating figure.

Much more could be said about this remarkable book. In addition to the uniqueness of the material (with the thirty performances transcribed and/or translated in the appendix to the volume), notes on its collection, a discussion of a semiotic methodology, and not least the author's careful and creative attention to nonverbal aspects of performance, it provides a model for future work in this and other specialties. For Africanists and folklorists, as well as scholars and students in many different areas, *Ewe Comic Heroes* will stand as a landmark study in oral tradition.

John Miles Foley
Center for Studies in Oral Tradition
University of Missouri

Preface

> Virtuous and vicious every man must be
> Few in th' extreme, but all in the degree;
> The rogue and the fool by fits is fair and wise
> And ev'n the best, by fits, what they despise.
> Alexander Pope

What more exciting topic than that which speaks to the vicious and virtuous natures which lie inside all of us? So it is that the subject of this study, the trickster hero in Ewe oral narrative performances, was chosen.

The trickster character is prominent in the cultural, particularly narrative, traditions of many different peoples throughout the world. Ture, Gizo, Wanto, Ananse, Wadjakunga, Velniṉš—are all examples of the many different cultural representations of the trickster figure. Comic and serious, stupid and clever, benevolent and evil, winner and loser—the trickster is a study in contradictions. The trickster cannot be pigeonholed, for he does not fit into any neat categories or definitions. The best way to learn about trickster is to observe him and experience him.

This study is an attempt to allow you, the reader, the opportunity to experience in some small measure the dynamic and exciting dramatic oral narrative performances of the Ewe people of West Africa. By so doing, it is hoped that you will gain new insight and appreciation into the highly developed and aesthetically complex narrative art forms found on the African continent, in this case, southern Togo and Ghana.

It is virtually impossible to discuss a performed dramatic art form without losing a good deal of the sounds, rhythms, and visual stimuli that make for lively and exciting performances. Nonetheless, that is the nature of analysis, and therefore, there are limitations one must live with. Every attempt has been made, however, to recreate and incorporate as many vital elements of performance as possible, including gestures, expression, body rhythms, and other components of nonverbal behavior.

This research was originally conducted as dissertation field work for the Ph.D. degree in African Languages and Literature at the University of Wisconsin–Madison. Over a period of 13 months in 1979–80 the research yielded 400 narratives collected among the Ewe speaking peoples of Togo and Ghana. A core of thirty trickster narratives was chosen as the basis for the present analysis.

The field work in Africa was funded by a University of Wisconsin–Madison Graduate School Fellowship and Travel Grant, and the writing of the dissertation was made possible by a fellowship from the American Association of University Women. Valuable technical assistance was provided by the University of Wisconsin–Madison African Studies Program and Indiana University which furnished recording tape.

Writing a dissertation feels at times like a long and lonely uphill climb. Surprisingly, so does the preparation of a manuscript for publication. Fortunately, in both cases there were colleagues and friends who lent their support, assistance, and guidance every step of the way.

The person who made this book possible is Professor Henry Louis Gates, Jr. It was his judgment and belief that this research offered a perspective worthy of being shared with a larger audience and one that could contribute to the study of oral traditions.

Professor Phil Noss, a friend and colleague from the University of Wisconsin–Madison, helped shape the present form of this work by asking probing questions and suggesting important changes. I took his advice and basically rewrote the original dissertation.

Professor Michael D. Lieber at the University of Illinois at Chicago provided an invaluable critique of the work in its early stages and channeled my thinking about the goals of the present book.

At the University of Wisconsin–Madison I worked with pioneer spirits and accomplished scholars who contributed in numerous ways to the study and preservation of African oral traditions. Professor A. Neil Skinner provided "*gliful*" insights while directing my dissertation and saw it to its conclusion. Professor Edris Makward, my adviser and friend, was there to give advice and support and was instrumental in making the research possible. Professor Harold Scheub played a major role in guiding my thinking about oral narrative process and made important theoretical and methodological contributions to the study of African oral traditions in general.

Yet, the real heroes of this study are the Ewe people. This study would not have been possible without Koblavi Ahadzi, Kɔdzo Gadagboe, Komlā Tɔnyo, the Klige family, and so many other great performers who shared their time, their traditions, and their artistry—*meɖe akpe na mi loo*!

The very difficult task of transcribing and translating were undertaken by Kofi Dumoga, Edem Adubra, and Adiko Mensa. The lion's share was done by Dr. Kudzo Dzantor, a rare friend whose patience, endurance, and commitment can never be adequately acknowledged.

Other friends and colleagues in Togo and Ghana deserve thanks for their hospitality and support: Victor and Yela Hodasi, the family Brassier, Laolitou Tankouta, Yao Tsolenyonou, and Professor Yao Amela; and importantly, the Université du Bénin and the Institut National de la Recherche Scientifique who creatively solved what appeared to be unsolvable logistical problems involving transportation and accommodations.

On this side of the ocean, family and friends provided moral support when spirits sank and resolve wavered. Karen, Niki, Oscar, and Lapsiṇa could always be counted on for inspiration and encouragement. Karen Nickels also deserves thanks for her help with some of the artwork in this manuscript.

Thanks also to Dr. John Foley and the staff at Garland Publishing, especially Amy DeAngelis, Chuck Bartelt, and Julie Threlkeld, who solved more than one technical difficulty in the preparation of this book. And a special thanks to the fine folks at Arvey Paper who helped solve a minor technical crisis.

Two very special people silently wondered whether this work would ever be completed, but with love and unswerving resolve they made it possible. I dedicate this book to my Mom and Dad.

Introduction

Throughout many parts of the world storytelling is a dynamic and popular form of entertainment appealing to audiences both young and old. These stories, more accurately called "oral imaginative narratives," contribute to the social well-being of people by expressing fundamental conceptual notions about life, how it is and how it could be. Other times, oral narratives are simply told for fun with no particular thematic or moral significance intended.

In many parts of Africa the oral narrative tradition continues to play an important role in the cultural lives of its people. In Togo, West Africa, this tradition is extremely rich and colorful. Everyone seems to know stories but only a few people are clearly recognized as masterful storytellers. Not surprisingly, the better storytellers tend to be elders whose wisdom and experience are reflected in the tales they tell. Meanwhile, generations of young would-be storytellers sit at the feet of the recognized masters eagerly listening, observing, and taking their turn at spinning tales, warmly encouraged by the circle of listeners.

A popular type of oral narrative enjoyed throughout the African continent is the "trickster tale." Some early scholars commonly referred to these oral narratives as "animal tales." In Togo, trickster tales are narratives involving deceit and deception. They are part of a broader category of oral imaginative narratives called *gliwo*. The feature that distinguishes trickster tales from other *gliwo* is the presence of the trick along with one or several trickster characters. While the focus is on the plot, not the character, the trickster character cannot help but draw attention to himself.

In discussing trickster narratives, there are three key aspects. First, these are performed narratives. This means that artist and audience together are involved in a performance, radically different from performance in the western sense where the audience passively watches what unfolds on the stage. The performer is not isolated somewhere on a stage. He or she is seated on a bench or chair, surrounded sometimes by a few, often by dozens of audience members who sing, dance, freely interrupt, and banter with the performer, who welcomes these interchanges as a sign of audience interest and approval. The performer's job is to manage the spontaneity and direct the various self-assigned roles, so that the performance retains its aesthetic integrity and does not become a rowdy free-for-all.

Second, trickster narratives function as a nonformal communication system. Within this context, trickster narratives communicate important messages to the listening audience through images and themes the performer evokes in the course of the performance. Often, the images are culture-bound, that is, specific to the Ewe culture, so that people not familiar with Ewe culture may not fully understand the themes or their significance in the story being told. Sometimes, themes in trickster tales appear to be somewhat superficial or missing altogether. In reality, themes operate on many different levels. Understanding how message is communicated in this particular art form provides insight into the way trickster narratives reinforce cultural values and beliefs and communicate socially accepted roles and models of behavior.

The third and final dimension focuses on the nonverbal aspects of narrative performance. Since it is very difficult to discuss nonverbal behavior in written form, most research conducted on African oral traditions to date does not to any great extent incorporate the nonverbal aspects of behavior into the analysis. Often, token mention may be made of the existence of the nonverbal dimension, but treatment of this important aspect is generally thin. The present research demonstrates how critically important nonverbal behavior is to the communication process and how crucial a role it plays in terms of the different "meanings" audiences may infer from the performance of trickster narratives.

It should be noted that we are dealing with an art form that is strictly oral in nature. No *gliwo*, including trickster narratives, have scripts. These are impromptu renderings that flow from the imagination of local artists. Certainly, the narratives are based on images and plots familiar to all who live in Ewe culture, but the order and manner of the telling of each tale is unique to each performer and performance. In cultures where the literacy rate is relatively low, verbal and nonverbal forms play an extremely important role in the communication process—far more so perhaps than they do in cultures with higher literacy rates.

It is the intent of this study to take an in-depth look at Ewe trickster narratives as both a performed aesthetic art form and a nonformal communication system. This study aims to look primarily at trickster narratives as they are performed in Eweland. Although the study is not comparative in nature, some other trickster traditions, in Africa and elsewhere, will be used to illustrate relevant points. The following chapters will treat various aspects of this dual framework.

Chapter One describes the present collection of trickster narratives, elucidating the circumstances of how this collection came into being, who the Ewe people are, and relevant aspects of their cultural background.

Chapter Two looks at the historical/mythological origins of the trickster character in an attempt to understand where the trickster character comes from, how widespread the trickster phenomenon is, and antecedents in other cultures and historical periods.

Chapter Three discusses the approach used in gathering the present collection and describes the framework in which this work is analyzed. Seminal concepts are introduced and terms are explained that elucidate the methodological approach used in this study.

Chapter Four discusses the formal features of Ewe trickster narratives. Attention will focus on the formal characteristics of the trick, namely the role of patterning, illusion, disguise, substitution, deception, and stealth; and opening and closing formulae.

Chapter Five sets forth a communication model that provides the framework for understanding how "meaning" is conveyed in trickster narrative performance, how themes are developed, and how they structure trickster narratives.

Chapter Six takes an in-depth look at the narrative style of one performer in particular, integrating both the verbal and nonverbal aspects of performance. It will be shown how the verbal and nonverbal systems of communication complement each other and interact sometimes in a rather surprising manner.

Finally, Chapter Seven situates the trickster in a broader context. Trickster's presence in widely diverse cultural and geographic areas raises the question as to what needs the trickster character meets in a psychological and symbolic sense. Several theories are explored concerning the Trickster's omniscient presence.

The appendix contains thirty trickster narratives in translation upon which the analysis is based. In addition, six narratives also appear in their original Ewe transcription to give readers a sense of the language and its many complexities.

EWE COMIC HEROES

CHAPTER ONE

The Collection

In total some 400 narratives were collected in southern Togo along with a representative sampling of narratives gathered in Ho, Ghana, in the Volta Region. The major portion of the collection was gathered in Kpalime and the Plateau region around Apeyeme and Wotrope (Fig. 1-1).

Kpalime is a small urban center of 20,000 people about 120 km. northwest of Lomé. It is the political and economic center of the Ewe-speaking region. Since an important focus of social and economic activity in Africa is the marketplace, it is not surprising that Kpalime has one of the largest and most popular markets in Togo. Additionally, Kpalime is an important agricultural center. It was chosen as the starting point for this collection because of its central location that provided access to many small relatively isolated villages in the surrounding areas.

The first performers were met as a result of a visit to the traditional chief of Kpalime, Tɔgbui Kofi Apetor III, who called a meeting of some forty elders. About fifteen elders actually came. Among these fifteen, five agreed to let me record their stories. Each storytelling session led to more introductions and more storytellers.

Among the Ewe, both men and women performed tales. More often than not, however, men were the primary storytellers. Women tended to be more reserved and thus, contact with them was more difficult. Once they came forth and proper introductions were made, women proved to be very adept storytellers, although stylistically different from men. While men tended to be more animated, and told, in many cases, raucously wild and bawdy tales, women were more subdued and deliberate in their telling. Controlling their audience

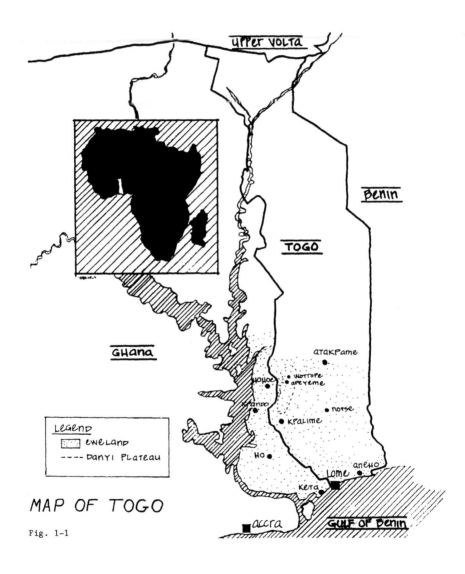

MAP OF TOGO

Fig. 1-1

through measured pacing, they tended to pay more attention to character descriptions and the motivational aspects of characters' actions.

The degree of skill varied, but Mr. Kponton, a Togolese historian and collector of musical instruments, observed that the most esteemed artists, both male and female, shared four criteria: they spoke well, had a large repertory of narratives, were not timid, and knew how to use gestures effectively.[1] Humorous narratives were received with unabashed merriment and laughter. More serious tales were often interjected to change the pace of the performance. A sign of appreciation for a well-executed narrative was the frequency with which audience members contributed songs, prefaced by the phrase *mele tefe* ("I was there").

Importantly, the Togolese government was committed to preserving these valued cultural traditions and played an important role in facilitating this research. To conduct this research, approval from local governmental authorities was required. In all instances, the local authorities were extremely cooperative and assigned me an "assistant" from the Ministère de la Jeunesse, Sport et Culture, who accompanied me during the course of my research. Mr. Laolitou Tankouta was a regional representative who served as guide, translator, and trusted friend in Kpalime.[2] Together we traveled to nearby villages on motorbikes, usually within a range of 15–20 km. from Kpalime. Many performances took place at night after dinner and just before bedtime. Other times, recordings were made on Sunday mornings and afternoons when people were not busy farming or doing other chores.

In the case of a family of cultivators in Klige Kodzi, a seven-day week was not adhered to. Their week was based on a five-day cycle.

---

[1] Personal communication, November 1979.

[2] Mr. Tankouta's official title was "animateur culturel," a government functionary with two years specialized training in Algeria and Cameroun to prepare him for working with rural youth in community projects and to train these youth in team sports such as soccer.

Second, his mission was to initiate local cultural projects designed to preserve local traditions. My project collecting *gliwo* was of extreme interest to local officials in the regions where I worked, hence the enthusiastic cooperation and assistance I received at all levels of government.

This family of performers agreed to tell stories on their day of rest, which fell on the fifth day. Their narrative sessions were remarkable because of the pageantry involved. They often began their sessions by beating big drums to announce the storytelling session. People flocked in droves from all around the village. I usually stopped counting the number of people in the audience when that number reached seventy-five. During the course of these sessions, as many as four generations in this family narrated tales, accompanied by a variety of musical instruments and much singing and dancing.

Several weeks were also spent on the Danyi Plateau, some 50 km. north of Kpalime and 915 meters at its highest point. There again, after clearing the necessary administrative and political channels, the local authorities assigned me another "assistant," Mr. Yao Tsolenyonou, to accompany and assist me in gathering narratives while in the Plateau region.[3]

In mock seriousness, people on the Plateau assured me their stories were better than those I had been told in Kpalime. It would not be fair to say that their stories were either better or worse. Rather, there were observable differences in the storytelling styles among the two groups of performers. As one proceeded farther into the rural countryside, the tenor of performances changed. The pace was slower, the atmosphere more relaxed, and the stories more elaborate. Also, some traditional practices were in evidence which were not observed in the Kpalime Region. In Wotrope, for example, to demonstrate what storytelling was like in the "olden days," a group of people recreated late one afternoon a setting that ordinarily occurred in the old days only at night. So it was that a fire was built and a man produced a musical instrument in the form of a long hollow stick with holes, which he played with a small flat object resembling a hollow rock or a large dried-out seed. With this instrument he accompanied two elderly women who took turns spinning cotton onto a spindle as they told their stories. Every so often, one of them would thrust the spindle into the lap of the other so that

---

[3]Mr. Tsolenyonou was also an "animateur culturel" in the Plateau Region. Mr. Tsolenyonou was particularly interested in my project because he was planning a storytelling festival to take place in the fall of 1979. A near-fatal auto accident in August 1979 severely blinded him.

she could join the men in a dance. The grace and dexterity with which citizens of seventy and eighty years of age danced and performed were magnificent. Storytellers aged ninety and over often surpassed the younger generation in enthusiasm and dynamism.

Who Are the Ewe People?

The origin of the Ewe people is recounted in a popular and frequently told narrative.[4] It was said that the Ewe nation was born in the seventeenth century in the walled city of Ŋɔtse, some 120 km. north of Lomé, in the south-central portion of Togo. Descended from Yoruba stock, the Ewe people migrated from western Nigeria, settling along the way until they finally stopped at Ŋɔtse. There, under the malevolent rule of their first king, Agɔkɔli I, the Ewe people suffered great physical hardship and cruel punishment, as King Agɔkɔli ordered them to knead mud embedded with jagged pieces of glass, rocks, and thorns. With this mud they were to build their houses. The people endured for as long as they could until one day the women conspired to douse the mud walls of their city with buckets of water throughout the course of the day. During the night when the king and his entourage were asleep, the inhabitants pressed ever so quietly through the weakened mud fortress and fled. This exodus scattered the Ewe people over the entire Benin Gulf coast and resulted in major Ewe settlements in Togo, Ghana, and Benin.

Ewe-related speakers in West Africa total roughly five million. In Togo, out of a total population of some four million people, the Ewes are over a third of the population. Together with closely related linguistic and cultural groups, such as the Mina, speakers of Ewe and related dialects are the linguistically dominant group. Additionally, in Ghana in the densely populated Volta Region where Ewe is spoken, there are roughly two to three million speakers. In Benin the

---

[4]Henry Kwakume, *Précis d'Histoire du Peuple Ewe* (Lyon, 1951), pp. 8–11.

linguistically related Fon population, who may understand Ewe but do not speak it, total an additional half million people.

Despite their widely differing colonial experiences, the Ewe people share similar traditional beliefs and practices.⁵ These beliefs are expressed in traditional narrative forms. Every ritual ceremony—whether it be viδeδe δe to (infant's outdooring), ŋkɔnana (name-giving ceremony), srɔ̃δeδe (marriage), or ku (death)—is accompanied by an invocation to the ancestors, a prayer, a dramatic reenactment of an event, or a song. The spoken word in Ewe society, as in most African societies, has an importance unequalled in industrialized societies. Walter J. Ong wrote,

> ... cultures which do not reduce words to space but know them only as oral-aural phenomenon, in actuality or in the imagination, naturally regard words as more powerful than do literate cultures. . . . Words in an oral-aural culture are inseparable from action for they are always sounds. . . . It is thus eminently credible that words can be used to achieve an effect such as weapons or tools can achieve. . . .⁶

It suffices to observe a palaver among village elders or a family conclave summoned to discuss an issue of great consequence to realize

---

⁵The French, British, and Germans were the major colonial powers in Togoland. For further information, see Robert Cornevin, *Le Togo Nation-Pilote* (Paris: Nouvelles Editions Latines, 1963).

The cultural unity of the Ewe people was frequently expressed in personal communications and is a concept that was officially sanctioned and encouraged by the Agbɔbɔzã Festival held annually during the first or second week of September in Ŋɔtse, the Ewe ancestral home. Ewe customary chiefs from Togo, Ghana, and Benin were usually in attendance. It was a four-day festival with speeches, ritual ceremonies, and dances, only some of which were open to the general public.

The sacred portions of the festival were performed at the original wall, traces of which are still in evidence. These ceremonies were performed by the elders, a group of seven or eight men specially selected for this honor. The convenor for each year's festival is the Chief of Ŋɔtse, the direct descendant of Chief Agɔkɔli I. It was he who decided the agenda of the festival, with the help of a group of some fifteen committee men and women.

⁶Walter J. Ong, *The Presence of the Word: Some Prolegomena and Religious History* (New Haven: Yale University Press, 1967), 12–15.

the importance attached to the spoken word. Legal issues in traditional courts are tried by oral evidence alone; a person's character and disposition are measured by the length and quality of the greetings extended in conversation; a person's good or evil intentions are assessed through certain formulae pronounced upon entering another's home.

Ewe Oral Traditions

The oral tradition in Eweland is venerable. Its richness stems from the wellsprings of belief and custom people seek to transmit to successive generations. Storytelling is rooted in the events of daily life of the Ewe people, in their triumphs and struggles, in their aspirations and hopes for future generations, and in their need to reaffirm ancestral ties. The stories people tell record the past and celebrate the present. A measure of the popularity of the storytelling tradition is the frequency with which one hears stories told in Eweland. Ewe people have stories for every occasion and never miss an opportunity to share them.

The oral tradition remains viable because of its importance as a primary communication system. The oral tradition continues to coexist with and flourish alongside the printed word. Mass media, technology, and European influences have altered the content of verbal art forms and the nature of images, but oral traditions continue to thrive and remain an important form of nonformal communication.

Ewe oral traditions assume many forms. History and genealogy are remembered and transmitted orally in ŋutinya, sometimes also called dzɔdzɔmenya. These narratives are considered to be "true stories." They may include documented history, legends, or anecdotes, such as those told by a group of fishermen in "Bé about their adventures while fishing at sea."[7] Moreover, dramatic art in Togo is a well-established art form that has tremendous popular appeal, as witnessed by the enthusiastic crowds who flocked to weekend performances of "concert parties,"[8]

---

[7] Konrad Collection, Tape III, October 28, 1978, Lomé.
[8] Alain Ricard, "The Concert Party as a Genre: The Happy Stars of Lomé," *Research in African Literature*, No. 2 (1975), pp. 165–179.

and to the more formally staged "cantatas," which are modern-day morality plays humorously executed and based on biblical themes.

Lɔdɔdowo (proverbs) are a rich source of traditional wisdom and are immensely popular with adults who use them as instructional devices to teach their children. Similarly, adzowo (riddles) are told by young and old alike to entertain as well as to test one another's mental alacrity. Alobalowo are dilemma tales frequently heard in conjunction with other fictitious stories told during storytelling sessions. Finally, songs are an important component of Ewe oral traditions, for songs accompany most rituals, whether a funeral, marriage, or celebration of a successful harvest.

Each narrative, song, prayer, or greeting is a celebration and affirmation of every individual's relationship with the ancestors, with nature, and with each other. The interrelatedness of the universe where each individual and each physical object has significance and an assigned role in the cosmic order is reflected in the oral traditions of the Ewe people and provides the framework for the beliefs so vital to the Ewe people's view of themselves and the world they inhabit.

It is in the context of a strong oral tradition that storytelling in Eweland must be viewed. In the course of a storytelling session, any number and combination of the different types of oral art forms may be heard. Often one form is alternated with another, such as *alobalowo* interspersed among *gliwo*. Sometimes an *adzo* or *lɔdɔdo* is interjected within the structural framework of a *gli* or *alobalo*. The diversity of oral art forms is a source of great pride to the Ewe people and it is for this reason that many men, women, and children could provide examples of the different forms when asked to do so.

By far, the most entertaining and lively popular art form in Eweland is the *gli* (pl. *gliwo*), the imaginative oral narrative. The *gli* is born in the moment of telling, the result of a complex interaction between performer, audience, the tradition, and the patterns of images used to express that tradition. No two stories are ever identical, not even the same story told by the same teller, because the creation of a tale is an act, a dynamic process. Isolated images are brought together, juxtaposed with other images according to the artistic vision of the performer at a given moment in time and shaped into a unique performance captured fleetingly in time and space.

The oral narrative experience owes its force and vitality to the reactions of the audience and the interrelationship between performer and audience. The performer's primary objective is to shape audience responses. In doing so, the performer is, in turn, guided and influenced by the audience. A passive silent audience is inconceivable in Eweland. At the heart of each performance is the constant interjection of comments and queries by audience members, and attendant responses and clarifications by the storyteller. The result is a dialogue, a harmonious collaboration between performer and audience in an artistic event.

The performance aspect of storytelling is vital. The written record of a performer's creation is but a shadow of the intricate web of images, themes, and meanings created by words, sounds, and gestures. The total effect can never be replicated and the potential for meaning is of a greater magnitude than that of words on a printed page. In the course of a performance the artist's words are punctuated by gestures, supplemented with animated body movements, and highlighted with vocal rhythms and inflections. The performer's body focuses the attention and responses of the audience. Through gesture, mime, and dance, the performer dramatizes narrative action and vividly injects life into his or her characters. Frequently, however, audience members, singly or in groups, momentarily arrest the narrative flow as they burst into song, and dance a few beats of the *agbadza*.[9] This interaction between performer and audience is one of the most tantalizing aspects of oral narrative performance and at the same time, a difficult one to describe and analyze.

Individual styles vary greatly from performer to performer. In the course of a performance the performer chooses from a wide repertoire of cultural images familiar to the entire audience. In Togo, people were often heard to remark, "I know that one. Let me tell it. I know it better." The readily identifiable surface features—plot sequence, characters, and moral endings—were known by everyone. A

---

[9]The *agbadza* is a popular traditional dance. Historically, it was a war dance.

performer's artistry lay in the aptness of the images used to create particular effects, the creation of sustained moods, the performer's particular use of his or her voice, body, instruments, and any other available tools to create musical rhythms and weave an intricate tapestry of images and themes.

Koblavi Ahadzi, a washerman in Lomé, relished creating humorous narratives and often joined the audience in laughter. His sense of timing was superb. With quick-witted repartees he could respond in quick succession to two or three comments from the audience and, without missing a beat, pick up the thread of his fast-paced narration. Moreover, he was an energetic and much-acclaimed dancer who used familiar dance steps to involve audience members, particularly children. Often, Koblavi would take a timid child by the hand and guide him or her through the proper movements.

Kɔdzo Gadagboe, on the other hand, a cultivator living on the outskirts of Kpalime, was the quintessence of restraint. His calm, totally unhurried manner belied a vast repertoire of facial expressions and gestures used to great dramatic effect. His artistry lay in his ability to create moods, usually reflective in character, and his skill in orchestrating tales often of a more serious nature. With his deeply resonant voice, finely sculptured hand gestures, and superb use of silences, he spellbound his audiences, limited usually to a mere handful of people because of the relative isolation of his farm.

Johnny Brofa[10] was a performer unequalled in creating ribald effects. During his performances people laughed so hard, they would beg him to stop. His blatantly suggestive gestures and carefree manner frequently brought him playful censure from women in the audience. But even they could not help getting caught up in the vortex of laughter he created during his performances. Brofa was a master of mime and often acted out the roles of the different characters who figured in his stories. In a tale about a monkey who grew a tail, every time he demonstrated how the monkey's tail grew longer and longer, the

---

[10]His real name was Komlá Tonyo Ŋgo. During one of his early performances he told a hilarious tale about a character, "Johnny Brofa de Whole Africa." "Brofa" became his nickname and that is how he was called during these storytelling sessions.

audience exploded into gales of laughter. Brofa welcomed distractions and incorporated anything and anybody into his performances. Once, he imitated the author taking pictures during his performances—to the great delight of everyone present. Although his performances resembled those of Koblavi in terms of content and animation, Brofa displayed a heightened sense of mimicry and used mime to create hilariously comic effects.

Women were in attendance at every session. Although, overall, women were far less animated than men, one performance in Lomé was an exception to this general rule. The performance of two women, Ami Mɔsɔde and her friend, both neighbors of Koblavi, began in a serene and low-keyed manner. When Koblavi joined the audience, he would interrupt and initiate dance sequences. In turn, the two women would stop their narrative, dance in very spirited fashion a few measures of the *agbadza* along with Koblavi, then regain their seats and resume the story, freely interrupting each other with songs and commentary as they continued their narration.

On the plateau of Danyi in the villages of Kpetɔ and Afia Ɖenyigba, women would join men to dance at appropriate moments in the course of the performance. In each case, however, it was only one woman, and she was invariably elderly. In other instances when women performed narratives, they were very sedate and hardly ever danced, and punctuated their narratives with sparse but carefully articulated gestures and body movements.

The physical and temporal settings were instrumental in creating the proper ambiance for storytelling to occur. In past times, the privileged moment for telling stories was after nightfall in the open courtyard under a full moon when the day's chores were completed and the evening meal cleared away. Women, men, and children would congregate to share a few relaxed moments together before going to sleep. Other times, adults would get together to share some palm wine or beer and entertain themselves after a hard day's work in the fields. Needless to say, the pressures of modern life and city living made storytelling more apt to occur in rural areas than in the cities. Yet, the oral tradition was very much alive, evidenced by the large numbers of young adults and children who knew lots of stories and eagerly offered to tell them at a moment's notice.

Educational Function of Storytelling

Storytelling in Eweland continues to be an informal means for reaffirming social and cultural values to both young and old. This educational dimension of oral narratives is significant in explaining their popularity as an expression of cultural and spiritual unity. Ewe *gliwo* are highly moralistic, often ending in a proverb or an aetiological explanation. For example,

> Megawɔ vɔe na vɔviwo o.
> (Therefore, it is not good to do evil unto others.)

or,

> Yiyi tae amewo nɔa nuwɔ ametɔwo ɖem ɖo.
> (It is because of Spider that people continue to marry invalids.)

> Ne emia ŋku be ye me le nuvɔ kpɔ ge o la, nunyui hã toa ameŋu va yi na.
> (He who closes his eyes in order not to see evil, fails also to see all else around him.)

Nonetheless, the overtly moral content of narratives in no way lessens the function of *gliwo* as an art form whose primary function is to entertain. Sometimes, messages present a model of proper behavior where justice is dispensed, as the bad guy is punished and the good guy is rewarded. Other times, however, the bad guy is rewarded with booty he obtained in deceitful ways, while the good guy is stripped naked of his goods and killed.

The moral endings and righteous themes cannot be taken at face value. The educational aspects of narrative performances are clearly secondary to their artistic and aesthetic entertainment function. As an art form, oral narrative performances utilize popular images of good and evil, reward and punishment, to weave themes only incidentally related to moral teachings. However, once the artistry of finely wrought stories is acknowledged, the educational, social, and historical aspects of oral narrative performances offer intriguing cultural insights.

Along with recognizing the primacy of the aesthetic dimensions of oral narrative art, it is equally necessary to refrain from pejoratively viewing these oral narratives as a facile source of entertainment for children and bawdy old men. They are a highly sophisticated art form. They represent an ancient and highly developed oral tradition relevant to and enjoyed by people of all ages and both sexes.

One senses the tremendous pride the Ewe people take in their rich cultural heritage expressed in this art form. Initiatives to preserve and enhance the narrative tradition are evident at all levels of society and people are deeply committed to passing on their heritage and keeping it alive. In the privacy of their individual compounds, at celebrations such as funerals, harvest festivals, and other communal events, stories are an important component. Storytelling is, in fact, a privileged moment where traditions are reaffirmed, ethnic identity strengthened, and the uniqueness of Ewe culture expressed.

Since parents no longer dispose of the requisite leisure time, and children spend much of their evenings doing homework and getting ready for school the following day, stories are heard less frequently in the compounds at night. The popularity of storytelling as an art form, however, is recognized and encouraged. Stories told in Ewe and Kabiye[11] continue to be heard on Radio Lomé. Schools also are doing their part to preserve these traditions by using primary school texts that include popular narratives. Teachers use these tales in their classrooms and often children can be heard telling stories to one another during recreational breaks.

The government, for its part, has created institutional channels for collecting, preserving, and encouraging storytelling. The Institut National de la Recherche Scientifique, under the auspices of the Ministère de l'Education Nationale, is responsible for collecting narratives throughout Togo and making the recordings and transcriptions part of the national archives. Togo's national

---

[11] Kabiye is spoken in the central portion of the country and is the mother tongue of President General Eyadema.

transcriptions part of the national archives. Togo's national commitment to the preservation of traditional art forms is further expressed by its continuing participation in Niger's Centre d'Etudes Linguistiques et Historiques par Tradition Orale in Niamey, the capital of Niger.[12]

---

[12]C.E.L.H.T.O. is a joint effort among several francophone African countries to preserve African oral traditions. Niamey houses the collection and supervises the archives. It depends on individual countries to make their collections available. Togo continues to participate in this effort.

CHAPTER TWO

Origins of Trickster

In the fantastic universe of oral narration where imagination and creativity operate freely, outlandish events can and often do happen. One character from whom we can expect anything is the trickster, who exercises full autonomy in thought and deed. Trickster's actions are as outrageous as they are predictable. There are no limits or moral judgments to inhibit him. Individual cultural expressions of the trickster may differ, but as a narrative character and social type he is familiar to audiences throughout the world.

The trickster figure is a popular phenomenon whose presence spans continents as well as centuries. Among the ancient Greeks, Hermes figured prominently, while among the Norse, Loki was a favorite culture hero and trickster. Christianity heralded the appearance of the devil, an often overlooked and unacknowledged trickster. In the Middle Ages, Reynard the Fox and Pantagruel enjoyed immense popularity. In more recent times, North American Indians continue to hold Coyote, Raven, Mink, and Blue Jay in high esteem as popular trickster heroes. In America Wile E. Coyote, Sylvester the Cat, Yosemite Sam, Bluto, the Blues Brothers, the Joker, Kingfisher, and Joe Isuzu are popular tricksters. Brer Rabbit and Brer Fox are tricksters par excellence among African Americans, while their narrative counterparts in much of West Africa are Spider, Hare, and Tortoise, among many others.

Among the Ewe of southern Togo there are many different trickster characters. Contrary to some African trickster traditions, where trickster is usually only one specific character, among the Ewe people, the trickster can be any animal.[1] Big or little, tricksters come in a variety of shapes and sizes. Antelope, Goat, and Mouse, for example, can all play the "trickster" interchangeably from narrative to narrative.

Yiyi the Spider is the most frequent and popular Ewe trickster. In true trickster-like fashion, he may adopt different names. As Yiyi in one narrative, he may appear as Wawuie, Golotoe ("roundish belly"), Ayiyi or Ayevi in another. He is one of the smallest creatures in the animal kingdom and that fact contributes to his guileful nature. His small size gives him access to nooks and crannies where larger animals cannot go.

Little is known about his physical characteristics other than a round belly and very rapid speech rendered comical by his nasal voice. He is married to Funɔ, and they have an unspecified number of children. His tricks are often motivated by the desire for food, either for himself or his wife and children, and by the desire for more wives, hence, by implication more sex and more children. His trickery, however, need not always be well motivated. Frequently, he deceives his adversaries for the sheer pleasure of deception. He fears no opponent and experiences defeat and reversals of fortune as easily as he does victories. Overall, Yiyi is a likable creature loved by Ewe audiences. And, even when he behaves badly, he is the source of great frivolity, since audiences expect him to behave in a perfectly incongruous and amoral manner. On those occasions when he does reap some benefits for his family or village community, the good he renders is often inadvertent and secondary to his primary purpose, which is to satisfy his own biological needs.

On the African continent, trickster characters are mostly animals, with the occasional presence of human tricksters. Marcelle Colardelle-Diarrassouba posited that in Africa there are two main cycles of trickster narratives, that of the Hare and that of the Spider. She divided their distribution geographically, noting that Hare predominated in the savannah regions of Sub-Saharan Africa, while Spider inhabited the narrative universe of the forest areas. There are obvious exceptions, such as Gizo, the popular spider of the Hausa people of Niger, but

---

[1] For example, among the Gbaya the trickster is Wanto, and in the Zande narrative tradition it is Ture.

according to Colardelle-Diarrassouba, Gizo shares more traits with Hare than he does with Spider.[2]

Spider is Hare's counterpart in other parts of the African continent. Whereas Spider is generally portrayed as greedy, self-serving, and constantly plotting against everyone, Hare usually sides with the weak and unfortunate. Even though Spider displays antisocial traits, he is nonetheless considered to be a hero and a very popular one at that. According to Colardelle-Diarrassouba, this different portrayal of heroes in the two cycles reflects the differences in the social and metaphysical concerns of the two types of societies. The Hare cycle primarily reflects concern with social class structure and the preservation of ancestral traditions, evident among the Wolof, for example. The Spider tradition, on the other hand, is more concerned with a metaphysical interpretation of human relations and a representation of forest life.[3]

Sacred/Religious Origins of Trickster Narratives

Scholars have long debated trickster's probable origins. There is no clear consensus among social scientists about how tricksters found their way into mythological systems and why they assumed the form they did.

Among the Ewe, as well as in many other African cultures, oral narratives are believed to have sacred origins.

> It is evident that the tale is not a simple secular story. The tale is not only a dramatization of men's history; it is a cosmic drama of the great myths of nature.[4]

More specifically, Agblemagnon documented the mythical origins of the *gli* in Ewe cosmology:

---

[2]Marcelle Colardelle-Diarrassouba, *Le Lièvre et l'Araignée dans les Contes de l'Ouest Africain* (Paris: Union Générale d'Editions, 1975), p. 142.

[3]Colardelle-Diarrassouba, pp. 191–99.

[4]N'Sougan Agblemagnon, *Sociologie des Sociétés Orales d'Afrique Noire Les Ewe du Sud-Togo* (Paris: Mouton, 1969), p. 140. Translations are my own.

> What we call *gli* (tale) comes from "Fetome," the birthplace of the gods and where men are born into the world according to their individual destiny. The laws of this world constitute the eternal knowledge of things. The tale is not merely an invention of man; it dates from time immemorial, born with the ancestors and the gods. It is the history of the ancestors, the gods, and the laws which have unified the world from the very beginning.[5]

A second theory advanced the hypothesis that *gliwo* were rooted in *Fa*, the science of divination.[6] In this purview, each of the sixteen signs in the divination system, made by casting palm nuts or cowrie shells, had sixteen stories associated with it, making a total of 256 stories, not including variants. Their primary purpose was to explain some event in the present, predict the future, or guide and protect the client from misfortune. Each of the 256 stories could be summarized in a proverb and if the *Fa* diviner did not wish to recount the whole story which the palm nuts or cowrie shells indicated, he offered a proverb instead. Two examples are:

> Sign I: Nothing can stop a dog from going to the market, not even the wind.
>
> Sign VI: Pepper said, "Who is as strong as I? Surely not the little millet!"[7]

The relationship between proverbs and oral narratives is a close one, for as Dr. Agudze observed, every proverb has a *gli* as its source of explanation.[8] There is a proverb, for example, which says, "Vagina said, 'Even if I am large, Testicles will not enter'." The story from which this proverb is said to derive is the following:

> Vagina had three friends, Penis and Testicles. Penis was very nice and friendly but Testicles were selfish and bellicose. Every morning the three friends went to work together in the fields. At noon they would stop and have lunch. One day lunch consisted of boiled yams,

---

[5] Agblemagnon, p. 141.

[6] Also known as *Ifa* or *Afá*.

[7] Bernard Agudze, "L'Homme et le Monde à Travers les Proverbes Togolais de Langue Ewe," Thèse de Doctorat, Paris, 1976, p. 440.

[8] *Ibid*.

Vagina's favorite. Vagina gulped down her portion and asked her friends to share their portions with her.

Penis obliged but Testicles refused. After lunch they chatted a while before returning to work, when suddenly the skies turned dark and rain began to fall. Where to hide?

"Don't worry," said Vagina. "I'll shelter you."

Vagina opened wide and invited Penis in. Testicles also begged entry, but Vagina would not open. They got drenched but Vagina still refused, saying, "Even if I am large, I will never let you enter."[9]

Agudze argued that far from being the degradation of a myth, *gliwo* were the vulgarization of science. Like biblical stories presented in cartoon form, sacred *gliwo* were popularized to reach the masses.

The tale has passed into the public domain through the efforts of priests encouraged by the public to popularize an esoteric science considered too secretive. Today many literatures which propose to study African tales commit, either from ignorance or prejudice, the serious error of neglecting this fundamental aspect of oral material. The tale is a sacred genre, the oldest of the sciences, jealously guarded by the priests.[10]

The religious origins of *gliwo* continue to exert their influence in Ewe beliefs, for it is said that people who tell stories in daytime will be blinded, and Fa priests are prohibited from telling stories in public. Similarly, the parents of twins, who are believed to be related to the gods, are prohibited from telling stories at any time.

In the mythologies of ancient civilizations, trickster characters also appear to have religious origins. In Scandinavian mythology, for example, Loki was frequently presented as a companion to Thor, the god of thunder, and to Odin, the leader of the gods and the god of battle, inspiration, and death. Loki was associated with the gods, but he was not a deity worshipped by humans, as were Thor and Odin. He was known, however, to rescue the gods, but at the same time, he mocked them and the goddesses who inhabited Asgard.[11]

---

[9]Agudze, pp. 467–8.
[10]Agudze, p. 481.
[11]Ellis Davidson, *Gods and Myths of Northern Europe* (Baltimore: Penguin Books), p. 177.

Loki was clearly associated with the realm of the dead to which he belonged. As a chthonic figure, he was linked with the giants at Ragnarok, the monsters who would slay the gods and destroy the human world. He was said to be the Father of Monsters and thus responsible for the creation of the terrible goddess Hel, the guardian of the realm of death.[12]

Loki's chief characteristic was his talent as a thief who stole and hid the treasures of the gods. He was mischievous rather than wicked when he stole the apples of immortality and cut off the wonderful golden hair of Sif, Thor's wife. Moreover, his exploits were all the more fantastic because of his magical ability to change his shape. Loki turned himself into a fly and stung a smith at the critical moment, then took the form of an old woman to prevent Balder, the immortal one, from coming back to Asgard.[13]

His fundamental ambiguity and the contradictory aspects of his character have puzzled scholars for centuries. Ellis Davidson wrote:

> Loki, the thief, the deceiver, the sharp-tongued scandalmonger, who outrages the gods and goddesses by his malicious revelations . . . yet who nevertheless seems to be accepted as a dweller in Asgard and a companion of the greatest gods is hard to comprehend.[14]

In Greek mythology, Hermes was Loki's counterpart. Both were thieves, mischievous pranksters, inventors of cultural objects, and messengers to the gods. In contrast to Loki, the trickster-like qualities of Hermes predominated; his culture-hero traits were present but they were of secondary importance. At times, he was a prankster stealing his mother's clothes while she bathed. Other times, he was best known as a "plunderer, a cattle-raider, a night-watching door way-laying chief," who stole Apollo's cattle the very day he was born.

Hermes' reputation as a thief was attributed to his skill as a trickster. He possessed the mysterious and magical ability to steal cattle, transform himself into mist and pass through a keyhole, camouflage the direction in which he walked by facing backwards, and charm dogs to

---

[12]Davidson, p. 178.
[13]*Ibid.*
[14]Davidson, p. 180.

sleep.[15] In cultures where rituals were regularly performed to alter the natural causal order, magic was a powerful weapon used to control nature. Those who held this awesome power were greatly respected and silently feared.

Hermes' magical prowess owed not only to his reputation as a cunning trickster but to his association with boundaries and boundary stones. Stone heaps known as "herms"—in honor of Hermes—typically represented the point of social and economic exchange between strangers. Since strangers were considered hostile forces, they had to be maneuvered and tricked, and magical safeguards invoked in order to counter and disarm their intrusive presence.[16]

If anything, the trickster is a complex phenomenon filled with contradictions which have baffled scholars for centuries.

> The trickster is greedy, selfish, and treacherous; he takes on animal form; he appears in comic and often disgusting situations, and yet he may be regarded as a kind of culture hero, who provides mankind with benefits like sunlight and fire. At times he even appears as a creator. He can take both male and female forms and can give birth to children. He is, in fact, a kind of semi-comic shaman, halfway between god and hero, yet with a strong dash of the jester elements, foreign to both, thrown in.[17]

These baffling contradictions promoted further comparison with the trickster on yet another continent. The trickster in North American Indian mythology was associated with the creation and transformation of the earth. He was pictured as a wandering hero, hungry, oversexed, and continually tricking animals and humans. Paul Radin, in his seminal study of the Winnebago, observed that the trickster had no fixed form. He appeared either as a hare or as an old man and was believed to have recreated the world after the flood. He introduced fire, flint, tobacco, and cultivated plants; he freed the world from ogres and monsters and assigned proper functions to the forces of nature.[18]

---

[15]Norman O. Brown, *Hermes the Thief* (Madison: University of Wisconsin Press, 1947), p. 46.
[16]Brown, pp. 32–37.
[17]Davidson, p. 181.
[18]Paul Radin, *The Trickster* (New York: Schocken Books, 1972), p. xxiv.

As Wadjunkaga, the tricky one, he was known for his salient and, for that matter, only physical attribute, an enormous penis. He was the chief of the tribe, who knew no principle of order and lived by his instincts alone. He took no responsibility for his actions and had no specific sexual identity, for he could transform his sex at will, and in fact, married the chief's son. He was an otherwise normal man, socialized into accepted social roles, but he vigorously protected himself against domestication and obligations. He was an inchoate being of undetermined proportions. Never uniquely good nor evil, he was a little bit of both. He had some divine traits but they were secondary to his roles as trickster and culture hero. Radin observed that most people postulated trickster's divinity, then questioned it, for he was always defeated by a real deity and was reduced to a semi-deity. Radin asked,

> ... whether trickster was originally a deity. Are we dealing here with a disintegration of his creative activities, or with a merging of two entirely distinct figures, one a deity, the other a hero, represented either as human or animal? Has a hero here been elevated to the rank of a god or was Trickster originally a deity with two sides to his nature, one constructive, one destructive, one spiritual, the other material? Or, again, does Trickster antedate the divine, the animal, and the human?[19]

Spider as a Symbol

Although the Ewe strongly believe in the sacred origins of their oral narratives, this research did not uncover any direct evidence that they believed that Yiyi the Spider was ever a deity or in any way associated with the gods, other than occasional mentions of Spider having created the sun, moon, and stars. Among other cultures, however, Spider's association with the gods is much stronger. The Ashanti, for example, believe that people were created by a big spider.[20] In Mali there is a

---

[19]Radin, p. 125.
[20]Robert Laffont, *Dictionnaire des Symboles* (Paris: Editions R. Laffont et Editions Jupiter, 1969), p. 50.

legend that refers to the Spider as a counselor to the gods, a "creator hero." In Micronesia, the spider Nareau is the first being and creator of humankind. Among the Bambara, the Spider represents the highest level of initiation, the knowledge that comes to that class of initiates who have achieved "interiority," the strength that comes from intuitive knowledge and contemplation.

In his research on the Kaka people of Cameroun, Paul Gebauer found that the spider is used in divination practices and its life is protected at all times. It is believed that anyone who kills a spider must in turn be killed, and anyone who chances upon a spider on a trail must turn around and seek another route. In this context, the spider enjoys important symbolic significance in that the spider's home and life underground, near the ancestors and spirits, give it a special wisdom and a privileged position in divination rituals.[21]

Not always, however, are the traits associated with the spider positive. In Colombia among the Muisca, the spider is believed to transport souls to hell, and among the Aztecs the spider symbolized the devil himself.[22]

Viewed across cultures, the spider's characteristics vary greatly. In Ewe society, for example, Spider is not viewed as a semi-deity like he is among the Winnebago, nor does he have the symbolic value Hermes had in Greek culture as the representative of a changing social and economic order. The Ewe Spider is primarily a comic hero who incidentally benefits humanity, but usually does so only when it suits him.

The choice of a spider character is particularly fitting. What better image can incorporate such a wide array of dimensions appropriate to the trickster figure? The image of the spider and his ability to spin a web from his own secretions lends itself to the conceptual notions of creation, destiny, instability, and even conflicting notions such as imprisonment and spiritual freedom. This rich tapestry of conceptual ideas makes the spider a prolific multivalent symbol whose properties offer many possibilities for interpretation.

---

[21] Paul Gebauer, *Spider Divination in the Camerouns*, Publications in Anthropology 10 (Milwaukee: Milwaukee Public Museum, 1964).
[22] Laffont, p. 37.

Spider is an apt symbol for expressing certain relationships between forces of the universe. In a narrative and aesthetic sense, Spider is privileged to act as a mediator between the supernatural world and the visible one, between unseen supernatural forces and imperfect humans. Importantly, trickster characters in general, and the spider in particular, symbolically represent the forces of nature and their links with the human sphere. In this sense, trickster narratives raise questions about human existence and suggest possible answers.

CHAPTER THREE

Methodology

Trickster narratives constitute a communication system of a unique kind. On the one hand, trickster narratives function as a nonformal educational system conveying and reaffirming traditional beliefs and values. On the other hand, they are a sophisticated and intricate performance art form with aesthetic rules and standards. The analytical approach used in this study is two-fold: first, to understand how the communication system works in Ewe trickster narrative performances and second, as a corollary to the communication process, to understand how meaning is transmitted and perceived by the audience. To do this, a model based on the complementary aspects of communication and signification will help elucidate the components of the performed oral narrative event. Central to this approach are several concepts, specifically sign/image relationships, nonverbal behavior, and a structuralist analytical approach to meaning.

Communication

Communication takes on special significance in the context of oral narrative performance. To help define and clarify the somewhat amorphous concept of communication, Roman Jakobson proposed a model of language and communication based on factors and functions.[1]

---

[1] Jacobson's original model has been slightly altered to demonstrate a more precise correspondence between factors and functions. For a description of these models, see Roman Jakobson, "Linguistics and Poetics," in Sebeok, ed.,

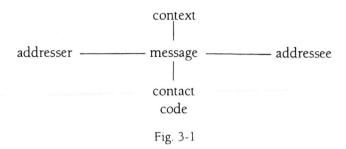

Fig. 3-1

Superimposed on this scheme of basic language factors is a hierarchical order of functions:

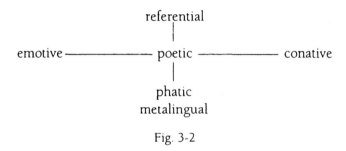

Fig. 3-2

Briefly, the "referential" or "cognitive" function is oriented toward the "context" and is the predominant function in ordinary discourse. The "emotive" or "expressive" function focuses on the "addresser" and reveals the speaker's attitude about what he or she is saying. The "conative" function is oriented toward the "addressee" and is expressed through vocative or imperative forms, such as "John! Drink!" The "metalingual" function is oriented toward the "code" in which speakers talk about the language or tradition reflected in the work, asking, for example, "What do you mean? Could you repeat that?" The "phatic" function correlates with "contact" or the invocation of ritualized formulae to maintain and prolong verbal interaction, e.g., "How are you? What's new? How's the family?" The "poetic" function focuses on the "message" or actual text of a discursive work of art. In oral narrative

---

Style in Language (Cambridge, Massachusetts: The M.I.T. Press, 1960), pp. 350–77.

performance the poetic function is perhaps dominant, emphasizing as it does the questions of selection and arrangement, metonymy and metaphor, and other stylistic effects.

Oral narrative performance is not, however, limited to the poetic function, for audience involvement encompasses the conative, emotive, referential, phatic, and metalingual functions as well. Tag endings, for example, which often feature a moral, involve "contact." Performers' attitudes and artistry embrace the emotive function. The poetic function, however, merits closer scrutiny in order to understand the semantic richness and imagery in narratives.

The poetic function of oral narratives reveals an important trait of language which differs markedly from the language used in factual information-oriented discourse. George Steiner, a philosopher and scholar interested in the evolution of language, noted that "language is the main instrument of man's refusal to accept the world as it is. . . . Ours is the ability, the need, to gainsay or "un-say" the world, to imagine and speak it otherwise."[2] Steiner observed the value placed on deception and mendacity in the classical world where, for example, Greeks took an aesthetic or sporting view of lying. He developed the idea of the creativity of falsehood, the organic intimacy between the genius of speech and fiction in saying "what is not."[3] Indeed, according to Steiner, language as "information" in any speech event is very small.

> . . . the great mass of common speech events, of words spoken and heard, does not fall under the rubric of "factuality" and truth. The very concept of integral truth—"the whole truth and nothing but the truth"—is a fictive ideal of the court-room or the seminar in logic. Statistically, the incidence of true statements"—definitional, demonstrative, tautological, in any given mass of discourse is probably small. . . .[4]

Steiner believes that language as communication in the "poetic" sense is primary:

---

[2]George Steiner, *After Babel* (New York: Oxford University Press, 1975).
[3]Steiner, pp. 219–220.
[4]Steiner, p. 220.

> We communicate motivated images, local frameworks of feeling. All descriptions are partial. We speak less than the truth, we fragment in order to reconstruct desired alternatives, we select and elide. It is not "the things which are" that we say, but those which might be, which we would bring about, which the eye and remembrance compose.[5]

The relevance of this conception of language and communication is vital to trickster narratives, for, more often than not, the "raison d'être" of the trickster character is lies, disguise, illusion, and deception.

Meaning

The second major component of the proposed communication model is signification, commonly referred to as "meaning." "Meaning" is viewed not as an object or representation of a mental image but as a signifying process. It is not an expression of equivalence such as $a=b$; rather, it is a function of relations, specifically, the correlation between expression and content. The question which needs to be asked is not "What does this narrative mean?" but rather, "How does this narrative mean?" that is, how do the images, in combination with each other, affect listeners' emotions, imagination, cognition, and sensory perceptions?

"Meaning" in trickster narratives will be discussed in the context of a structuralist perspective. Structuralism posits fundamental binary oppositions between images which establish poles of meaning around which themes are built. Thematic development in Ewe trickster narratives may appear to be quite simple but looked at closely, they may be quite intricate and complex. Ambiguity and metaphor play important roles in the signification process and are key elements to the aesthetic complexity and beauty of performed Ewe trickster narratives.

Underlying the notions implicit in the communication process is the concept of the "sign." At its simplest level, a "sign" is something that stands for something else. Charles Peirce, who revived interest in semiotics in the early twentieth century, developed the basic concepts

---

[5] *Ibid.*

of semiotic inquiry, the study of "signs." Peirce defined a "sign" as a triadic relation:

> A sign is in a conjoint relation to the thing denoted and to the mind ... the sign is related to its object only in consequence of a mental association, and depends upon habit.[6]

Accordingly, a sign is always interpreted as a sign of something by some interpreter, and this in turn, becomes a sign of something else. This interrelationship of signs occurs at every level of culture and in all forms of communication.

Ferdinand de Saussure, on the other hand, viewed the sign as a diadic relation between an acoustic image (*signifiant*) and a concept (*signifié*). He insisted on the arbitrariness of the relation between *signifiant* and *signifié* and viewed language as a system, that is, a network of reciprocal opportunities. Whereas de Saussure's theory referred specifically to verbal language, Peirce's theory encompassed all forms of communication, both verbal and nonverbal, and thus, had somewhat wider application. Both theories, however, stressed the relational aspect of sign systems and paved the way for considering the "sign" as a function correlating expression and content. The concept of "sign-function" explains how a given object of a concept can stand for many other objects and concepts which create ambiguity and semantic richness in language.[7]

Peirce made another significant contribution to semiotic theory by developing a typology of signs based on the varying relationships signs form with the objects to which they refer. Peirce distinguished among three different types of signs: symbols, index, and icon. "Symbols" he viewed as having an arbitrary and conventional relationship with the objects to which they refer. An "index" was viewed as conveying a relationship based on causality, such as berries on a holly tree, which

---

[6]Quoted in Sebeok, ed., *Sight, Sound, and Sense* (Bloomington: Indiana University Press, 1978), p. 216.

[7]Umberto Eco, "Looking for a Logic of Culture," in Sebeok, ed., *The Tell-Tale Sign* (Netherlands: The Peter De Ridder Press, 1975), p. 15.

suggest a hard winter.[8] An "icon," on the other hand, resembles that which it stands for and usually has a natural or cultural link. The sun and moon representing day and night, for example, are "icons," while the dove representing peace would be a "symbol."

In nonverbal communication systems, signs are also the basic constituent units. Body movements and gestures can be differentiated as symbols, indices, and icons. Like signs in verbal communication, the function of body movements and gestures is determined by usage and these have meaning only in relation to other signs, never in isolation. Cicourel in a study based on the deaf concluded, "We should not equate gestural signs to words or lexical items, but recognize that (these) signs index and organize other unmarked information differently."[9]

Nonverbal communication conveyed through body movements and hand gestures is generally subordinate to the auditory system. In fact, in oral narrative art the nonverbal system cannot exist independently of aural-oral systems. Interestingly, Leach observed that the syntax of nonverbal language is a great deal simpler than that of spoken or written language.[10] On the other hand, William Stokoe argued that, unlike oral signs, gestural signs have more information attached to them than the verbal sign and act as indicators of more details.[11]

---

[8]Edmund Leach further distinguished between "index" and "signal." He defined an "index" as being static with no time dimension, while a "signal" involved cause and effect sequences in time. For example, a forest or river would be an "index" for the metaphysical discrimination between this world/other world, while the performance of a ritual would be a "signal" triggering a change in the metaphysical state of the world.

For this study, both notions are combined in the term "index." For more details, see Edmund Leach, *Culture and Communication* (New York: Cambridge University Press, 1976).

[9]Aaron V. Cicourel, "Gestural-Sign Language and the Study of Nonverbal Communication," in Jonathan Benthall and Ted Polhemus, eds., *The Body as a Medium of Expression* (New York: E.P. Dutton and Co., Inc., 1975), p. 228.

[10]Leach, p. 11.

[11]Quoted in Cicourel, p. 197.

Birdwhistell, a pioneer in kinesic research, did not consider gestural signs as inherently richer in significance, but he did note the similarity between gestures and word forms in language.

> The kinesic system has forms which are astonishingly like words in language . . . there are body behaviors which function like significant sounds, that combine into simple or relatively complex units like words, which are combined into much longer structures or structural behavior like sentences or even paragraphs.[12]

In oral narrative performance the nonverbal system clearly plays a complementary role to the aural/oral system, although the relationship between the two systems can be quite complex. Nonverbal systems normally reinforce and emphasize the significance of the spoken word, but occasionally, nonverbal systems convey divergent or opposing significations from those of the verbal system. The two systems are closely intertwined and both are vital for a full appreciation of oral narrative performance.

Structuralist Approach to Meaning

Trained as we are in the West to probe the meaning of all that we see, read, or hear, it is appropriate that we look at the "meaning" of trickster narratives as well. A pioneer in the field of social anthropology, Claude Lévi-Strauss investigated mythic process in the oral narratives of South American Indians. As a champion of paradigmatic/synchronic structural analysis, Lévi-Strauss viewed culture not as the sum of its tools and artifacts, but as a system of relationships encompassing the material as well as the moral, religious, mythic, and aesthetic aspects.[13] Instead of viewing society as a set of functions, he proposed the idea of society as a system of communication whose meaning is conveyed through an

---

[12] Ray R. Birdwhistell, *Kinesics and Context* (Philadelphia: University of Pennsylvania Press, 1970), p. 80.
[13] Claude Lévi-Strauss, *Structural Anthropology* (Garden City, New York: Doubleday, 1963), p. 9.

aggregate of signs, hence a structure.[14] Each structure, he posited, had a code, which, when deciphered, revealed categories of thought unconsciously experienced but rationally conceived.

In trying to understand myths and mythic process in general, Lévi-Strauss based his structuralist approach on the binary opposition between terms such as culture/nature and life/death. He viewed these oppositions as an organizing principle of myth as well as culture. Although his primary field of interest was anthropology, his heuristic principles and insights into structural organization are relevant to trickster narratives, which are, in fact, a type of mythological system in themselves.

The privileged role that mediating terms play in Lévi-Strauss's approach is reflected in trickster narratives as well. Lévi-Strauss asserted that all mythic systems involve a mental operation based on the reconciliation of contradictory terms. According to Lévi-Strauss, this conflict of terms is solved by mediating terms. In mythic systems in general, mediators may take many forms. Heroes, gods, and animals are frequent mediators. Similarly, divine twins, hermaphrodite gods, and trickster characters also figure prominently as mediating agents. As essentially ambiguous figures, trickster characters are deeply involved in the processes of mediation and transformation, which are important operational principles of trickster narratives.

The terminology particular to structuralist theory has been largely shaped and influenced by two disciplines, anthropology and linguistics. Historically, there has been a relative lack of terms available to literary critics and others interested in oral narrative systems from an aesthetic point of view. Harold Scheub, in the course of extensive research among the Xhosa people in South Africa, made a significant contribution to structuralist aesthetic criticism by introducing several seminal notions in the study of oral narrative performance as aesthetic systems.[15]

---

[14]Octavio Paz, *Claude Lévi-Strauss, An Introduction* (New York: Dell Publishing Co, 1970), p. 9.

[15]Harold Scheub, *The Xhosa Ntsomi* (London: Oxford University Press, 1975).

Image

The first of these notions is the "image," which Scheub defined as "a visualized action or set of actions evoked in the minds of the audience by verbal and nonverbal elements arranged by the artist, requiring a common experience by both artist and audience."[16] Images are the basic units of an aesthetic narrative system whose function is to evoke an emotional response from an audience. In linguistic terms, the analog of the "image" is the "sign" as described by Charles Peirce and Ferdinand de Saussure. Artist and audience share a common repertory of images/signs which the performer calls forth in the minds of the audience to shape and guide a performance. This process requires the active participation of audience members both emotionally and cognitively.[17]

Since words are the vehicle for evoking and controlling the various images, the performer's skill in handling words and images and using the multiple connotations suggested by these images is paramount. By the same token, an audience's sensitivity to the subtleties of language, as well as to the numerous clues a performer emits, determines to a large extent the audience's level of involvement in and enjoyment of a particular performance.

Patterning

The second notion Scheub emphasized was that of "patterning." As a narrative moves from conflict to resolution, the linear sequencing common to most narrative art reveals a number of recurring elements. The operational mechanism for any pattern is repetition. Repeated elements, by virtue of their identical, isomorphic, and contrasting characteristics create patterns of images. Patterns viewed in isolation have virtually no significance to speak of, but patterns in relation to one

---

[16]Harold Scheub, "Oral Narrative Process and the Use of Models," in *New Literary History*, VI, No. 2 (Winter 1975), pp. 353–78.
[17]Scheub, "Oral Narrative Process," p. 353.

another ultimately constitute and reveal the thematic content of narrative performance.

The possible combinations of different narrative patterns are endless. A pattern at its simplest level may contain a single structure. A narrative told in Plymouth, Tobago, for example, consisted of a single pattern repeated many times:

> Once upon a time there was a king. He had his only daughter. A different fellow went in order to get the daughter to marry 'im. So he said, the king said, the only fellow that will get the girl to marry 'im mus' give a story without knowin'. The one fellow came and he started the story. He said he went in a place and there was some locus' . . . locus' among corn. So the locus' they start to remove the grain of corn . . . to remove the grain of corn.
>
> One locus' came and took a grain of corn.
> Another locus' came and took another grain of corn.
> Another locus' came and took another grain of corn.
> And another locus' came and took another grain of corn.
> And another locus' came and took another grain of corn.
> And another locus' came and took another grain of corn.
> And another locus' came and took another grain of corn.
> And another locus' came and took another grain of corn.
> And another locus' came and took another grain of corn.
> And another locus' came and took another grain of corn.
> And another locus' came and took another grain of corn.
> And another locus' came and took another grain of corn.
>
> (Performer laughs)
>
> The king got tired. And he tol' the fellow he can get the daughter and marry her. And that was the end of the story.[18]

Repeating the same basic element a total of twelve times, varying only his intonation and rate of delivery, the performer, Mr. Bertie Ford, played on the audience's anticipation of the pattern's coming to an end. The performer, by prolonging the image of the locust taking one more

---

[18]This narrative was told to the author in the summer of 1976 during field research on oral narratives in Trinidad and Tobago, funded by a grant from the Latvian American Association.

grain of corn, modulated and heightened the audience's sense of anticipation. The result was sheer delight as the audience realized they were being teased and manipulated good-naturedly by the performer, who knew his audience extremely well.

Scheub identified three basic narrative patterns in all. The "expansible image," illustrated above, consists of a single repeated structure. It may be a song, a phrase, or a repeated action. An image is repeated as frequently as is necessary and desirable to develop a narrative plot. Although in most cases the final repetition is altered to bring the narrative to an end, the above example from Tobago closed without such resolution. The narrative ended abruptly, triggered by the performer's judgment that his audience had had enough and that he had exhausted the laughter-provoking potential of that particular structure.

The second type of narrative pattern is the "patterned-image set." In this case, two similar sets of images are brought together, with the second image set differing slightly from the first. As Scheub explained, "It is in the difference that the point of the narrative is made; it is in the slight difference between two identical image sets that the humor or pathos of the narrative is generated."[19] Trickster narratives are often of this type where trickster establishes a pattern intended to dupe another character, but he himself is duped instead.

The third type of narrative pattern is the "parallel-image set," which contains two or more contrasting image sets juxtaposed to reveal similarity between image sets. This type of patterning is the most complex of narrative patterns and may result in metaphorically rich and often complex themes.[20] All three types of narrative patterns will be illustrated in the course of this analysis.

---

[19] Harold Scheub, "Parallel-Image Sets in African Oral Narrative-Performance," *Review of National Literatures*, 2, No. 2 (Fall, 1971), p. 222.

[20] For a fuller description and discussion of this type of narrative patterning, see Scheub's "Oral Narrative Process," "Parallel-Image Sets," and *Xhosa Ntsomi*.

Variant Analysis

Finally, central to the analytical framework is the concept of "variant analysis." Variants are narratives having one or more episodes in common with at least one differing episode. Variants are a useful tool for comparing thematic development and stylistic effects within narratives. The present collection of thirty Ewe trickster narratives contains five groups of variants. These are:

(1) "Lizard Loses His Tongue" (1.2.5)
    "The Chief and His Two Daughters" (28.2.6.)
    "Spider and the Kente Cloth" (5.1.3.)

(2) "The Bird with Seven Heads" (1.2.6.)
    "Spider Refuses the Chief's Daughter" (30.2.2.)

(3) "Spider and the Mill" (5.1.8.)
    "Spider Removes the Mill" (10.2.1.)

(4) "Spider and the Stone with Eyes" (5.1.10.)
    "Spider and Rat" (54.1.8.)

(5) "Monster and Antelope" (21.2.4.)
    "Monster Flogs Spider" (29.1.5.)

Transcription

The thirty narratives in this collection were transcribed verbatim using standard Ewe orthography. Detailed differences and stylistic variations in performers' speech are reproduced as closely as possible. As a result, these transcriptions may not necessarily reflect proper Standard Ewe grammar. Readers should be careful not to judge these texts as "bad" Ewe but understand that faithful transcription of the spoken word was the intended goal.

The appendix contains translations of the 30 trickster narratives used in this analysis. Full Ewe transcriptions of six narratives have also been provided. These are: "Rabbit and Crocodile" (1.1.1.), "Lizard

Methodology

Loses His Tongue" (1.2.5.), "Spider and the Mill" (5.1.8.), "Spider Removes the Mill" (10.2.1.), "Hyena, Goat, and Leopard" (10.2.2.), and "Goat in the Village of Animals" (18.1.1.).

Audience responses such as laughter are fully marked and narrators' pauses, false starts, and self-corrections are indicated. Audience comments appear in parentheses and all foreign words are italicized.

CHAPTER FOUR

Formal Features of Trickster Narratives

The Ewe people do not formally distinguish between trickster and non-trickster narratives. The closest one can come to eliciting specifically a trickster narrative is to ask an Ewe audience for "a story about Yiyi" or "a story about Ayevi."[1] In response, one will probably hear a trickster narrative where Yiyi is the main protagonist. Unprompted, however, Ewe performers tell both trickster and non-trickster tales, making no formal distinctions between them.

Ethnic research conducted by Herskovits among the Fon, Finnegan among the Limba, Tremearne in Hausaland, and Evans-Pritchard among the Zande—similarly reveals no separation of categories among these groups. Bruce Grindal observed among the Sisala of Ghana, for example:

> While trickster motifs are found in many Sisala tales, there is no generic term for trickster or trickster tale; instead, tales are usually named after the main protagonist. However, tales about spider, rabbit, and monkey most closely approximate our definition of trickster tales.[2]

Among the Akan people, spider stories are known as *anansesam* (Ananse tales), whereas the Azande spider stories are called the *sangba ture* (Ture tales). In each case, these names are given to stories with or without spider's presence and are used for trickster as well as non-trickster tales. It is difficult to determine whether these terms were ever exclusively limited to spider stories, but it is possible they were never

---

[1]"Ayevi" is another name for Spider.
[2]Bruce Grindal, "The Sisala Trickster Tale," *Journal of the Folklore Institute*, 9 (The Hague: Mouton, 1972), p. 173.

intended to be anything more than a convenient label for oral imaginative narratives in general.

Among the Ewe, certain formal and structural characteristics are shared by "trickster" narratives. These are: framing devices, specifically, opening and closing formulae; the particular sequencing of events; one or more tricks based on illusion and narrative patterning; songs; the concept of "taboo" with respect to food, sex, excrement; and moral endings. Several key terms are essential to discussing trickster narratives. These include "formal features," "structure" and "structural relationships," "theme," and "image." In the pre-war period, literary criticism typically viewed literature as a reflection or explanation of historical, social, or psychological phenomena. The emphasis was on meaning derived primarily from outside the work of art. With the advent of the formalists and later, the structuralists, literary criticism was oriented toward viewing form and content as inseparable, and the meaning in a work of art was conceived of as being the work itself. Both the formalists and structuralists made significant contributions to understanding narrative process.[3] Their findings resulted in basic distinctions between "plot" and "story" and between "paradigmatic" and "syntagmatic" organization of verbal art.

For our purposes, this discussion will define the formal features of narrative art in terms of syntagmatic organization, that is, the diachronic or linear relationships among images. Opening and closing formulae, events or sequences of images within the story, and the association of certain actions with specific characters are the most obvious formal features.

"Structure" is a more ambiguous concept. On the one hand, syntagmatic features of all narrative art are part of a structure in some

---

[3]For more information about formalist criticism, see essays by Boris Tomashevsky and Victor Shlovsky, translated by Lee Lemon and Marion Reis in *Russian Formalist Criticism* (Lincoln: University of Nebraska Press, 1965). For information about structuralist criticism, see Claude Lévi-Strauss, *Structuralist Anthropology*, trans. Claire Jacobson and Brooke G. Schoepf (New York: Doubleday, 1963); Vladimir Propp, *Morphology of the Folktale*, 2nd ed. (Austin: University of Texas Press, 1968); Roland Barthes, *S/Z* (New York: Hill and Wang, 1974).

Formal Features of Trickster Narratives

sense. On the other hand, structural relationships in a paradigmatic sense refer to similarities or differences among corresponding images. These relationships become apparent when images are repeated. It is in the repetition or patterning of images that corresponding relationships, based on identity, similarity, and opposition are revealed.

"Theme" also is a function of the paradigmatic organization of narrative art. It is an analytical construct intuitively perceived and consciously interpreted by the audience. Boris Tomashevsky defined "theme" as:

> ... what is being said in a work (that) unites the separate elements of a work. The work as a whole has a theme, and its individual parts also have themes. ... To be coherent, a verbal structure must have a unifying theme running through it.

He further observed,

> Selection of an interesting theme is not enough. Interest must also be maintained, attention stimulated. The theme does both. The emotion attached to the theme plays a major role in maintaining interest.[4]

Although themes may exist on several levels, "theme" will be defined as the idea that ties the narrative together and lies beyond the descriptive images of the plot. Accordingly, "theme" is revealed by the structural relationships within the narrative and is integrally associated with the metaphoric process which reveals thematic content.

Additionally, the terms "story," "tale," and "narrative" will be used interchangeably and refer to the description of events. "Plot," on the other hand, is a compositional feature and refers to the structure or arrangement of events.[5] In our frame of reference, "plot" is interrelated with "theme." While there can be a plot with no theme, there cannot be a theme without plot.

---

[4] Lemon and Reis, trans., pp. 63–65.
[5] Lemon and Reis, trans., pp. 119–22.

Opening Formulae

Opening formulae in trickster narratives signal to audiences a break with everyday events. In the Ewe tradition the opening formula for all narratives is *mise gli loo* ("listen to a story") to which the audience responds *gli ne va* ("let the story come"). This brief introduction is like the setting of a dramatic stage whose curtain is about to rise. It corresponds to house lights being dimmed as the stage lights are brought up. The major difference with a Western stage is that in Eweland the houselights go down with the setting of the sun and the stage is lit by the bright glow of the moon in the dark tropical sky and sometimes, by the incandescent light of a kerosene lamp.

The start of a narrative performance is signaled by the performer calling for the audience's attention and their encouragement to proceed. An enthusiastic response encourages the performer to continue. A half-hearted and mediocre response is a signal that audience expectations are not very high.

The introductory formula is followed by *Gli tso keke va dze Yiyi dzi* ("The story rises, travels, and falls on Spider"). The effect created is that of a disembodied force traveling of its own volition, moving down from the heavens and over the rivers, mountains, and valleys until it lands on the chosen narrative characters. The downward motion of the narrative as a disembodied spirit reminds the audience of the narrative's origins in *Fetome*, the world of beyond where the ancestors dwell, and dramatically points up the narrative's "élan vital" for which the performer is but a vehicle.[6] It is as if the narrative has a life of its own, which the performer merely interprets for the audience.

The phrase *va dze* ("falls on") further evokes a religious connotation. In the course of certain religious ceremonies Ewe devotees often fall into a trance. When this happens, they say, "*Etrɔ dze edzi*" ("The spirit has fallen on them"). As soon as the trance begins, the chosen individual appears as if he or she is animated by an invisible force, resulting in an altered state in which extraordinary events may occur.

---

[6]N'Sougan Agblemagnon, *Sociologie des Sociétés Orales d'Afrique Noire: Les Ewe du Sud-Togo* (Paris: Mouton,1969).

Formal Features of Trickster Narratives

Similarly, in narrative performance the performer possesses the power to create an altered state for his or her listeners, transposing them from everyday reality to an imaginary world where fantasy reigns.

The Ewe people believe that the storytelling tradition is rooted in an esoteric science, geomancy, and that the stories themselves are messages from supernatural forces and their intermediaries, the revered ancestors. Consequently, the performer, who interprets these messages, is believed to have special "magical" abilities. The really expert performers are so highly esteemed that audiences attribute to them quasi-divine talents and skills.

The audience participates in the illusion of the free-falling "narrative spirit" as members witness the narrative's falling and selecting narrative characters. The audience witnesses this process by rejoining, "*Edze dzi*" ("It falls indeed"). There is a tacit understanding between audience and performer that what they are about to hear is a "lie"—an illusion collectively shared between audience and performer. Although the limits of human imagination appear to be endless, performers who give too free reign to their imagination are corrected and rebuked for "lying." Such challenges to narrative plausibility clearly imply that the narrative world of "lies" has, nonetheless, an internal order and consistency whose limits must be respected.

A universal characteristic of all imaginative narratives is the creation of an illusion rooted in a temporal framework. "Once upon a time," *il y avait une fois*, "a long time ago"—all recall an unspecified but anterior time period, presumably a golden age of antiquity when wondrous things happened. This link with antiquity is an important element in Ewe narrative traditions as well because it reaffirms the interrelatedness of human existence with the religious and natural spheres. In African and Caribbean narrative traditions the same effect is created through temporally based images. Crowley, for example, observed in the Bahamas the following opening formulae:

> Bunday! Once upon a time, a very (wery, werary, berry, or merry) good time, a monkey chew tobacco and he spit white lime . . . wasn't my time, was in old people time when they used to take fish scale to make shingle and fish bone to make needle.

Or,

> This was not my time, in old people time, when children used to pee in the pumpkin wine and call it seasoning.[7]

Among the Ashanti, emphasis is put on the fictitious nature of narrative performance:

> We do not mean, we do not really mean (that what we are going to say is true).[8]

Some narrative traditions evoke no particular images in their opening formulae at all, using instead a simple linguistic marker. For example, the Hausa say,

> A tale for you. Let it come and pass by.[9]

Similarly, the Xhosa say,

> It came about, according to some tale, that . . . [10]

Concluding Formulae

By the same token, the concluding formula in Ewe narratives reinforces the illusion of a lie having been told:

> This is what I was deceived with and this is what I deceive you with.[11]

This phrase openly acknowledges the fictitious nature of the story, underscoring the active participation of listeners and tellers in the

---

[7] Daniel J. Crowley, *I Could Talk Old Story Good: Creativity in Bahamian Folklore* (Berkeley: University of California Press, 1966), p. 33.

[8] R.S. Rattray, *Akan-Ashanti Folktales* (Oxford: Clarendon Press, 1930).

[9] Connie Stephens, "The Relationship of Social Symbol and Narrative Metaphor," Diss. University of Wisconsin–Madison, 1981, p. 321.

[10] A.C. Jordan, trans. *Tales From Southern Africa* (Los Angeles: University of California Press, 1973).

[11] Other concluding formulae heard on occasion were: "The yam is cooking in the fire. Bring it so that we may peel it and eat it." Or, "My voice has fallen down."

creative storytelling process. The allusion to deception may be loosely translated as "coaxed," "tempted," or "enticed with." Common to all these connotations is the image of being lured, as if by an invisible magnetic force.

The listeners' response "*Woezɔ loo*" ("You are very welcome") reaffirms their complicity and creates the illusion of a "journey." *Woezɔ* is the traditional greeting given to a traveler who has just arrived. In this case, the narrator is welcomed back from the narrative journey he or she just undertook. The more enthusiastic the expression of greeting, the more appreciative the audience members are of their narrative voyage and successful return. Importantly, the audience's pleasure is not vicarious. Rather, audience members participate directly, adding their own comments and music, guiding and shaping the performer's unfolding tapestry of words, images, and gestures.

In the Volta Region, the Ewe-speaking region of Ghana where narratives were also gathered, a variation of the closing formula prevailed. Instead of the disclaimer, "This is what I have brought to deceive you with," the performer often attributed the tale to an elderly woman:

> When I was going, an old lady called me. When she called me she gave me this story and asked me to narrate it to you all.

The reference to an older person passing by in the story is an important clue to understanding the role that tradition and the elders play in the Ewe socio-religious order. The Ewe world view is typical of many African peoples in that the elders are ancestors, the revered forebearers of life and keepers of traditional beliefs and customs. The traditions of the people, their rituals, religion, festivals, and artifacts are all part of the legacy elders have left to younger generations to teach, guide, and protect them. The stories people tell are among the most precious possessions they have to express deep cultural bonds. Suggesting the ancestral origins of the *gli* transposes the symbolic significance of stories to a higher plane. The link with revered ancestors not only reinforces the tale's sacred origins but expresses the respect the Ewe people have for their ancestors and the storytelling tradition.

In the Volta Region a second audience response varied from that found in southern Togo. Instead of welcoming the performer back from the fictitious voyage, the audience applauded and praised the performer:

> You have the mouth for telling.

The audience's critical standards are revealed, suggesting that not everyone can spin a good tale. It was not uncommon for audiences to tell a performer, "You made it up" and terminate his performance with a simple and unenthusiastic, "*Yooooo.*"

In other cultures, concluding formulae form an interesting array of variations. In the Bahamas, for example, performers say:

> From that to this . . . old people's back do be bent so; (or) Cat does chase dog. I was passing by and I say and the kick he kick at me . . . causing me to come here tonight to tell you this big lie.[12]

The Azande, by contrast, conclude with:

> I came here and saw men quarreling and as I went to calm them, one of them made for me at once and hit me hard, and as I cried out he took a bit of meat and put it in my hands, and I brought it and placed it on top of the doorway here; child go and fetch it.[13]

Frequently, concluding formulae reinforce the image of a "lie" or add a bit of nonsense, such as witnessing a quarrel on the way to "deliver" the tale. Sometimes there is no attempt to create any illusion at all, such as Xhosa tales which end with:

> End, end, little tale.

The Hausa often conclude with:

> That's all for that story. This with peace.

but an alternate variation injects an element of illusion:

> I ate the rat, not the rat ate me.[14]

---

[12] Crowly, p. 36.

[13] E.E. Evans-Pritchard, *The Zande Trickster* (Oxford: Clarendon Press, 1967), p. 55.

[14] Neil Skinner, ed. and trans., *Hausa Tales and Traditions*, Vol. 1 (New York: Africana Publishing Corp., 1969).

Morphology of the Trick

The trick is the focus of all trickster narratives. By definition, it is a device or strategem used to deceive another.[15] The trick not only defines the structural relationship between characters, it is the central organizing device which focuses dramatic action and shapes the emotional response of audience members. The more successful and outrageous the trick, the greater the audience's delight and enthusiastic reaction. The trick is the key element of the plot which focuses the audience's reactions and serves as a barometer of the audience's appreciation of the performance.

The trick is characterized by two structural features: (1) patterned or non-patterned images and (2) the creation of an illusion to deceive an opponent.

Patterning

The trick has as its structural grid a series of repeated elements which create a model. Harold Scheub observed that the simplest model is built on "patterned images," which consist of two or more similar sets of images.[16] Scheub explained:

> ... in a West African Dahomean narrative, Trickster Yo seeks an animal for a ceremony that his chief is preparing. He finds an elephant and invites that creature to play a game. "You tie me in the basket," Yo proposes, "and when I tell you that the rope hurts, you untie me. Then when I tie you, and you tell me that the rope hurts, I

---

[15] Laura Tanna, "The Art of Jamaican Oral Narrative Performance," Vol. 1, Diss. University of Wisconsin–Madison 1980, pp. 324–5.

[16] Harold Scheub, "Parallel-Image Sets in African Oral Narrative-Performances," *Review of National Literatures*, 2, No. 2 (Fall 1971), p. 222.

will untie you." This is the model, the verbal statement of the pattern that is now to be repeated. . . . [17]

If the model were repeated in an identical manner, there would be no change in the narrative. The model, however, is not followed exactly and the slight alteration in patterning causes the elephant to be caught. It is in the shift of images, in the juxtaposition of similar but not identical images that the dramatic point of the narrative is made.

Scheub explains that the first part of the trick proceeds as Yo proposes, but the second part is built on an illusion. Yo makes Elephant believe that the pattern "you tie me and I'll tie you" will occur as described. It works for Yo when he is tied and released by Elephant. But built into the model is a deception. Yo lies about the outcome awaiting Elephant, for Yo has no intention of releasing Elephant.

A variety of different trickster narrative structures can be generated based on patterned-image sets. A variation of the "you tie me and I'll tie you" pattern can be repeated in reverse order. For example, Yo may describe the model, the adversary tries it, and is released. When Yo himself enters the boiling pot, the intended dupe may alter the model by not releasing Yo, thus causing Yo to suffer the fate of the intended victim.

Patterned image sets are one of the most common devices used to structure tricks in oral narratives. They have the potential for weaving complex themes based on metaphorical associations.[18] In this collection, relatively few narratives of the "you tie me and I'll tie you" type were recorded. Rather, a popular variation is serially imbedded tricks. In "Spider the Trader" (23.2.2.), for example, a sequence of exchanges results in Spider adroitly engineering the exchange of a pfennig for a rooster which, in turn, is traded for a ram, and so forth until Spider successfully obtains seven maidens.

---

[17]Harold Scheub, *The Xhosa Ntsomi* (London: Oxford University Press, 1975), p. 155.

[18]Scheub, *Ntsomi*, p. 155.

Formal Features of Trickster Narratives

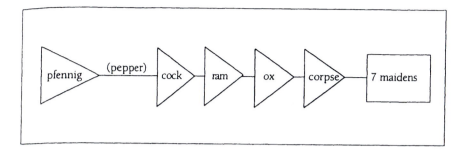

Fig. 4-1

In "Spider Brings Disharmony into the World" (23.2.3.), Spider devises a scheme for creating hostility among his fellow creatures. A repeated series of patterns results in the invited guests killing one other in turn.

> Spider rushed to Rooster and asked him to come tomorrow morning to clear his farm for him. He needed his help. This was very necessary. Rooster said, "Have you asked anyone else? If you ask Hawk, I will not come." Spider said, "No, how could I ask Hawk? You are the only one I asked."
>
> As soon as Spider got up, he went to Hawk and said, when morning breaks, he should come and work with him, by all means.

Another variation in narrative patterning consists of a single expansible image.[19] In "Frog and Horse" (9.1.6.) the two animals decide to have a race. Frog deceives Horse by posting identical frogs along the road. The winner is as predictable as Frog is clever. Horse's shock and utter disbelief each time that he finds Frog ahead of him on the road are a source of delight for the audience. Repetition of the same expansible image—Frog at the signpost and Horse's resultant disbelief—constitutes the plot of the narrative. Each repetition pushes the narrative ahead as it gathers momentum and increases the comical effect until final resolution is reached.

---

[19]Scheub, *Ntsomi*, p. 5.

A similar narrative device is used in "Rabbit and Crocodile" (1.1.1.) and "Spider Decorates Eggs" (30.1.2.) which operate on the illusion that "one is many." In "Rabbit and Crocodile," Rabbit is asked to bring the baby crocodiles to their mother for suckling. The repetition of bringing the same baby each time constitutes the narrative plot. The single expansible image crystallizes the irony of the mother crocodile's ignorance which turns to horror as she realizes that Rabbit has eaten five of her children and is, in fact, bringing her the same baby crocodile each time.

In yet another example, "Spider Decorates Eggs," Spider is given eggs to decorate. He decorates only one egg and eats the rest. When he is asked to show his work, he produces the same egg each time. In this narrative the expansible image is actually part of a larger more complex narrative, but taken by itself, it may constitute a complete narrative. Narratives of this type do not concentrate on conflict between characters. Instead, they exploit the aesthetic potential of the expansible image which is the essence of the trick. This, in turn, focuses the emotional response of the audience. Each repetition builds the intensity of the audience's anticipation of the resolution. The resolution may consist of trickster's defeat or his escape, as the audience eagerly awaits each new twist. What appears to be a simple narrative pattern is rooted, in fact, in a complex narrative technique requiring considerable artistic skill to make it work.

Another popular pattern structuring tricks in Ewe narratives consists of a patterned-image set seeking closure. "Spider and the Stone with Eyes" (5.1.10.) and "Spider and Rat" (54.1.8.) illustrate this pattern. In "Spider and the Stone with Eyes" Spider finds a magic stone which commands anyone who calls the stone by its proper name, "Stone-with-eyes," to die on the spot. Spider establishes a model by pointing to the stone and asking animals, "What is that?" As soon as the animal answers, it falls dead. Squirrel, however, refuses to cooperate. Assuming trickster's role, he repeats the established model and asks Yiyi, "What is that?" Yiyi answers the question in spite of himself, completes the pattern, and falls dead.

In "Spider and Rat" a similar pattern is based on counting yam mounds. Whoever utters aloud the number "seven" will die instantly.

Formal Features of Trickster Narratives

The dramatic interest in this narrative pattern lies in the juxtaposition of contrasting images. A trick usually occurs where there is an alteration in the established pattern of images. In this case, however, the tension lies in the disparity between an established pattern—counting to seven, followed by death—and Spider's valiant effort to refrain from completing the pattern. He is tricked because he substitutes himself for the intended victim. Spider falls prey to his own impatience and fierce competitive spirit to prove that his *juju* powers are superior to those of Rat.

The structural patterns of trickster narratives are created from repeated images. Repetition, however, can assume various forms. The importance of repetition in oral narrative performance cannot be overemphasized. As Scheub noted, "Repetition is the basic aesthetic principle of performance." Western audiences may find the great amount of repetition wearisome and offensive to their artistic sensibilities, but Scheub observed:

> ... there is nothing at all offensive about the splendidly rhythmic use of images and songs, repeated again and again.

Indeed, the rhythms of performed verbal art are so dynamic and powerful, they modulate audience energy and interest from mild passive receptivity to energetic displays of dance, song, laughter, clapping, and other body movements.

Not all trickster narratives are built on the same model. Patterning distinguishes narratives in useful ways. Images relating to the trick, for instance, may be patterned serially as in "Spider the Trader" (23.2.2). In this narrative there is no change in the relationship between Spider and his victims. He repeats the same basic pattern, acting as a death-dealer and blaming innocent creatures. In "Hyena, Goat, and Leopard" (10.2.2.), however, patterning defines three sets of relationships as Hyena, Goat, and Leopard plot against each other, while the basic repeated images dramatize the transformation of excretory substances into ambrosiac delights. In "Spider in the Village of One-armed Men" (21.1.3.) Yiyi repeatedly disguises himself in a variety of colored robes to deceive his wife and stop her from leaving him. In each case, the images involving the trick are patterned both visually and rhythmically, creating richly dramatic effects through the use of repetition.

"Nyanuwufia" (54.1.4.) offers an interesting structural grid for examining patterned and non-patterned tricks. This tale is one of the few narratives that appears to have essentially human characters. The main character, however, is far from being an ordinary human. His extraordinary name, Nyanuwufia ("Know-More-Than-the-Chief"), strange birth, supernatural ability to communicate while in the womb, and his insolent challenge to the chief—all make him a supernatural being. Like his animal counterparts, he is well-suited to the role the tradition bestows upon trickster figures. In one episode the chief plots to kill Nyanuwufia by sending him on a bogus mission and flattering him by giving him a lovely *kente* cloth to wear. It is the chief's relentless attempts to kill Nyanuwufia that are the repeated element. Each of the four main episodes has as its core a cluster of images related to trickery, but the images within each cluster are not patterned in themselves. They are not built on repeated elements like those in the "you tie me" motif, nor are they serially embedded like the "one pfennig buys seven women" type of narrative. The overall structure of the narrative combines structural characteristics of both patterned and non-patterned narratives, creating a tightly woven and artistically pleasing performance.

Illusion

The second formal feature of the trick is its function to deceive. To understand the dynamics of the trick we must look at the various devices narrative characters use to devise and perform tricks. One of the possible consequences of a trick is to reverse the outcome which trickster's intended victim expects. Spider, for example, expects Squirrel to release him from a trap, but Spider is trapped instead. Squirrel thus alters the outcome expected by Spider.

Other times, tricks are used to veil the trickster's real motives, thus making possible an action which would ordinarily be difficult or impossible to perform. In "Spider and the Beans" (51.2.5.) Yiyi attends his mother-in-law's funeral and eats the beans prepared for the funereal repast. By feigning enormous grief over his mother-in-law's death, he creates the illusion of mourning and draws attention away from his real motive, eating the beans.

A trick, whether it is in the form of verbal deception, disguise, or substitution, usually works by virtue of the illusion it creates. Charles Morgan observed,

> Illusion is the suspense of dramatic form.... The suspense of form, by which is meant the incompleteness of a known completion, is to be clearly distinguished from common suspense—suspense of plot— the ignorance of what will happen ... suspense of form is, as I understand it, essential to the dramatic form itself.[20]

In trickster narratives suspense on the plot level is often minimal. The audience is thoroughly familiar with the narratives, having heard them many times before. In most cases, the plot is predictable. For example, we know that Yiyi will try to hide the fact that he has eaten all the beans and, in all likelihood, will be discovered. If the plot were the primary criterion of a good story, most stories would fail miserably. It is the affective involvement of the audience that elevates the tale from a mundane bit of nonsense to entertaining drama. Audience members primarily experience the stories through their emotions and feelings, and in the course of the actual telling, they suspend their disbelief. Although intellectually they are familiar with the sequence of events, each telling is, in fact, a new and different experience.

The element of illusion captures the audience's interest and intensifies their affective involvement. In dramatic performances illusion functions on two levels, the formal and the thematic. Morgan refers to the formal level when he discusses illusion as "the suspense of form." The key elements are anticipation, fulfillment, and closure. The illusion of an imminent outcome guides the performance and brings artist and audience into a close symbiotic relationship with each other as the artist evokes a continuous range of possible feelings from sorrow to comic relief. The illusion is created in the act of telling. When the narrative is completed, the illusion is over. Charles Morgan said,

---

[20]Charles Morgan, "The Nature of Dramatic Illusion," in *Reflections On Art*, ed. Susanne Langer (New York: Oxford University Press, 1961), p. 98.

> What form is chosen ... matters less than that while the drama moves, a form is being fulfilled.[21]

Illusion functions on a thematic level through the tensions generated in the complex of images related to the trick, of which there may be more than one in a narrative. This tension is expressed in the opposition between characters' erroneous or at least limited perception of reality and the audience's perception of "informed" reality, altered by the performer to let audience members know only what he or she wants them to know. In the process of objectifying oral narratives, performers introduce and embellish thematic elements associated with appearance and reality. The relationships between these images result in aesthetic tensions vividly experienced by the audience. If meaningful relationships among images were not perceived by the audience, all there would be is a series of disjointed images, much like shaggy dog stories with no beginning and no end. Images viewed in meaningful relationship to each other, however, form contrastive patterns which allow illusion to operate and themes to develop.

Illusion is the mechanism which allows the trick to produce the outcome desired by the person performing the trick. Disguise, substitution, and verbal deception are the three major operational devices used to produce illusion in trickster narratives. These devices are by no means mutually exclusive and each trick may blend elements of all three devices. Typically, however, one of the three devices predominates and is the key organizing mechanism in the trick. These devices are not unique to oral narrative performances. Their importance in trickster narratives, however, lies in their marked regularity and centrality in structuring the trick.

Disguise

One of the most popular devices trickster characters use to execute tricks is disguise. Often, disguise takes the form of trickster changing his physical appearance such as shaving his head or donning a certain

---

[21]Morgan, p. 98.

article of clothing. In "Spider Decorates Eggs" (30.1.2.), Yiyi first shaves his head, then dresses up as a Hausaman in his efforts to avoid capture. In "Nyanuwufia" (54.1.4.) the young child outsmarts the chief by exchanging his *kente* cloth for a poor man's cloth, thus sending the chief's son to his death.

In "Spider in the Village of One-armed Men" (21.1.3.), Yiyi loses his hand in a buffalo's anus and tries to hide the fact from his wife. Yiyi, proud and fearing humiliation, wraps his arm in white linen and tries to stop his wife from leaving him and look for a normal husband with both arms intact.

> As the woman went along one path, Yi Gogoe took another, wrapped his arm in white linen and intercepted her on the way. He lifted his bandaged arm and said, "We are all people of cut-off arms here at Adā."

His disguise is successful because his wife does not recognize him. He repeats the same trick, bandaging his arm first in red, then in indigo cloth. His wife eventually is convinced that she might as well return to her one-armed husband, since men everywhere appear to be invalids.

In this narrative Yiyi extrapolates from the particular and makes it the norm. The illusion of normalcy is created from an abnormal situation. The illusion is all the more provocative because of the colorful images brought together in sharp relief. It is as if the bandaged arm were alternately emblazoned in red, white, and blue. These images are so powerful that the colors short-circuit the woman's other sensory perceptions so that she cannot see beyond the colorful banners waving before her; nor does she see through Yiyi's trick.

In "Spider Pounds Fufu" (51.1.5.) Adzanyi (Spider) pretends to die. The performer does not elaborate how Spider feigns his death, but we do know that he creates a successful illusion:

> So one day Spider came and said he was ill. He was ill for a very long time and then "died." He lay very still and very flat. They went and made a coffin for him. Spider said that if he dies, they should take a mortar and pestle and bury them with him.

Safely buried in his coffin with his prized yams, mortar, and pestle, Spider rises from the dead, pounds and eats *fufu* to his heart's content.

Disguise, not as obvious in these narratives as in the preceding ones, nevertheless establishes tension between two sets of images related to life and death.

In order for the performer to involve the audience in the dramatic unfolding of the narrative, it is important that audience members be privy to the disguise mechanism. The performer exploits the audience's perceptions of appearance and reality and creates a sense of complicity between trickster and the audience. This complicity is a key factor in engaging the audience's emotions and affective responses. By allowing the audience to witness Yiyi's deviousness and clever trickery, audience members vicariously reap Yiyi's rewards and suffer his fate. Conceivably, if the audience were fooled along with the other characters in the story, the audience's surprise might be greater. However, Morgan observed,

> ... this formal suspense has the greater power if we know beforehand ... what the formal release will be.[22]

Substitution

Substitution is an equally familiar device used to create illusion. In "Frog and Horse" (9.1.6.) the race between the two animals is built on the illusion of one person being many. As in previous examples where disguise is the primary operating mechanism, in this narrative the audience's privileged knowledge of the nature of Frog's trick makes Horse's plight all the more pitiful. The audience cannot help but want to warn the naive but good-natured Horse. However, the repetition of frogs jumping out to greet Horse at each signpost along the road is comical. This comic effect owes not only to the clever execution of the ruse but to the apt choice of opponents as well. The performer of this narrative fully exploits the incongruous situation where the swiftest of domestic animals, the horse, is pitted against the slowest and most awkward of creatures, the frog.

---

[22] *Ibid.*

Formal Features of Trickster Narratives

An intriguing example of the substitution motif occurs in "Hyena, Goat, and Leopard" (10.2.2.). In this narrative Hyena attempts to kill Goat, using substitution to create an illusion.

trickster	mediator	intended dupe
HYENA	LEOPARD	GOAT
	Illusion: excrement is tiger-nuts	

The tables are turned as Goat is tipped off about Hyena's intentions and Goat turns trickster:

trickster	mediator	intended dupe
GOAT	LEOPARD	HYENA
	Illusion: urine is honey	

This tightly woven narrative is built on a series of parallel but inverse relationships between Goat and Hyena:

Hyena : Leopard : Goat : : Goat : Leopard : Hyena

Hyena and Goat are avowed enemies. Hyena attempts to kill Goat, but Goat succeeds in killing Hyena through Leopard, who is the actual death-dealer. The illusion, based on the substitution of nonfood (excrement and urine) for real food (nuts and honey), makes this reversal between Hyena and Goat possible.

This is achieved through the opposition between images of food and nonfood which, in turn, define the parallel relationship between Hyena and Goat. Second, the illusion created by food/nonfood images enables Hyena and Goat to manipulate Leopard as their mutual foil, who in this case, mediates between life and death. This deceptively simple narrative based on three characters revolves around the substitution of nonfood for real food and establishes, in turn, the binary opposition between life and death. The result is an intriguingly complex narrative where character roles are in constant flux.

Verbal Deception

Another frequently used device to create illusion in trickster narratives is verbal deception. This usually takes the form of lies but can include flattery, persuasion, and cajolery—all of which are intended to deceive, but to varying degrees.

Trickster characters in Ewe oral traditions are masters of verbal artistry. In "Spider and Death" (10.2.3.), Spider is aware of the potency of words and consciously uses them to his advantage. He adopts his most charming demeanor to strike up a friendship—albeit false—with Antelope. Antelope obeys Yiyi when he tells her to open the door for the "friend" who is knocking. The friend is none other than Death, who knocks Antelope on the head and kills her.

In "Spider the Trader" (23.2.2.), Yiyi displays his cleverness and superior powers of persuasion as he convinces the chief that the chief's ram ate Yiyi's rooster, which Yiyi himself strangled. In like manner, Yiyi strangles the ram and convinces the chief that the chief's ox gorged the ram to death. Yiyi's creative manipulation of language and his ability to deceive allow him to gain control of his adversary. Controlling his opponent is what makes trickster's ruses successful. Nonetheless, trickster does not always win. Sometimes, when the illusion is unmasked, he may be duped, shorn of his power, and killed.

In the earlier examples of trickster narratives in antiquity, we saw tricksters display magical and supernatural abilities. Hermes, for example, was able to transform himself into a mist and pass through a keyhole, while Loki was able to slay giants. African tricksters are equally adept. Yiyi, for example, pretends to be a diviner and prescribes cures for illness. He "cures" through the medium of language, creating a convincing and effective illusion of expertise. In "Spider Commits Incest" (23.1.3.), Yiyi prescribes his own "cure," that is, intercourse with his daughter, which metaphorically "cures" him but literally kills her. His power lies in words and his expert ability to fashion an illusive reality through linguistic means.

Similarly, in "Spider Propels Animals from a Tree" (2.1.5.), Yiyi promises a quick trip to unsuspecting victims who agree to be propelled from the branches of a tree. Yiyi entices his dupes with

Formal Features of Trickster Narratives

seductive but empty words, incorporating a formula believed to have magical properties. Because the spoken word is a powerful instrument and trickster's greatest skill is to deceive, it is no wonder that the Ewe trickster often displays the qualities of a master linguist.

In other African narrative traditions this trait is similarly evident. In a Wolof narrative, for example, the mere choice of names becomes a powerful weapon to counter Hyena's attempt to starve Hare.

> The hare arrived there (Hyena's compound) and said, "Salaam Alekum." The hyena replied, "Alekum Salaam." Then the hare asked, "Uncle Hyena, I am looking for a host farmer." It asked, "Are you swift?" and it replied, "Yes, I am very quick." The hyena asked, "What is your name?" The hare replied, "Bisimilahi" ("In the name of Allah") is my given name, "Wahumala" ("I am not talking to you") is my surname.
>
> The hyena would go behind the compound and prepare to eat its meal alone out of sight of the hare. Before it began, however, the hyena mechanically prayed to Allah to bless its food. As it did so, it pronounced the hare's name as if to call it and partake of the meal.
>
> You know, when you are eating you get used to saying "Bisimilahi" before you eat. The hyena whispered "Bisimilahi" . . . and the hare came and said "Yes?" and ate the hyena's food.[23]

Songs

Ewe oral narratives are often characterized by songs interspersed within the narrative performance. Athough songs occur frequently, they do not have to be present in either trickster or non-trickster narratives. This is in contrast to oral narrative systems in other African cultures. Among the Yoruba, as well as the Gbaya, for instance, there are two categories of prose narratives, those with songs and those without. In the Yoruba classification system, stories with songs are called *alɔ*, while *itan* are stories without songs, or at least songs are not an integral part of the

---

[23]Emil Magel, "Caste Identification of the Hare in Wolof Oral Narratives," *Research in African Literatures*, Vol. 12, No. 2 (Summer 1981), p. 197.

performance.[24] Similarly, the Gbaya distinguish between the *lizaŋ*, a parable with no song, and *tô*, a narrative with songs.[25]

The more flexible classification of songs in Ewe narratives in no way implies that songs have diminished importance in narrative development or in the dramatic quality of narrative images. The musical accompaniment which songs provide injects a melodic counterpoint to the narrative tempo created by verbal rhythms. Songs heighten audience involvement by inviting the audience to join the singing, usually intoned by an audience member, and they lend color and brilliance to the performance.

In Ewe narratives, songs figure in about half the thirty narratives and serve a variety of functions. Frequently, songs disclose or comment upon events in the narrative. The song's irruption momentarily stops the narrative flow and focuses attention on a particular aspect, relationship, or event. In "Spider and the Beans" (51.2.5.), for example, the song draws attention to the bottomless pit over which Spider must jump. While singing, Yiyi recapitulates the events leading up to the missing *fufu* balls. The song actually advances the plot because it prophesies Spider's fate as he prepares to jump. Spider's nasalized rendition of the song underscores his humorous pretense that the song is about someone else and highlights the irony of his situation and trepidation about leaping over the pit.

In "Spider and Death" (10.2.3.), Spider challenges fate through a song:

> Death wants to eat,
> Death wants to eat,
> Death will never eat me.

As songs typically create sharp aural impressions, this song vividly suggests the Mephistophelean relationship between Spider and Death.

The song in "Mouse and the Adzigo Drum" (5.2.1.) serves as a personal lament and foreshadows events. In this narrative, Mouse

---

[24] Deirdre Lapin, "Story, Medium and Masque: The Idea and Art of Yoruba Storytelling," Diss. University of Wisconsin–Madison, 1977, p. 31.

[25] Philip Noss, "The Performance of the Gbaya Tale," in *Forms of Folklore in Africa*, ed. Bernth Lindfors (Austin: University of Texas Press, 1977), p. 18.

Formal Features of Trickster Narratives

rallies the audience's sympathy as he sings of his plight trapped under a heavy pot.

> 'Kpako, 'kpako, corn-making pot,
> I am trapped.
> 'Kpako, 'kpako, corn-making pot,
> I am trapped.
> I wanted to do this, wanted to do that,
> I wanted to do this, wanted to do that,
> Listen, I am trapped.
> Come, lift up the heavy pot,
> I am trapped.
> Come, lift up the heavy pot,
> I am trapped.
> The heavy pot covered me,
> My *adzigo* drum mates shall beat me today,
> I am trapped.

Since Mouse is charged with leading the drumming and dancing at his mother-in-law's funeral, his narration in song is in keeping with his given role as song-master. Like Hermes, Mouse manipulates his colleagues through song. He orchestrates their running back and forth to the house and eventually releasing him—all through the powerful medium of the song.

A second major function of songs reveals Spider's character. In "Spider Pounds Fufu" (51.1.5.), Spider shamelessly mocks his wife's stupidity in believing his ploy, while he delights in his own cleverness:

> Funɔ and her children are such fools,
> Funɔ and her children are such fools,
> Are mortar and pestle buried with the dead?
> It's pounded, it's mashed, it's taken out.

Not always is trickster's mockery aimed at others. In "The Chief and His Two Daughters" (28.2.6.), Spider pokes fun at himself. Having cleverly discovered the names of the chief's daughters, Yiyi fashions a horn to help him remember the girls' names. Predictably, the harder he plays, the quicker he forgets. The song exploits the humor of Yiyi achieving the exact opposite of what he intended. But lest we feel too sorry for the miserable Spider, in true trickster-like fashion he immediately turns the situation to his advantage.

Songs in Ewe trickster narratives are a dramatic device for focusing attention on elements within the story that the performer considers important. Usually a song comments on one or more events or relationships within the story. Sometimes it exploits the comic elements of the trickster character as he engages in good-natured mockery of himself or of a gullible victim. Songs inevitably heighten the dramatic quality and entertainment value of the performance.

Food/Sex/Excrement

A salient feature of Ewe trickster narratives, as well as many other West African trickster traditions, is the predominance of images related to food, sex, and excrement.

Images dealing with food, sex, and excrement, and the conflicts associated with these elements are rooted in nature and culture. They never appear in the narrative setting shorn of their cultural context and significance. In Ewe society, as in most Sub-Saharan societies, famine is a constant threat and cause of great suffering. The predominance of imagery related to food and famine, hence, reflects a concern with basic human needs.

Another popular motif reflecting basic human needs is sex. Closely tied to sex are images of excretory substances. Not only is there an abundance of these images in Ewe trickster narratives, but they often serve as metaphors for each other. In "The Chief and His Two Daughters" (28.2.6.), for example, honey is associated with the winning of two wives, hence, their sexual favors. In "Hyena, Goat, and Leopard" (10.2.2.) excretory substances are disguised as honey and nuts and used to entice Leopard to kill, first Goat and then, Hyena.

Underlying the predominance of images related to food, sex, and excrement is the concept of taboo. A "taboo" is a psycho-social construct associated with those objects and beliefs held sacred by a group of people. For example, in some societies eating certain animals such as pork or dog is considered taboo, as is fornicating with one's sister or mother, or pronouncing certain words. These things are simply not done for fear of provoking harmful acts from a supernatural force.

Moreover, the prohibitions associated with taboos are closely allied with the notion of what is sacred. The sacred is marked by boundaries that are a source of conflict and anxiety.[26] Boundaries by definition are "dirty" in the sense that "dirt is matter out of place."[27] The concepts of dirt and pollution are powerful ones and have deep psychological roots. Social distinctions and social roles, the metaphysical enquiry of what is part of one's being and what is not, and the social implications of what people eat and what they do not eat are all concerned with boundaries and gateways of the human body, the focus of taboos.

The trickster figure in general is often associated with the concept of taboo. Laura Makarius sees trickster as the prototype of the ritual violator of taboo,[28] as does Barbara Babcock-Abrahams:

> Since the sacred is the result of the violation of taboo, trickster is a sacred being and the founder of ritual and ceremonial life of his society precisely because he violates taboo for the profit of his group.[29]

The trickster figure in Ewe narratives predictably violates interdictions. The Ewe people have numerous taboos, such as eating snake, digging the ground without appropriate prayers, whistling at night, or speaking to someone on the way to the toilet. In the narrative universe the trickster revels in breaking taboos. He has no qualms about killing little children or old grandmothers, commiting incest with his daughter, or filling rooms with his own excrement. His exploits violate sacred norms—albeit in amusing fashion, but they are imbued with symbolic meaning stemming from the importance of the taboo construct.

---

[26]Edmund Leach, *Culture and Communciation* (New York: Cambridge University Press, 1976), p. 34.

[27]See Mary Douglas, *Purity and Danger* (London: Routledge and Kegan Paul, 1966).

[28]Laura Makarius, "Ritual Clowns and Symbolic Behaviour," *Diogenes* 69 (Spring 1970), p. 66.

[29]Barbara Babcock-Abrahams, "A Tolerated Margin of Mess: The Trickster and His Tales Reconsidered," *Journal of the Folklore Institute*, Vol. XI (The Hague: Mouton, 1974), p. 164.

Moral Endings

The formulaic endings of trickster narratives invariably include a moral or a proverb. They are a persistent feature within the trickster narrative tradition, and one which some scholars readily dismiss as merely "tag" endings. They are a stable feature of oral narratives, but their importance varies depending on whom one talks to. When asked what a particular narrative is about, Ewe people inevitably pointed out the educational function of storytelling, "Stories are used to teach children how not to behave, that is, don't do as Yiyi does."[30]

Often, the ending is explanatory in nature, recounting, for example, why the spider is found on the ceiling or why people marry invalids. Usually, the moral has some bearing on the story, but occasionally, the relationship is spurious. "The Bird with Seven Heads" (1.2.6.) ostensibly deals with a monster who makes Spider his slave. The narrative ends, however, with a bizarre explanation about why turkey's nose is so long. The ending appears to be irrelevant to the logical flow of the narrative. Since moral endings are part of the conventional formal structure of narratives, they may be tagged on regardless of any logical connection. In this instance, the performer used the irrelevancy of the narrative ending to heighten the comic effect.

Such endings can be interchanged with little or no harm done to the content of the narratives, or to the structural relationships among characters. There are standards of acceptability, however, so that "just any old moral ending" cannot be appended. For example, it would be difficult to imagine that "Spider in the Village of One-Armed Men" (21.1.3.) could end with the explanation of why turkey's nose is so long. When audience members were asked if a different ending would be acceptable, the typical response was, "The narrative does not go that way."

The rules for appropriate endings are codified in the canons of narrative performance, mutually defined and determined by the

---

[30]Paraphrased answer in response to the question, "What do these stories mean?"

audience and performer. Long-standing familiarity with the narratives and the audience's habit of hearing narratives told in a particular way are an important element in the formulation of these artistic standards. The rules governing conventional features of narrative performance are not easily verbalized because they are intuitively perceived, but the performer's artistic latitude is quite large. Daniel Crowley, in his study of Bahamian narratives, for instance, observed:

> These morals are almost never serious but provide an opportunity for the narrator to make a humorous or shocking statement in opposition to the point of the story. An example is, "Mister, I say, you shouldn't do that girl like so," after a man had righteously executed his daughter for murdering her two children and hiding their graves.[31]

Ewe performers delight in shocking their audiences in a playful manner, but they often used the moral endings to conclude on a more serious note. "Spider Commits Incest" (23.1.3.) playfully shocked the audience with the irony of Spider's actions, but the moral ending brought the narrative back to a serious social and moral plane as audiences were reminded, "That is why fathers do not have sex with their daughters."

As noted earlier, the Ewe people are fond of proverbial sayings and parables and never miss an opportunity to interject popular words of wisdom in everyday conversation. The moral summations may appear to be arbitrarily appended tag endings, but they are not extraneous in an artistic and aesthetic sense. The audience anticipates these conventional devices, for they permit the performer to display his or her ingenuity. Although the absence of a moral may not detract from the overall plot and development of the narrative, the absence of a moral at the end of a narrative would definitely be noticed and would call into question the performer's ability to spin a good tale.

---

[31]Crowley, p. 35.

CHAPTER FIVE

Metaphor and Meaning in Trickster Narratives

Formal properties of trickster narratives may help identify and describe the category of trickster narratives, but formal properties alone do not shed much light on questions of meaning and interpretation. "Meaning" is a problematic and heuristic concept provoking scores of debates and theories but eliciting little consensus among scholars.

A seminal work in the study of meaning was C.K. Ogden and I.A. Richards's *The Meaning of Meaning*. These two pioneers offered twenty-two definitions of the word "meaning" from different theoretical viewpoints. These included:

- an intrinsic property
- the connotation of a word
- the place of anything in a system
- that to which the use of a symbol refers
- that to which the user of a symbol believes himself to be referring.[1]

These definitions reflect the different criteria and frames of reference offered by specialists in various disciplines. A philologist, for example, may define "meaning" in terms of truth and falsehood, while a literary critic may focus on readers' aesthetic responses.

"Meaning" in oral narrative performance is not a homogeneous concept and hence, may benefit from perspectives gleaned from various disciplines with differing but related points of view. Understanding the

---

[1]C.K. Ogden and I.A. Richards, *The Meaning of Meaning* (New York: Harcourt, Brace, and Co., 1938), pp. 186–87.

meaning of any of the narratives in the present collection involves discerning the relationships among many interrelated variables. Ultimately, "meaning" is the final step of the communication process and not the starting point.

"Meaning" is an interactional concept referring to relationships among constituent parts. Conceptually, it has a triadic structure:

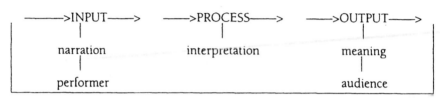

Fig 5-1

The narrator provides the input, i.e., the narration of the tale, including the entire cast of narrative characters involved in the plot, and the provocative and humorous exchanges between performer and audience. Through a series of narrative stylistic devices the performer manipulates the characters into relationships with each other. The narrator consciously seeks to create patterns of images exploiting the cognitive and affective functions of language to create desired effects.

Regardless of how technically skilled a narrator may be, narratives must be interpreted and understood by the audience in order for them to perceive any "meaning" at all. In this sense, performer and audience are in complementary relationship with each other. Words strung together to form thoughts and ideas have no foreordained immutable "meaning." On the one hand, audience members react individually to the artist's words, gestures, and rhythms. On the other hand, audience members as a group experience and react to the performance event. Hence, "meaning" is as much an individual as a collective phenomenon strongly influenced by the cultural context in which a narrative is performed.

As narrative "meaning" unfolds, the teller actively evokes images for the audience to interpret. A schematization which implies the separation of roles between listener and teller is misleading. The performance relies on the active participation of both audience and performer. Although there is a difference in emphasis and degree in the roles narrator and audience play at various stages of the performance, the interchange is a dynamic and continuous one. Consequently, "meaning" is continually in the process of being created until the performance ends.

Since we are dealing with trickster narratives, our primary concern is with discourse. Narrative discourse does not consist of truth theorems or proofs of logic. Rather, it comments on aspects of human activity and does so through allusion. In trickster narratives few direct observations are made, for example, about human relations. Instead, such information is conveyed through analogical processes where parallels are drawn between images. "Meaning" as an interpretive act offers a wide range of possible signification that varies from performer to performer, narrative to narrative, audience to audience.

In this chapter, a semiotic model of inquiry into Ewe trickster narratives is proposed. A semiotic model is not intrinsically better than any other model. The function of a model is not to propose an analytically "correct" structural description. Rather, it describes how sequences and images have form and ultimately create "meaning." The model which follows is based on the concept of "sign-function" and posits the belief that "meaning" in a work of art is rooted in interrelated patterns of images. It is in the interstices of these multiple patterns that key relationships are specified and significance is perceived.

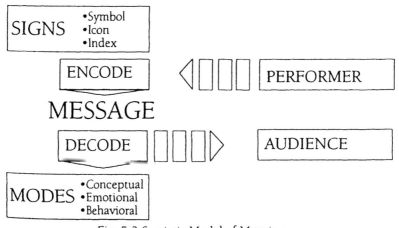

Fig. 5-2 Semiotic Model of Meaning

The proposed model is process-oriented. "Meaning" results from the interaction of signs, performer, and audience. The performer encodes the signs as "messages" which the audience decodes as "meaning": cognitive, emotional, and behavioral.

Several key concepts underlie this model. "Text" is the artist's interpretation and experience of the words and actions communicated in performance. In the realm of narrative performance, a performer's text is his or her rendition of a story featuring both the discursive and non-verbal elements of storytelling, including pauses, random remarks, mispronunciations, self-corrections, gestures, dance movements, and other rhythms. The text is transferred into the written mode for reasons of necessity and convenience but no inherent link between the two forms is presupposed. The written text is intended only to reproduce for the reader as near an approximation as possible of the original performed event.

"Signs" are the building blocks of text. They are the elementary linguistic units and images a performer evokes in the minds of the audience through words and gestures.

Distinguishing among different types of signs, there is the "index" based on a cause and effect relationship which orders the audience's anticipation of events. For example,

> Yiyi saw Wawuie return with food.

The "icon" is based on a perceived resemblance between the sound-image and the concept. For example, the sound an Ewe rooster makes when crowing is,

> kɔkɔliakɔɛɛ!

A "symbol" has an arbitrary or conventional relationship between its expression and content. Honey, for example, in Ewe narratives is often a symbol for sex. Images that are symbols tend to be characters or objects and have strong connotative potential, such as food or excrement.

"Code" is the set of internalized rules used by the performer and understood by the audience to transform one medium of a sign system to another.[2] Specifically, the Ewe language is the code used by narrators in this collection.

"Message" is the nexus of relationships among signs. It is the locus of patterned images and narrative devices that the narrator employs to juxtapose images and create intricate webs of meaning. "Message" is not synonymous with "meaning." It is part of a communication process that is dual in nature. Indices, icons, and symbols are encoded by the performer as "message," while the encoded message is decoded by the audience and simultaneously interpreted and understood as "meaning."

Moreover, "meaning" has three dimensions or modes of communication: cognitive, emotional, and behavioral. The cognitive mode is what the audience conceptually interprets as "theme." The emotional mode centers on the audience's affective responses, such as laughter, joy, and sadness, and includes as well, nonverbal responses such as clapping, dancing, and facial expressions. The behavioral mode includes those higher order lessons the audience members understand as proper behavior and which they internalize into proper modes of conduct. Since the three modes are closely intertwined, it is only for the purpose of analysis that the modes will be separated and discussed as independent aspects of "meaning."

In this chapter, we will focus primarily on the conceptual mode, that is, the cognitive perception of images which the audience interprets and understands as "theme."

Theme

Often, thematic content in narrative art is based on oppositional concepts such as justice and injustice, life and death, harmony and disunity. Or, themes can refer to categories of relations such as proper relationships among kin, concern with the natural order, social harmony, and respect for traditional values. In each case, a concern with the normative order is implied. For example, the concern with life

---

[2]D.J. Allerton, *Essentials of Grammatical Theory* (Boston: Routledge and Kegan Paul, 1979), p. 21.

and death may not appear to be a particularly compelling theme, but the concepts of life and death refer directly to the reaffirmation of the natural order and may function in some instances thematically.

"Theme" is primarily a cognitive function. For the most part, cognitive meaning remains preconscious. When prompted, audience members may clearly state the thematic content of a narrative but that occurs rarely. The reason for this is that cognitive elements of meaning lie under the surface. Empson observed,

> I do not think that (all) these meanings should pass through the mind. . . . What is gathered is the main form and rhythm, and a general sense of compacted intellectual wealth, of an elaborate balance of variously associated feeling.[3]

Thematically, traditional narratives explore human behavior and those organizing principles which structure society and create order from chaos. Accordingly, trickster narratives provide an implicit scheme for ordering human behavior by providing a paradigm of proper behavior.

Trickster figures consistently transgress accepted social norms and abuse the established order. Trickster engages in amoral acts of the most outrageous kind—he assassinates grandmothers ("Goat in the Village of Animals"), he lies to his mother-in-law about stealing *fufu* ("Spider Jumps Over the Pit"), and he enters into marriage under false pretenses ("Spider and the Kente Cloth"). By proposing incorrect models of behavior, the narrator actually presents normative ideals and values in negative form. The audience members, intimately familiar with trickster figures and trickster narratives, interpret the social categories and provide appropriate positive response patterns. In essence, trickster narratives make intelligible certain cultural belief patterns, values, and ideals and form a charter by suggesting normative opposites.

In most cases, trickster's antisocial behavior is punished. Spider's incestuous relations with his daughter lead to her death ("Spider Commits Incest"); marrying the chief's daughter under false pretenses

---

[3]William Empson, *Seven Types of Ambiguity* (London: Chatto and Windus, 1931), p. 94.

leads to Spider's own death ("Spider and the Kente Cloth"); lying about stealing *fufu* leads to Spider's ignominious fall into the pit ("Spider Jumps Over the Pit"); stealing Yiyi's intended wives leads to Lizard's painful assault by bees ("The Chief and His Two Daughters"). The perils of improper behavior and social relations among friends, in-laws, husbands and wives, fathers and daughters—are a major thematic preoccupation in these narratives.

Social criticism and the concern for normative behavior is made all the more palatable by the animal guises trickster characters wear. The criticism and warnings aimed at human folly are more readily accepted by audience members when the social concerns are couched in narrative terms and the allusions are implicit rather than direct.

Metaphor

The complex web of themes spun in the course of narrative performance operates according to laws inherent in the semiotic process. Images that function as signs in verbal art enter into patterned relationships as they are brought into proximate relationship with other images and create metaphors. In this juxtaposition of patterns, individual images and groups of images assume significance as the audience discerns relations of analogy (metaphor) and contiguity (metonymy). Metaphoric process, which constitutes the phenomenon of sign transformation, utilizes the potential ambiguity inherent in all signs. As a structuring principle of sign transformation, ambiguity enables signs to function as symbols, which in turn, are perceived as narrative themes and add aesthetic richness and rhythmic vitality to the narrative.

Ambiguity, which in the language of science may give rise to untenable contradictions, in narrative art often creates fortuitous dramatic effects. Ambiguity is a structural tool and a transformational device that strengthens a sign's potential aesthetic value. Drawing upon the multiple aspects of metaphoric process, such as ambiguity and symbol formation, let us examine how metaphor operates in Ewe trickster narratives.

An underlying belief in all cultural systems is the existence of correspondences between disparate phenomena on several planes of reality.[4] This view posits the indissoluble unity of the universe. Schneider advances this argument by observing that rhythms and modes allow relationships to be established between different planes of reality. These rhythmic patterns are based on spatial, numerical, or positional similitude; cause and effect, and other metonymic relationships. Cirlot wrote,

> ... phenomena are brought together by virtue of their having a "common rhythm," hence one finds that such elements as the following are correlated: musical or cultural instruments and implements of work; animals, gods, and heavenly bodies; the seasons, the points of the compass, and material symbols; rites, colours, and offices; parts of the human body and phases in animal life.[5]

The exploitation and juxtaposition of common rhythms among objects, forces, concepts, and images of these phenomena relate directly to metaphoric activity in oral narratives. In "Monster Flogs Spider" (29.1.5.), for example, the opposition between nature and culture is symbolically embodied in the characters of Spider and Monkey respectively. Spider, who is hotly pursued by Monster, finds a welcome helpmate in the form of Monkey posing as a blacksmith. Spider is limned as an untamed natural force fleeing for his life, while Monkey, skilled in the art of smithing, helps Spider outwit and defeat Monster. Metaphorically, nature and culture join forces to restore harmony which has been temporarily disrupted by the intrusive and unwelcome presence of the monster.

Dissecting this brief narrative into its component parts, it becomes apparent that the relationship between Spider and nature is based on the analogous comparison of two objects with a common rhythm, in this case, untamed force. On the other hand, the symbolic association "Monkey/culture" is based on a metonymic relationship specified in

---

[4] J.E.Cirlot, *A Dictionary of Symbols*, trans. Jack Sage (London: Routledge and Kegan Paul, 1967), p. xxxiii.
[5] *Ibid*.

terms of the general (culture) and the particular (Monkey as blacksmith).

The interpretation of metaphorical signs relies on culturally accepted rules. The principles governing these rules reflect the dual function that metaphor serves within the cognitive and the affective domains. The cognitive function of metaphor structures human thought by juxtaposing images and is a primary and readily observable phenomenon. Yet, to define metaphor as a cognitive structure alone is to overlook metaphor's directional impulse. Admittedly, metaphor is a cognitive structure, but it derives its power and thrust from evoking an emotional response.

The operational view of metaphor used in this analysis is based on a paradigm developed by Philip Wheelwright for studying the tension in metaphorical structures. Wheelwright discusses at length the features of tension in language systems. In verbal language systems semantic tension operates on many levels. He analyzes metaphor in terms of concrete and abstract meanings. Borrowing I.A. Richards's terminology, he uses the concepts of "tenor"—the inchoate abstract idea (semantic content)—and "vehicle"—the concrete element described (semantic carrier). Together, "vehicle" and "tenor" are fundamental and consistent units of all metaphorical expression.[6]

Etymologically, the word "metaphor" implies motion (phora) and change (meta).[7] The relationship between tenor and vehicle creates a third term, the concept of an idea different in significance from either of its two constituent parts. The combination of the two terms is greater than the sum of its parts. In the interplay between "tenor" and "vehicle," a dialectical transformation of constituent parts occurs. This is the "interaction view of metaphor" proposed by Max Black. It posits a system of associated commonplaces shared by both the tenor and vehicle.

In the example Wheelwright offers —"man is wolf"—the wolf's perceived fierceness and scavenger nature are viewed in relation to the

---

[6]I.A. Richards, *The Philosophy of Rhetoric* (New York: Oxford University Press, 1965), pp. 99–101.

[7]Philip Wheelwright, *Metaphor and Reality* (Bloomington: Indiana University Press, 1975), p. 69.

principal subject, man. It is immaterial whether these characteristics are true. What is essential is that they are readily and freely evoked.[8] Since metaphor selects only certain features within the total range of possible associations, excluded in this case would be features such as a wolf's presumed link with dead humans, his color, or his developed sense of smell. Thus, in the "interaction" view, metaphor organizes features of the principal subject or tenor by selecting, emphasizing, or suppressing certain traits. These attributes or features may be culturally specific or universally shared, or they may express established arbitrary commonplaces.

The interaction view is in sharp contrast to the "substitution" theory of metaphor, which views metaphorical expression as merely a substitution for a literal expression. Importantly, it suggests an "improper" or "abnormal" use of the literal expression, hence the popular definition of metaphor as "saying one thing and meaning another."[9]

Similarly, the "comparison" view of metaphor, closely related to the "substitution" theory, suggests an underlying resemblance between two terms where the similarity is implied rather than stated, as it would be in a simile or comparison.

The inadequacies of both the substitution and comparison views of metaphor are obvious. If metaphors were nothing more than substitutions, we would have no difficulty understanding or explaining the following example from T.S. Eliot:

> ... frigid purgatorial fires
> Of which the flame is roses, and the smoke is briars.[10]

Since the association between the images (flame/roses, smoke/briars) is not readily apparent, the metaphoric process actively creates relationships that require interpretation based on similarity between images. In this respect, metaphorical expression is not a

---

[8] Wheelwright, p. 40.

[9] Max Black, *Models and Metaphors: Studies in Language and Philosophy* (Ithaca: Cornell University Press, 1962), p. 31-32.

[10] T.S. Eliot, "East Coker," *The Complete Poems and Plays 1909-1950* (New York: Harcourt, Brace, and World, Inc., 1971), p. 128.

Metaphor and Meaning in Trickster Narratives

substitution for a formal comparison or a literal statement of any kind. It is a dynamic and interactive process with its own distinctive capacities and limits.[11]

Food/Sex Metaphors

In Ewe trickster narratives sex and food are two of the most frequent categories of images. One of the most vivid illustrations of food used as a metaphor for sex occurs in "The Chief and His Two Daughters" (28.2.6.). Food in this instance is the honey which Spider uses to trap Lizard so that Spider may reassert his role as husband and punish Lizard for stealing Spider's intended wives. In this metaphor, honey (as vehicle) conveys two underlying and interrelated ideas, sex and a trap (tenor). An exquisite juxtaposition of images exploits the trap/sex and trap/honey dichotomies by repeating these dual images a number of times in slightly differing contexts.

Spider's scheme to win back his wives consists first of enticing the two women with the irresistible and delicious taste of honey. Honey's sweet ambrosia seduces the women and leads them to threaten Lizard with divorce if he does not provide them with the honey they desire. Spider's ability to provide honey, compared with Lizard's failure to do so, implicitly refers to Spider's sexual superiority, which Lizard seeks to emulate. The honey pot is Spider's key to victory and Lizard's downfall as he naively and painfully thrusts his tongue into the beehive.

Not only does Spider use honey to seduce the women, he traps Lizard himself with the desire for honey, thereby vanquishing his rival and affirming his own physical prowess over Lizard and winning back his wives. The sexual implications of honey are unmistakeably based on the attributive properties of both sex and honey as being "sweet" and eagerly desired by marriage partners.

This structurally simple narrative achieves complexity through the layering of images related to the trap. In effect, Spider ensnares one of the women, Akpalaboŋ, in a trap as she attempts to straddle a log

---

[11]Black, p. 37.

blocking the path in which Spider has carved a hole and inserted his penis. Although no explicit mention is made of honey as Spider seduces the woman, we are told of the sweetness of the seduction,

> She was held there enjoying it and
> she would not move away.

Later, Spider falls into a hole whose rain-soaked walls prevent his exit. The cavernous pit with slippery walls is reminiscent of a womb-like structure and conducive to evoking the sexual union Spider so eagerly awaits.

The honey pot evokes the image of a trap, which, in turn, stands in metaphorical relationship to sex, for it is not uncommon to hear sex referred to as a "trap." The image-vehicle of honey is fairly bristling with connotative secondary meanings, calling forth a host of related images, suggesting sexual union.

The intricate structuring of this narrative through the dual metaphors of honey and trap creates an aesthetic layering of metaphorical complexity. It obscures, however, the more basic underlying theme the narrative develops. The tripartite configuration of actors—Spider, Lizard, women—actually discusses in imaged fashion the relationship between husbands and wives, as well as appropriate and acceptable behavior between friends. Lizard is the culprit who violates both sets of relationships. Lizard becomes, in essence, a surrogate husband as he steals Spider's intended wives and mistreats Spider's first wife, Funɔ, whom Spider mistreated as well. As husband to the two young women, Lizard fails to adequately fulfill his conjugal duties and is thus properly punished. The dual images of the "honey pot" and the "trap" structure the narrative's development and provide the tension and unity among images so that the narrative themes may be disclosed. In this sense, metaphoric activity reveals and underscores the abiding moral and social concerns of Ewe society. The stated moral of the narrative, "This is why Lizard knocks his head on walls," is but a humorous aside not to be taken too seriously when considering the full import of this narrative.

Comparison with a variant narrative, "Lizard Loses His Tongue" (1.2.5.), illustrates how narratives with apparently similar images develop different themes. Both narratives have the following episodes in common, focused on Spider's desire for a wife:

- Spider tricks girls into revealing their names
- Spider asks Lizard to serve as his surrogate in marriage
- Lizard steals Spider's intended wives
- Spider seeks revenge

There the resemblance ends. In "Lizard Loses His Tongue," Spider cuts out the chief's tongue and places the blame on Lizard. The chief's severed tongue and Spider's bloody knife focus attention on the image of blood. Blood as metaphorical vehicle evokes the sacred authority embodied in the figure of the chief. The conflict in the narrative, apparently between Lizard and Spider, is actually between Spider and the chief. In effect, Spider challenges and displaces the chief as the authority figure in his household and in the village. By severing the chief's tongue, Spider metaphorically assumes the stature of "chief" through newly formed marriage ties.

The central metaphors in the two narratives operate somewhat differently, resulting in different themes. In "The Chief and His Two Daughters" the metaphoric relationship between honey and the trap placed the emphasis on proper marital relations defined through sex. In "Lizard Loses His Tongue," however, the focus is on power and the realignment of social roles.

A second narrative structured along categories of food is "Hyena, Goat, and Leopard" (10.2.2.). This narrative relies on elements of deception and illusion to create purposeful ambiguity in two sets of images: nuts as excrement and honey as urine. The two food images, nuts and honey, are in parallel relation to Goat and Hyena through the imaged association between nuts and Goat's excrement on the one hand, and honey and Hyena's urine on the other. Ostensibly, the story is about Hyena and Goat's efforts to kill each other, but the illusion involving categories of food and non-food actually focuses attention on the marital relationship between Goat and Leopard.

This narrative portrays the problems and paradoxes of marriage. Goat and Leopard are married but their marriage is fragile and fraught with difficulties, for the differences between them are great. By nature,

Goat and Leopard are incompatible. Goat is a domesticated animal who has been put into the service of humans and is therefore associated with culture. In contrast, Leopard is a wild animal whose normal habitat is the bush. He does not normally live in harmony with humans and therefore, represents untamed nature.

The union between Goat and Leopard is unnatural and tenuous at best. It is based on illusion and deception, as evidenced by Leopard's believing Hyena's deception that tiger nuts are really Goat's excrement and by Goat's attempt to control Leopard through the illusion that honey is Hyena's urine.

The tension inherent in this unnatural union is paralleled in the nature of the tricks. The attempt to create the illusion that non food (excrement and urine) is real food (tiger nuts and honey) parallels Goat's attempts to domesticate Leopard through marriage.

Although Leopard is the mediator in a narrative sense, metaphorically, Hyena mediates the reconcilation between Goat and Leopard. Once Hyena is killed, the imbalance of the natural order is corrected and marital harmony is restored.

Although this example is constructed on the relationship between honey and nuts (vehicle) and marriage (tenor), the dynamic of images is complex. Purposeful ambiguity in the symbolic interplay between the images of honey and urine and nuts and excrement results in a finely balanced treatment of the theme of marital discord.

Food/Life-and-Death Metaphors

A large portion of Ewe trickster narratives deals with life and death. This is not surprising, since the images of life and death are fundamental to the natural order. Through transformation, diffusion, and concentration, the images of life and death can be represented in multiple ways. Metaphoric and symbolic processes create tensive relationships between images, lending richness, depth, and significance to these basic images.

Often, Ewe trickster narratives feature food motifs, which, not surprisingly, are related to the theme of life and death, as well as to sex.

Categories of food continuously shape structural relationships creating a dialectical tension between images. In "Spider and the Beans" (5.1.2.5.), for example, Yiyi attempts to mourn his mother-in-law's death. In spite of his ravenous appetite, he announces to the mourners his refusal to partake of any food during the course of the funeral, weeping loudly instead. Yiyi's refusal to touch food serves two functions: (1) to publicly display his grief, and (2) to demonstrate his love for his wife. In both cases, he seeks to affirm his social role in the community and prove his devotion as a good husband.

Although the context is a funeral, the image of food effects a paradoxical twist. Food, which is the sustenance of life, is at the same time a primary ingredient of funereal ceremonies and thus signals death. The ambiguity in the food metaphor,

Fig. 5-3

reaffirms life in the face of death. While the lack of food in reality can lead to death, its prominent role in the funeral ceremony also marks the end of life.

The tension inherent in the images of food/life/death is based on the relationship between food as a source of life and the attributive principle of food as a marker of death in the funeral ceremony. This narrative explores the ambiguity in the image of food in relation to life and death and uses the inherent tension in the triad of images to explore social relations in the community.

Interestingly, food in this narrative functions as a "conjunctive" symbol, that is, a symbol that can be interchanged with other symbols, rather than a "disjunctive" more localized particular symbol that cannnot be easily substituted for another. Specifically, the beans and rice that Yiyi scoops into his hat and places on his head can be interchanged with other categories of food. In other narratives we learn that Yiyi covets different food items, particularly yams and ground nuts.

Beans and rice, however, are an apt choice in this narrative because the heat used to cook the beans burns Yiyi's head, leaving him bald. Appropriately, the liquid consistency of the beans heightens the comic effect of the hot beans streaming down his head and face.

"Spider Pounds Fufu" (51.1.5.) also illustrates the interrelationship between images of food, life, and death in Yiyi stories. In this narrative Spider has a coffin made and asks to be buried in it along with a mortar, pestle, salt, pepper, and yams. Spider's feigned death permits him to rise from the dead and pound *fufu* to his heart's content. Again, ambiguity in the images of life and death creates a series of paradoxes involving the images of the coffin, food, and tarbaby.

The first paradox is established as the opposition between life and death is expressed in the image of the coffin. The coffin is an outward manifestation of death based on the metonymic relationship between corpse and container. The coffin, in turn, stands in metonymic relation to yams and other foodstuffs buried with Spider. Amusing paradoxes are built on the following sets of oppositional images:

- Spider is buried alive
- Food, the sustenance of life, is buried with him
- Spider rises from the dead to steal yams and pound fufu

A second set of paradoxes unfolds as the narrative continues:

- Buried (dead) food sustains Spider's life
- Spider steals food (life) from his family
- Spider is trapped by a "dead" object disguised as a live human

The illusion of death (Spider in the coffin) is counterposed with the illusion of life (tarbaby, a lifeless stick figure). On the other hand, food, which normally sustains life, leads to deprivation and death for Spider's wife and children because of Yiyi's extreme greed. The three metaphorical relationships revolve around the ambiguity implicit in each image:

Metaphor and Meaning in Trickster Narratives 85

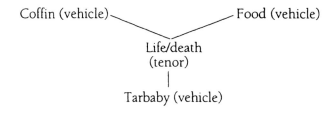

Fig. 5-4

Paradoxically, in the convoluted and inverted social order evoked in the narrative, what is normally associated with death results in life and what should bring life brings, in fact, death. The tension generated by the oppositional forces of life and death structures the narrative into a metaphysical battle of life against death, as Spider pits himself against the social order.

A final narrative explores somewhat differently the metaphorical relationship between food, life, and death. In "Spider Removes the Mill" (10.2.1) and its variant, "Spider and the Mill" (5.1.8.), the metonymic order between the mill and the grain it grinds structures the relationship between life and death. Yiyi, in a period of famine, is in pursuit of food. Yiyi is shown a mill which grinds by itself, and despite injunctions to the contrary, transports it home.

An immediate spatial opposition between bush and home establishes the poles of the narrative. The mill in the bush is an abundant source of food, while famine ravages the homestead. By transporting the mill home, Yiyi causes the images of life and death to blend in uneasy unison. The mill is placed squarely in the middle of a death-like environment. The tension between life and death is rendered all the more acute by Yiyi's excruciating pain as the mill's roots penetrate into his head, requiring his head to be cut off. By providing food for his children, Yiyi and the mill are life-givers. Yiyi sacrifices his life so that his children may live. But the mill, by killing Yiyi, is also a death-dealer.

In this narrative, the mill, as an ambiguous symbol of both life and death, is counterposed with Yiyi who is somewhat more strongly associated with life-giving images.

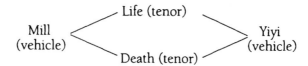

Fig. 5-5

The mill ultimately transforms death into life through the mediation of Yiyi. Yiyi, by sacrificing his own life, allows the village and his family to live, hence mediates between life and death.

In terms of thematic development, the opposition between the images of life and death is crucial. The spatial polarities between bush and home, aligned with the life and death qualities of the mill impart new significance to both the bush and the mill. In a sense, the bush via the mill is transported to the homestead where it provides food and supports life. Metaphorically, the bush has been domesticated and tamed as it is brought to the homestead to feed the famished villagers.

In the examples just seen, one image, food, simultaneously suggests opposite meanings. In other narratives, dissimilar images are brought into parallel relation with each other so that images which initially appear to be disparate, fuse and are ultimately experienced by the audience as being identical.[12] This type of patterning called "diaphoric patterning" is rooted in parallel-image sets and is often characteristic of non-trickster narratives. When it does occur in trickster narratives, potentially complex thought-provoking themes may be created.

"The Bird with Seven Heads" (1.2.6.) combines two apparently unrelated episodes. The introductory images are non-trickster in nature and describe the actions of a bird with seven heads who terrorizes a village. The adults fail to rid the village of the vulture, but a little boy armed with a bag, sword, and a club succeeds in doing so. The second half of the narrative deals with Spider and a monster. This portion of

---

[12] Harold Scheub, "Parallel-Image Sets in African Oral Narrative-Performance, "*Review of National Literature*, 2, No.2 (Fall 1971), p. 222.

the narrative can stand alone and does so, in fact, in a variant, "Spider Refuses the Chief's Daughter" (30.2.2.).

In "The Bird with Seven Heads" Spider has a ram which he does not want to share with anyone. Monster comes along, eats Spider's ram, and in the process makes Spider his slave. The bird in Part One and the monster in Part Two are intrusive evil forces which bring death. Both are strange-looking fantastic creatures. The bird has seven heads and "looked like a cloud descending. When he hovered over a building . . . the building fell." The monster, on the other hand, rises like a phoenix from a bunch of fallen grapes, only to steal Spider's ram and prevent Spider from having a single morsel. A blending of images occurs as differences between the bird and the monster slowly diminish and the similarities between them are brought into sharper focus.

A merging of images occurs on a second level as well. The little boy and Spider are actually mirror reflections of each other. They have in common their small size, the impact of their actions on their milieu, and the nature of their task—to kill a large and powerful fantastic creature. The little boy, who lives in the human world, saves the village from impending disaster. Spider, on the other hand, straddles both the human and animal worlds, and saves, by implication, the animal world from the danger the monster poses. Both possess magical instruments which they use to achieve their goals. The boy uses a magical bag, a club, and a sword to kill the bird. Spider, in turn, uses a magical incantation to first punish, then kill the monster. Metaphorically, Spider and the boy take on the same identity as both rid their environment of an intrusive destructive force.

"Goat in the Village of Animals" (18.1.1.), one of the longest, most complex, and intriguing narratives in the collection, establishes a number of different relationships among a large cast of characters. The opening images establish conflict between the Short Man and the village of animals. The adversarial relationship casts the Short Man as a life-threatening force who beats the mighty animals to a pulp and steals their food. Simultaneously, Goat, in relation to the other animals, is an outsider because of his small physical stature and because he is a benign and passive grass-eater compared to his larger meat-eating fierce companions.

The relationship betwen the Short Man and Goat is brought into sharper focus as Goat becomes a successful hunter surpassing in ability his larger companions. The animals who initially insulted Goat and threatened to expel him from the village suddenly fear Goat because of his successful exploits as a hunter. The images of the Short Man and Goat continue to blend as each one begins to control the village through fear. We see, for example, the villagers fleeing from the Short Man, as they similarly flee from Goat in the latter half of the narrative.

The narrative unfolds along an axis of images associated with food, life, and death. The Short Man is associated with death, but he enters the second village hidden in a life-giving object, the grinding stone. Ironically, the animals, who are presumed to be good and noble providers, hence life givers, plot to kill Goat. Goat, on the other hand, a normally benign peace-loving creature, ends up destroying legions of fellow animals.

The predominance of food-related activity in the narrative develops a second set of images which fleshes out the theme. In this narrative where animals fight for their survival, the concern with food focuses attention on the manner in which they obtain and prepare food. In the first two villages, hunting and food preparation are collective activities. In a spirit of mutual concern for each other, the animals share their food and take turns guarding the village from thieves. In the third village, Goat is pitted against the collective. He does what they tell him to do, but because he does it too well, they seek to kill him. The thematic import lies in the tension generated between the two contrasting poles of conceptual thought, that is, the collective versus the individual, big vs small, animal vs human, and life vs death. This purposeful ambiguity involves the audience in a virtual conundrum. Dramatic irony results from the ambiguity inherent in images, and characters who appear to be different, in actual fact, mirror each other very closely.

Symbolic Expression and Ambiguity

In trickster narratives ambiguity plays an important role in structuring relationships between images and is a key component of the metaphoric process which ultimately develops themes.

In Ewe trickster narratives there are two different types of ambiguity. "Conjunctive ambiguity" occurs when separate meanings are jointly effective in interpretation.[13] Such is the case when oppositional complexes such as life and death are expressed in a single image such as the mill. "Conjunctive ambiguity" lends itself to the creation of comic effects when antithetical traits such as the wise and foolish, crafty and bungling, good and evil, the ridiculous and sublime are juxtaposed in a single image.

"Disjunctive ambiguity," on the other hand, features opposite meanings as alternatives in the process of interpretation.[14] Symbols often have meanings far enough apart so that they do not interfere or overlap with each other in a given context. One such example is that of excrement and its associated image of flatus. Excrement operates as a symbol in at least three narratives. In "Hyena, Goat, and Leopard" (10.2.2.) the metonymic relationship between an animal and its bodily function is used as the ploy to trick Leopard and Hyena.

In a second example, "Goat in the Village of Animals" (18.1.1.), Goat is given a *juju* which allows him to kill prey by farting bullets. It is not specified whether the bullets themselves are excrement or a magical substance. What is important is that the excretory function serves as the basis for a comparison with weaponry. The fart-triggered bullet which captures the explosive quality of the bullet as weapon and flatus as bodily function merges the two allusions into a unique comic symbol.

In a further example, "Spider Decorates Eggs" (30.1.2.) utilizes two related images of excrement. In the first instance, Spider decorates an egg, eats the rest, and leaves a room full of feces in his wake. In the

---

[13] Ernst Kris, *Psychoanalytic Explorations in Art* (New York: International Universities Press, Inc., 1962), p. 247.

[14] Kris, p. 245.

second instance, Pig excretes into the faces of his companions which quickly causes them to release him. Both images operate on the principle of disjunctive ambiguity. In the first case, the symbolic relationship between feces and the decorated egg is based on the inverse relationship between value and non-value and uses the concern with beauty and decoration as a motif to reveal the thematic concerns of the narrative.

Emphasis is placed on Spider's talents as a decorator, a motif reiterated when the animals enlist Spider to decorate their teeth. Spider's concern with beauty and decoration is, in fact, only a disguise for his more mundane concern with food. Substitution of his feces for the consumed eggs serves as a sort of trademark, similar to the thief who leaves his feces on his victim's doorstep. At the same time, the repulsive image of excrement contains certain ironic ambiguity in that feces are also considered to be private jewels in the same way that gold is often associated with excrement.[15]

In the concluding part of the narrative Pig's imprudent instructions to his friends cause his snout to be trapped in a hole while Yiyi slices away at it with a sharp knife from inside the hole. The louder Pig yells, the deeper his companions push him into the hole. Excreting in the faces of his companions ensures Pig's release. In this instance, excrement is associated with freedom, for the act of excreting causes the animals instinctively to pull away. This natural distancing effect associates freedom in a physical sense with the cessation of cruel and undeserved punishment in a metaphysical sense. Thus, the image of excrement in this narrative operates on a dual level linking two separate ideas, that of beauty and freedom. These separate and distinct associations are not integrated in any thematic sense. As a disjunctively ambiguous image, excrement is a symbol with a semantic field of alternative interpretations which simultaneously exclude, yet complement each other.

The thematic concerns in this particular narrative, centered on the cooperation and discord among animals, are reinforced in the image of excrement. On one hand, excrement as a narrative device provokes

---

[15]Cirlot, p. 99.

Metaphor and Meaning in Trickster Narratives

great hilarity and has an obvious sensory impact on the audience's sensibilities. On the other hand, it is used to symbolize an inverted social order where excrement is substituted for beauty, beauty leads to torture, pleas for assistance result in abandonment, and actual assistance leads to unbearable suffering and pain. In all three examples,

- excrement as food
- excrement as weaponry
- excrement as agent of freedom and substitute for beauty

the image of excrement operates as a disjunctive symbol whose semantic field is unique across narratives. A disjunctive symbol suggests different meanings from one narrative to the next or different meanings within the same narrative. Both types of symbols, conjunctive and disjunctive, abound in Ewe trickster narratives and both types contribute equally to the drama, humor, and wisdom of these narratives.

CHAPTER SIX

Style in Performance

As Ewe performers weave their tales of tricksterish fantasy and delight, their audiences are not passive observers. Rather, they are involved participants who anticipate trickster's every move, cheer him on in his exploits, and chide him when the occasion demands. The audience is the backdrop for the story-telling session, but more importantly, audience members are an integral part of the performance. The skilled artist engages the audience, encouraging members to participate in the performance by singing, dancing, and freely interrupting and conversing with the performer as he or she performs.

The performer involves the audience by evoking and engaging their emotions. In Chapter Five we looked at the conceptual mode of meaning, that is, the way performers create cognitive and symbolic meaning through the use of images and metaphors. We now shift our attention to the audience's internalization and interpretation of these images through their emotional involvement in the narrative communication process. Accordingly, this chapter focuses on the emotional and behavioral modes of meaning, two key dimensions of the communication model introduced earlier.

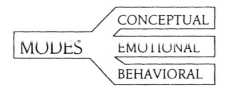

Fig. 6-1

In contrast to the conceptual mode of meaning where themes tell us what the story is "about," the emotional mode is more difficult to express in words, since emotions, by definition, are experienced. Performers have at their disposal a wide range of feelings and emotions they can evoke in audience members such as joy, sadness, sympathy, surprise, grief, compassion, and most important for trickster narratives, laughter.

Closely tied to the emotional mode of meaning is the behavioral mode. This encompasses the nonverbal aspects of performance as the artist stimulates and evokes emotional responses in audience members through the use of gestures, facial expressions, body movement, and dance. The audience, in turn, responds to the performer's cues, often singing, dancing, clapping, laughing, and otherwise commenting on the artist's performance. Again, since these elements of performance are experienced through the visual and tactile senses, it is exceedingly difficult to capture and discuss the nonverbal dimensions in writing. An attempt shall be made to do so, however, with the help of a notational system designed to account for those nonverbal aspects of performance germane to this study.

The stories narrators weave have a profound impact on the feelings and emotions of their listeners. The narrator has the ability to involve his or her listeners in the performance or to distance and alienate them. How successfully a performer engages the audience depends on the individual's unique talents and artistry, hence personal style.

In this chapter we shall take a detailed look at the artistry of a particular performer, one of many fine artists represented in this collection. The performer is Koblavi Ahadzi, an Ewe born in Bé, the old section of Lomé near the ocean. He made his living working as a security guard at the Libyan ambassador's residence and as a washerman other times. Koblavi was in his mid-forties at the time of this research and a popular storyteller greatly appreciated by Ewe audiences.

I met Koblavi one evening when I called on Chief Adjalle, the elderly and then ailing Chief of Lomé, who agreed to convene a storytelling session at his compound. Surrounding the Chief, who was seated in a large reclining wooden chair, were several children seated

Style in Performance

on the concrete floor and a handful of teenage girls and older women standing unobtrusively in the background.

As the shadows of the day grew longer and night swiftly fell, the light from a kerosene lamp greeted the dozen or so men, who arrived and assembled on two long benches facing the Chief. Each new arrival greeted the Chief in turn and took his place on the bench. As the storytelling began, one man, sporting a white t-shirt with four bright red stripes, made an immediate impact on the group with his rapid-fire speech, animated gestures, and unique ability to provoke unabashed peals of laughter. This was Koblavi.

Subsequently, I visited Koblavi many times for storytelling sessions that lasted anywhere from forty-five minutes to one and a half hours. Koblavi always invited everyone he could find who was not busy at the moment to enter his compound and participate in the storytelling session. He lived in Lomé, the large bustling capital of Togo, in a compound well enclosed behind a tall concrete wall. Since neighbors could not see what went on behind the wall, they did not come in uninvited to spontaneously join the storytelling, as they would have in a more rural setting. Children by the dozens, however, always seemed to find their way into the compound and into the circle of listeners.

On one occasion, Koblavi donned an attire that contrasted with his usual street garb. His normal workday outfit consisted of western-style long pants and a sleeveless undershirt which he wore while washing and ironing clothes in his compound. When the moment for storytelling came, he quickly improvised a head-tie and wrapped a meter-long cloth around his waist which reached down to his knees.

It is a custom among the Ewe people to mark all important occasions by covering everyday clothing with a traditional wrap called avɔ. This is a custom followed by both men and women on occasions of ritual importance. Koblavi, by following this custom, conveyed the importance of the storytelling event in the spiritual lives of the Ewe people.

The audience, seated in an open courtyard, consisted of three men on Koblavi's right and three children on his left.

Fig. 6-2

On this particular occasion, I arranged, with Koblavi's permission, to bring a video camera into the compound to tape the performance.[1] "Borrowing" electric current from the bar next door in exchange for a round of beers, I was able to record on video tape a forty-five minute storytelling session during which Koblavi told the same trickster tale he had told several weeks earlier.

The story he told was a familiar one, "Spider Removes the Mill" (10.2.1.), which recounted how a mill was uprooted from the bush and moved to the homestead to provide a steady source of food for Yiyi and his family. It is a popular narrative throughout Eweland and other parts of West Africa. The narrative is simple in structure, as are most trickster narratives, but whose comic potential was fully exploited by Koblavi.

Koblavi's keen dramatic flair breathed life into this narrative, injecting much humor and creating frequent laughter. Koblavi's artistry was most clearly revealed in his depiction of characters, choice of images, and use of language; through paralinguistic features such as pauses, and through kinesics, more commonly known as nonverbal behavior. To a large extent, Koblavi's portrayal of Spider and his adventures in the bush shared many common features with other Ewe performers' artistry and renditions of popular trickster narratives. Some

---

[1] The video equipment was kindly lent to me by the American Cultural Center in Lomé, thanks to Mr. Bob Lagama, director of the Center at the time.

characteristics, however, were unique trademarks of Koblavi's artistry alone.

Character/Situation

Koblavi's portrayal of Yiyi complemented the familiar depiction of the mischievous spider by accentuating his stock-in-trade attributes of insatiable hunger and skill at deception. Yiyi was shown as (1) motivated primarily by the desire for food, (2) having no patience to wait his turn to get food, (3) determined to trick Agɔsu into showing him the way to the mill, and (4) set on removing the mill from the bush in order to ensure a steady source of food for himself and his family. These traits served to make a caricature of the prankish spider by isolating and exaggerating his greed. As a caricature, he was obsessed by food and was doggedly determined to employ whatever means necessary to satisfy his craving.

The exaggeration of his insatiable desire for food made a normal human trait, hunger, appear robotic and machine-like. Bergson observed how laughable the human body is when it resembles a machine.[2] Although cognitively, everyone knew that Spider was an animal, metaphorically and emotionally, audience members perceived Yiyi's behavior as being human. His singular pursuit of gastronomic pleasure reduced him to an automaton. This is what Freud called the "deflection of life towards the mechanical," the belief that a living thing should never repeat itself, for wherever there is repetition or complete similarity, we always suspect some mechanism at work.[3]

Koblavi tempered the caricature of Yiyi by injecting a poignant twist. He added a heroic dimension to Yiyi by portraying him as somewhat of a culture hero as well. He did this by attributing to Yiyi a loftiness of purpose in the final scenes where Yiyi in a magnanimous gesture commands his wife to cut off his head for the sake of his

---

[2]Henri Bergson, *Laughter: An Essay on the Meaning of the Comic*, trans. Brereton and Rothwell (New York: MacMillan, 1911), p. 29.

[3]Sigmund Freud, *Wit and Its Relation to the Unconscious* (New York: Moffat, Yard, and Co., 1917), p. 337.

family's well-being. The pathos of this act was reinforced by the allusion to the famine causing his children to starve. The suggestion of Yiyi as a benevolent hero was ironic, however, in view of the unheroic traits he displayed in the rest of the narrative, hence diffusing the pathos of his plight.

Yiyi as a comic hero was framed in a highly comic situation. Narrative events focused on Yiyi's attempts to trick both Agɔsu and the mill. There were five different tricks by which Yiyi attempted to gain an advantage over his opponent. Although he ultimately lost, he enjoyed at least partial success, which added to his stature as a clever and worthy adversary, not merely a bumbling fool.

Yiyi's opponent was Agɔsu and his goal was to convince Agɔsu to lead him to the mill. Since Agɔsu had already agreed to do so, Yiyi's actions were prompted by his impatience to get to the copious source of food. His quest was rendered more plausible and legitimate by the performer's allusion to the famine conditions and threat of starvation in the village, but even this mitigating detail did not veil Yiyi's excessive impatience and immoderation. In fact, Yiyi's true greed was underscored. The performer could conceivably have portrayed Yiyi as being satisfied with collecting the flour and then leaving, as the other animals did. Instead, the juxtaposition of the starving children with Yiyi's insatiable greed rendered the comic irony of Yiyi's plight all the more acute.

Yiyi's first attempt to fool Agɔsu was to wake him in the middle of the night and tell him it was dawn. This half-hearted attempt to create the illusion of dawn was unsuccessful, so Yiyi tried again. The second time, Yiyi devised an elaborate ploy and set his house on fire to create the illusion of daylight. This act was all the more incongruous because of the extravagant effort made to create this illusion. The comic sense of this act lay in the distortion of the function of both nature and culture. Fire, which is a force of nature whose normal function is to provide heat, was misused to create merely light instead. By the same token, the house which was intended to provide shelter and warmth was destroyed for the sake of procuring food. This act heightened Yiyi's keen desperation and single-minded dedication to his all-consuming goal in life—the procurement of food.

The absurd act of burning his house emphasized Yiyi's own mortality and human weakness. By taking a force of nature, fire, Yiyi sought to create the illusion of sunlight, also a force of nature. Yiyi's attempt to perform a godlike act underscored his failure to appropriate divine power. The result was playful ridicule of his pretensions to greatness and reaffirmed his frail powers and humble origins.

Yiyi's third attempt to trick Agɔsu consisted of crowing like a rooster to convince Agɔsu that morning had indeed arrived. Once again, Yiyi distorted the familiar by imitating a rooster and almost fooling Agɔsu into believing that he was a rooster. At this point, Koblavi's almost perfect imitation of a crowing rooster thoroughly delighted the audience.

In comparison with Yiyi's three previous attempts to deceive Agɔsu, Yiyi's fourth attempt to trick Agɔsu into revealing the location of the mill was partially successful. In this episode, Yiyi cleverly pierced a hole in Agɔsu's sack, filling it with ashes which left a trail as Agɔsu walked toward the mill. Undaunted, when Agɔsu discovered the hole and dumped the ashes, Yiyi quickly devised a counter scheme.

The fifth and final trick consisted of feigning an assault by roving thugs. The rapidity with which Yiyi recovered from his previous failed attempts to lay a trail of ashes and his immediate execution of a counter ploy underscored Yiyi's superiority over his foe. Yiyi's small, yet glorious victory was all the more sweet because Agɔsu was a worthy opponent. The audience delighted in Yiyi's success over Agɔsu, whose momentary gullibility heightened the audience's own feelings of superiority. As Freud aptly observed, "... it cannot be denied ... that our laughing is the expression of a pleasurably perceived superiority which we adjudge in ourselves in comparison with others."[4]

The second half of the narrative focused on Yiyi's attempt to remove the mill from the bush, resulting in a contest between opponents of equal strength and determination. The first time Yiyi tried to remove the mill, the mill rooted in Yiyi's head. The second time, he took the precaution of first putting a tray on his head. All the elements were in place for the development of pure slapstick, which Rapp called

---

[4]Freud, p. 314.

"thrashing laughter,"[5] as Yiyi and the mill struggled fiercely and crashed loudly to the ground. Audience members identified with both duelists, but in victory there was a temptation to identify with the winner. Yiyi was clearly the hero because he sacrificed his life and successfully transported the mill from the bush.

Koblavi moulded the audience's sense of expectancy and anticipation through the use of repetition. This was most clearly evidenced in the five attempts to trick Agɔsu, a substantial number of patterned repetitions even for a trickster narrative. This copious repetition was juxtaposed with the change in the nature and degree of intensity of Yiyi's tricks. The result was a skilful choreographing of the audience's emotions ranging from sadness, pity, and empathy to laughter, surprise, admiration, and delight.

Finally, Koblavi skilfully used exaggeration to distort the familiar and render the incongruous laughably plausible. As Yiyi sought to fool Agɔsu, he attempted to transform night into day, make fire appear to be sunlight, and create the illusion that he was a rooster. When Yiyi did battle with the mill, he once again distorted the function of the natural world by expropriating the mill, a phenomenon of the natural world, and appropriating it for his own personal benefit. By removing the mill from its natural environment and implanting it into the human realm, Yiyi underscored the conflict between culture and nature and his own role as an "agent provocateur," thereby blurring the distinctions between nature and culture, human and animal, the real and the illusory. Yiyi's ability to juxtapose the incongruous and distort the familiar was in large part the basis for his success as a comic hero. Both a caricature with exaggerated traits and proportions and a superior duelist with whom the audience could identify, Yiyi made the audience laugh because they saw themselves reflected in Yiyi.

---

[5]Albert Rapp, *The Origins of Wit and Humor* (New York: E.P. Dutton and Co., Inc., 1973), p. 11.

Language/Style

Typically, language reflects the performer's origins, cultural influences, and immediate social environment. Two performers born in the same region, living in the same village, telling the same story to the same audience will more than likely tell the story in different ways. The differences result from differing language styles.

Style is not used in the sense of an ornament or trapping, nor is it limited to the spoken word. Rather, style is the product of a social situation and the relationship between language users.[6] Style as it relates to Koblavi's performance has two dimensions: first, verbal speech patterns, and second, paralinguistic and nonverbal features. Koblavi's speech was most notably marked by extremely rapid delivery. This resulted in a great deal of elision between words. People outside of Lomé had difficulty understanding him but in his milieu in Lomé, audiences had no trouble at all.[7] Even to an outsider, his vivacity and lively demeanor translated clearly. Moreover, his rapid delivery was interspersed with an effective use of pauses. Throughout his narration, Koblavi maintained a high level of suspense by first dropping his voice, thereby seeming to bring his narration to an abrupt halt, then, after sustaining a lengthy pause, he would suddenly resume his narration in his usual quick pace.

Koblavi made use of different tempos of narration to distinguish between characters. When Agɔsu was speaking, Koblavi spoke slowly and deliberately, corresponding to Agɔsu's mature bearing and years of experience. This contrasted with Yiyi's clipped and breathless speech. The panting quality of Yiyi's speech vividly conveyed his impatience to get to the mill and his determination to let nothing stand in his way.

Equally characteristic of Yiyi was his nasalized speech, purposefully exaggerated by Koblavi and emphasizing the growing tension in Yiyi's comic desperation:

---

[6] Raymond Chapman, *Linguistics and Literature* (New York: Littlefield, Adams, and Co., 1973), p. 22.

[7] When a tape of his performance was played to Ewe speakers not from Lomé, they admitted having difficulty understanding Koblavi.

Éwɔ lā vɔ lā!
(The flour will run out!)

and

Mākɔ yī ăʃēmē nē wōātū wɔ̄nā nyē ŋtɔ
nyē ɗēkā mānɔ ɖāɖā.

(I'll take it home with me so that it
will grind flour for me when I cook.)

Audience Rapport

An important distinguishing trait of Koblavi's narration was the close rapport he had with his audience, evidenced by his continuous dialogue with audience members, who responded with amusing observations. For example, before the narrative formally began, an audience member teased Koblavi that he was an old man (he was only 45). Koblavi responded with a long drawn out exaggerated laugh which caused everyone else to laugh because the laugh seemed to sustain itself quite independently of its originator. The laugh appeared to have a life of its own as it went on and on. It was a magical sound that drew everyone into the circle and created a bond among listeners. Koblavi commented that a man standing near the store, outside the circle of listeners, was not laughing, when an audience member quickly brought him back to the story, telling him,

EDZE DZI.
(It fell on him (Yiyi).)

The constant banter between Koblavi and the audience served several purposes. It emphasized the intimate warm feelings in the group and suggested a playful collusion between performer and audience in the shared creation of an imaginary reality. Moreover, the dialogue underscored the fact that the audience was participating in an imaginary event and, collectively, there was a tacit understanding that the events would be treated as believable and real. Lastly, the audience members served as sharp critics of the performer, demarcating the

Style in Performance

aesthetic parameters of Koblavi's performance and determining the acceptable limits of the narrator's selection and juxtaposition of images.

As Koblavi's accomplices in the creation of the imaginative tale, the audience challenged Koblavi's claims of veracity and candor. Repeatedly, audience members jestingly teased Koblavi with statements such as,

> L'EKPO ETEFE!
> (As if you saw the whole thing!)

or,

> EFO KƆMLÃ MIA BLE GE' GBE!
> (Brother Kɔmlã is really going to deceive us today!)

The constant juxtaposition between the imaginary realm of the tale and everyday reality was a prevailing pattern that underscored the shared set of expectations and closeness among audience members. Their familiarity and participation in a communal creation further prompted Koblavi to remind his audience,

> Ne ameaɖe kpɔ tefe ne eha ɖe le,
> ne no dòdò loo!"
> (If any of you were there, you should
> introduce songs!)

This further drew the audience closer together and reaffirmed the nature of the storytelling event, reminding the audience that the tale belonged to them as well and that they must participate if the tale was to succeed. The familiarity enjoyed between performer and audience was a necessary condition for laughter to occur.

At times, the audience echoed Koblavi's words and actions, thereby embellishing the storyline,

> EZI KAKA ÐE ... OBOBOBOBOBOBOBOBOBOBOI!
> (He pounded it ... obobobobobobobobobob oboi!)

> EVƆ! EYI TSI NENEA!
> (It's all over! Yiyi will remain like that forever!)

> A, DƆ LE WUI MADZO TƆTE GBƆA!
> (Hunger is killing him, but he should wait!)

Other times, the audience advanced the storyline by prompting Koblavi,

> ETE BIAE BE FIKA. . . .
> (The mill asked him where. . . .)

by correcting him,

> VƆA ŊKEKE AME ATƆE LOO!
> (It was really five days!)

or, by reaffirming what Koblavi had just said. For example, when Koblavi crowed like a rooster, the audience, obviously pleased with the imitation, said,

> KOKLOE KU ATƆI
> (Just like cock crowing!)

These audience comments were a measure of the audience's enjoyment of the narrative, hence a signal for the narrator to continue.

Lastly, audience members at times injected off-the-wall comments which by their sheer abstruseness provoked laughter,

> EYIA ŊUTƆ AFƆKA ADE LE ESIE! OHO!
> AFƆ WOAME ENE ME KOE!
> (Spider himself has six feet. Oh no! It's four!)

When asked, listeners found it difficult to explain why this last comment provoked hilarity, especially since the spider has, in fact, eight legs. The answer ostensibly lay in the metaphorical allusion to Yiyi's boundless determination and incessant trips to Agɔsu's door to awaken him. Allusion was made to the fact that Yiyi, despite his persistence and tenacity, was an animal just like the rest.

Repetition

Perhaps the most significant trait of Koblavi's narrative style was his use of repetition. Yiyi's repeated attempts to trick Agɔsu were discussed previously. Yet, another striking display of repetition was Koblavi's use of verbal phrases, adverbs, and exclamations. He was extremely adept, for example, in taking the adverb *kaka* meaning "much" or "very" and

Style in Performance

by reduplication, creating unusual dramatic effects. Koblavi said, for example, "Spider followed the trail of ashes *kakakakakaka*." Shortly thereafter, he used the same adverb again, "He followed the ashes a long way *kakakakakakakakakakakakakakakaka*." But this time he turned the phrase into a virtual melody, modulated in pitch, syllabic duration, and rhythm.

k̄a k̄a k̄a k̄a k̄a k̄a k̄a k̄a k̄a k̄a k̄a k̄a k̄a k̄a k̄a k̄a

Fig. 6-3

The correspondence between the sound and the image of Yiyi following the long trail of ashes caused wild laughter and prompted a hearty "*OOOOOOOOOOOOOO!*" meaning "You are surely exaggerating. We don't believe you!"

Koblavi was an absolute master of reduplication. No performer met in Togo during the course of this study rivalled him in using this device, much less produce sounds in such rapid succession. His knowledge of his audience and his instinctive ability to gauge how far to exploit this particular technique were clearly evident.

Koblavi's knowledge of his audience further allowed him to satisfy the audience's appreciation of exaggeration. Koblavi put exaggeration to good use when describing Yiyi's reaction to Agɔsu's bountiful cache, when he exclaimed, "*Obobobobobobobobobi*" signifying, "Will you just look at that!" Similarly, Koblavi described Yiyi putting the flour in his sack,

> Wòlɔe kaka yibe goloa yɔ. Wozi ɗe eme, zi ɗe eme, di kpo toe etoe etoe kaka . . . ebe yɔ.
>
> (He collected and collected until his sack was full. He packed and packed it; he pounded it, pounded it, pounded it . . . until it was full.)

The repetition of the verbal phrases,

> . . . Wozi ɗe eme, zi ɗe eme . . .

and

    ... di kpo toe etoe etoe

not only conveyed the vigorous and harried movement of Yiyi greedily stuffing his bag with flour, but the exaggerated intensity of the action suggested that stuffing alone was not enough. He insisted on *pounding* it to make more room!

Ideophones

The final characteristic of Koblavi's verbal narration was his use of ideophones. Ideophones are a phenomenon in African languages which invite differing interpretations as to their structure, function, and origin. Their importance has long been recognized by scholars of African languages and oral traditions. William Samarin, for example, remarked,

> Eloquence is undoubtedly best measured only by native speakers of a language. Nonetheless, I daresay that a masterful use of an African's language is probably always correlated with a generous use of ideophones.[8]

Their importance has long been acknowledged but only a handful of scholars has done serious study on this topic. Professor Daniel Kunene published an exhaustive study of ideophones in Southern Sotho. He suggested that the ideophone is a dramatization of actions or states, and that it served a predicative function primarily dramatic rather than narrative in nature.[9] Kunene also suggested coining the term "dramalogue" for the concept of ideophone, thereby adding to the perplexity surrounding this phenomenon.

Samarin, in his study of the Gbaya language in the Central African Republic, suggested that ideophones function as adverbs and are

---

[8]William J. Samarin, "Perspectives on African Ideophones," in *African Studies*, 24, No. 2 (1965), p. 117.

[9]Daniel P. Kunene, *The Ideophone in Southern Sotho* (Berlin: Verlag von Dietrich Reimer, 1978), pp. 2–3.

characterized by their ability to enter into construction with verbs. Yet unlike most adverbs, they can occur as attributives of nouns as well.[10] He rejected the characterization of ideophones as being onomatopoeic and descriptive in nature because such labels were simplistic and too vague.[11]

Although only a linguist could speak with authority about the morphological and phonemic structures of ideophones in the Ewe language, it would appear that ideophones differ from each other by their degree of specificity in reference to their predicates. Furthermore, they can be distinguished by perceived differences in the size, shape, speed, state, or condition of certain objects in motion to which they refer.[12]

In "Spider Removes the Mill" (10.2.1.) eleven different ideophones were used. Koblavi began, for example, "The tale flew *vuduvudu* and landed *kpàm!*[13] Next, as Agɔsu walked, he saw a mill grinding by itself *eglì glì glì!*[14] and he proceeded to collect a big sack of flour *ti!*[15] Determined to wake Agɔsu, Yiyi crowed like a rooster *kɔkɔliakɔɛɛ,*[16] then thrashed a bale of thatch *ekpû!*[17] to which the audience echoed *gbì!*[18] Yiyi was successful in locating the mill which sounded *keðe keðe*

---

[10] Samarin, p. 118.
[11] Samarin, p. 119.
[12] *Ibid.*
[13] *vuduvudu* suggests the running or flying movement of someone heavily enveloped in something such as many layers of clothing. The image is that of the tale running blindly and stumbling into Yiyi.
[14] This suggests a heavy grinding noise made, for example, by two stone surfaces rubbing against each other. *Glì glì glì* contrasts with *glí glí glí* which suggests something scattering.
[15] *Ti!* suggests the sound of something falling. In this case it refers to the sack stuffed full of flour falling to the ground. Although Koblavi does not say the sack falls, it can be imagined that when Yiyi tried to lift the sack, he could not, and so the sack fell making that sound.
[16] Compare this with:

kekereke	—Kpalime region of Togo
coquericot	—France
"cock-a-doodle-doo"	—U.S.A.

[17] *Kpû!* is the sound of someone being beaten.
[18] *Gbì!* connotes something heavy falling.

keɖe but when he tried to put it on his head, it fell di![19] He struggled with the mill again but this time they both crashed to the ground gbli![20] Finally, Funɔ cut off Yiyi's head gbé![21] and the story ended.

Six of the eleven ideophones referred to hitting, cutting, or falling motions. Kpàm, gbì, dì, ekpû, gblì, and tì connoted powerful, heavy, vigorous or frenzied movements; gbé was associated with an effortless sharp clean motion suggesting the trenchant blade used to cut off Yiyi's head. Only one ideophone in the narrative was truly onomatopoeic, kɔkɔliakɔɛɛ, the imitation of a rooster crowing. The other examples were associated with running or flying, vuduvudu, and grinding, gli and keɖe keɖe.

As in the case of audience comments, ideophones are not humorous in themselves. They are literary devices used to heighten dramatic tension, to accentuate certain actions, and to draw attention to certain images and deemphasize others. Ideophones convey fine nuances of meaning that exploit the tonal properties of the Ewe language. The sound symbolism and secondary associations attributed to ideophones suggest that ideophones are governed by conventional formulae and usage rather than being the result of a performer's creative whim and fantasy. If a sweet smelling flower, for example, were described in Ewe as lililililililì, the audience would undoubtedly protest vigorously.[22] Ideophones are, in effect, an enormously effective and efficient tool performers have at their disposal to develop the privileged relationship shared between narrator and audience in a culturally defined context. Not surprisingly, Koblavi generously peppered his performance with these effective dramatic devices.

---

[19] Keɖe keɖe keɖe is the sound of two objects rubbing against each other in rhythm, while dì! suggests a heavy object falling, such as a stone.

[20] Gbli! connotes two or more big masses falling in succession, not simultaneously. Gbli! also conveys the sound of a big object such as an elephant walking, suggesting its large size and perceived stature.

Compare, for example, the sounds of various objects falling, in descending order of size, weight, and loudness:

gbli!, gbì!, dì!, ti!

[21] Gbé! suggests a sharp clean cut requiring little effort.

[22] Lílílílílílílílí refers to something sweet-smelling, while lìlìlìlìlìlìlì refers to something foul-smelling.

Kinesics

If ideophones are a key to understanding subtleties of meaning, nonverbal images are equally significant. A performer like Koblavi utilized copious gestures, facial expressions, and body movements to express many subtleties of meaning. The following analysis, based on a video recording of "Spider Removes the Mill" (10.2.1.) illustrates Koblavi's virtuosity, the complexity of his art, and points up the staggering difficulties analysis presents.

In the video tape, it was puzzling that the audience did not laugh at those parts of the narrative that appeared to this author to be particularly funny, nor did the narrator's gestures seem to correspond to what could be considered the high points of the narrative. At first, these findings were attributed to the presence of the video camera and its perhaps inhibiting effect on the audience's reactions. A variant of this narrative, "Spider and the Mill" (5.1.8.) told by Koblavi several weeks earlier to a different audience showed a similar pattern of audience reactions. It appeared that something else was the cause of these discrepancies. Showing the tape to an Ewe speaker confirmed these suspicions and brought to light a suprising disclosure.[23] A detailed study of the nonverbal elements of narrative performance challenged certain assumptions about the Ewe concept of humor and led to a fascinating area of research.

The study of nonverbal aspects of performance presents a colossal challenge because of the difficulty in transposing nonverbal elements to written form. A system of notation satisfying the criteria of adequate representation and easy comprehension, despite attempts made by scholars such as Laban, Birdwhistell, and others, are still elusive. For the sake of convenience and clarity in the present analysis, stick figures were used as a notational device. The following analysis, with commentary, focuses on hand gestures and some body movements because more highly sophisticated techniques and equipment would be required to do more extensive analyses.

---

[23]Professor Yao E. Amela from the Université du Bénin in Lomé provided invaluable insights about the video recording of narrative 10.2.1.

As the following schematization illustrates, all of Koblavi's gestures generally fit into three categories: emblems, regulators, and illustrators.[24] "Emblems" are conventional gestures having a shared meaning which can be used as pause markers, thought connectors, or indicators of change in topic, such as,

Frame 6:"Woɖo koa" (Once there)

"Regulators" are related to the performer's exchanges with the audience, such as,

Frame 25: "Ne ameaɖe kpɔ teʃe ne eha ɖe le, ne no dòdò loo!" (If any of you were there, you should introduce songs!)

"Illustrators" are tied to the performer's pattern of speech and can be further broken down into six categories: demonstrators, ideographs, deictic motion, kinetographs, pictographs, and narrators. They are used to repeat, substitute, contradict, or augment information the performer conveys through his words.

"Demonstrators" accentuate and emphasize particular words; "ideographs" suggest the direction of a thought; "deictic motion" points to objects; "kinetographs" depict bodily action; "pictographs" present a visualized picture of the referent. "Narrators" augment the story line by adding new, additional, or contrary information to that already conveyed by the narrator's words, for example,

---

[24]The typology presented here is based in part on work done by Paul Ekman and Wallace V. Friesen, "The Repertoire of Nonverbal Behavior: Categories, Origins, Usage, and Coding," *Semiotica*, I (The Hague: Mouton, 1969), pp. 49–98.

Style in Performance 111

Frame 27: "Fɔfɔme yewoafɔ adzo loo."
(At dawn they will go.)

The words said, "At dawn they will go," but the gesture indicated that the destination was very far away.

The broad category of illustrators served a dual function which Scheub called "complementary" and "supplementary" systems of gesturing. He defined "complementary" gestures as being rooted in mimetic and representational forms, while "supplementary" gestures were more abstract, having lost their initial relationship to mimed gesture.[25] "Illustrators" are by far the largest category of nonverbal behavior in Koblavi's repertory and created most of the humorous effects in his performance.

The following analysis seeks to describe and interpret the elusive but critically essential nonverbal dimension of narrative performance. Initially, the purpose for doing this analysis was to illustrate in graphic form the richness of the nonverbal elements. Moreover, it was hypothesized that the nonverbal elements, in this case, gestures, served a complementary function, that is, that words and gestures closely corresponded with one another, embellishing, emphasizing, and illustrating the spoken word. As the analysis developed, a different pattern unfolded. The types of gestures in Part One of the narrative appeared to differ significantly from those in Part Two. Astonishingly, a new level of meaning encoded in the nonverbal sign system was revealed.

The tale "Spider Removes the Mill" (10.2.1.) is presented below in excerpts. Only those parts of the narrative that are accompanied by gestures are included. The full text of the narrative can be found in the appendix.

---

[25]Harold Scheub, "Body and Image in Oral Narrative Performance," in *New Literary History*, Vol. III, No. 3 (Spring 1977), p. 362.

Key: E = Emblem, R = Regulator, DM = Demonstrator, I = Ideograph, DC = Deictic, K = Kinetograph, P = Pictograph, N = Narrator

EWE TEXT	GESTURE	TYPE	COMMENTS
Part One			
(1) Yiyi kple viawo (Yiyi with his children)		P	Neutral gesture accompanying narration
(2) wókple viawo (together with his children)		DM	Emphasizes it was *all* the children
(3) be wóaku (dying)		N	The reason they were dying was because there was no food and famine had overcome them.
(4) Eyi nɔvi (Yiyi's brother)		DM	Emphasizes that it was Yiyi's brother who went
(5) ... tsɔ àðè ... tsɔ tu gbeðeka ðo gbe (decided to go hunting, took a gun, went into the bush)		K	Depicts the three actions
(6) woðo koa (once there)		E	Connecting thought
(7) ŋkeke wuiðeke (11 days)		I	Neutral gesture accompanying narrative
(8) wógblɔnɛ 'ma (that's how the story goes)		R	The audience protests, "The story indeed requires 11 days."

Style in Performance

(9) ŋkeke wuiðeke sia (11 days it is)		R	He insists, "Yes, that's what it is."
(10) eglì! eglì! eglì!		K	The sound the mill made while grinding
(11) ... tu wɔ gɔrɔɔ (it ground a heap of flour)		P	Refers to the heap of flour
(12) Eto koe va (Buffalo arrived)		I	Neutral gesture as narration continues
(13) lɔ wɔa (he collected flour)		K	Neutral gesture accompanying narration
(14) Ha va (Pig arrived)		K	Intensity of gesture increases
(15) lɔ wɔa (he collected flour)		DM	Emphasizes he collected a *lot* of flour
(16) ... megava o (no one else came)		DM	Emphasizes that *no one* else came
(17) ... lɔ wɔa (he gathered flour)		K	Shows how Agɔsu gathered flour
(18) gãa ɖe (big)		DM	The sack of flour was *very* big

(19) ti!		DM	The sack was so heavy that if it fell, it would sound ti!
(20) Kɔ va aƒeme (he returned home)		DC	Shows the direction in which he went
(21) koa (then)		E	Connecting thought
(22) kpɔtoe ƒu gbe (he threw the rest on the ground)		K	Shows how he threw the flour
(23) Obobobobobobo!		N	Implies, "This is too much. This isn't right."
(24) nu nuyuie tso (he took the goodies)		DM	Agɔsu had gotten so *much* food
(25) . . . kpɔ teƒe ne eha ɖe le, ne nɔ dòdò loo! (If any of you were there, you should sing!)		R	Interaction with the audience
(26) ne yewoayi (they should go)		DC	Emphasis is on the act of going, not the destination
(27) Fɔfɔme yewóafɔ adzo lòo (At dawn they would go)		N	Indicates how far they would have to go
(28) Fɔfɔme ɖo vɔa (Dawn approached)		I	Neutral gesture as narrative continues

Style in Performance

(29) ga wuiɖeke (11 o'clock)		DM	As if to say, "It's only 11 o'clock."
(30) meke haɖe o (day had not yet arrived)		DM	Emphasizes the incongruity of the situation
(31) tɔ dzo yi be xɔ (torched his house)		K	Expansive gesture depicting the act of torching
(32) xexeme katã kɔ nɛɛ (torched his house)		DM	Hands raised even higher. Emphasized that the whole sky was lit up
(33) "Agɔsu, kɔkɔkɔ, ŋu ke, midzo." ("Agɔsu, kɔkɔkɔ, it's day. Let's go.")		DM	Emphasizes that it's time to go
(34) Ne koklo neku atɔ gbɔ. (Let the rooster crow first.)		I	Neutral gesture accompanying narration
(35) Kɔkɔliakɔɛɛ! (Cock-a-doodle-doo!)		K	Slaps his knees 8 times after he crows, imitating the flapping wings of the rooster
(36) Kɔkɔliakɔɛɛ! (Cock-a-doodle-doo!)		K	Raises his shoulders while crowing, again imitating the rooster
(37) va mlɔ anyi (went to sleep)		DC	Shows the direction in which he went

(38) Ga me ko eʄo ga fɔʄɔme ga ene. Ne Agɔsu dzoa, Eyi dɔ alɔ. (He got up early, at 4 o'clock. When Agɔsu got up, Yiyi was still asleep.)		I	Neutral gesture
(39) . . . me kpɔe o (he didn't see him)		N	Indicates he was *thoroughly* discouraged
(40) Me yia? (Not so?)		E	Audience interaction
(41) . . . tsɔ wɔa gbɔe (Agɔsu again brought flour)		DM	Emphasizes how *again* he brought *lots* of flour
(42) Etsɔ mia yi (Tomorrow we will go)		N	Agɔsu assures Yiyi, "Have no fear . . ."
(43) Wogbɔ va ɖa ɖu . . . tsi wotsɔ ʄu gbe . . . lɔ ɖu ke (Agɔsu returned, prepared food, threw the rest on the ground)		K	Indicates the 3 actions
(44) mādɔ̄ kpɔ̄ (I will go to sleep)		DM	Slaps knee twice, emphasizes decision to go sleep at the gate
(45) . . . kɔkɔkɔ-kɔkɔkɔ (definitely, by all means)		DM	Slaps knees alternately; emphasizes his resolve.

Style in Performance

(46) aƒeme mɔnu (doorway of the house)		E	Connecting thought; gesture occurs in the pause following text
(47) (AFƆ WOAME ENE MA KOE) (HE HAS ONLY 4 FEET)		R	Audience interaction; claps 3 times in pause after audience comments. Koblavi finds this comment particularly funny and expresses his pleasure to the audience.
(48) Agɔsu ƒe goloea he no (took Agɔsu's bag and punched a hole in it)		DM	Emphasizes Yiyi punching the bag
(49) yi mlɔ anyi (he went to sleep)		DC	Shows the direction in which he went to go to bed
(50) wòdze eyome kakakakava yi ɖɔ (he followed him until he arrived at his destination)		DC	Koblavi uses his finger to trace the route
(51) Agɔsu va kpɔ . . . be "Yɔ yɔ yɔ kpɔ Yiyi flum ɖa" (Agɔsu realized and said, "Look how Yiyi has tricked me!")		N	Suggests a menace lurking behind Yiyi
(52) . . . tsɔ kpeteame vuvu kakaka . . . (. . . he took the bag and put his hand in it and shook the bag)		DM	Right hand slaps right knee, emphasizes shaking the bag

(53) edze mɔ (he took to the road)		I	Neutral gesture accompanying narration
(54) Ko dzo yi afia ʄo do nenea kakaka-kakakakakakaka (He left following the trail of ashes a long long way)		DM	4 times slaps knee with right hand, 7 times slaps knees with both hands. Emphasizes the length of the trail of ashes.
(55) . . . afia vayi se. Wotsɔ afia kpɔtɔa lɔ kɔ anyi, (, , , ashes stopped. The ashes had been poured on the ground.)		K	Shows where the ashes were
(56) O!		N	Indicates surprise
(57) Eblem! (You must be joking!)		N	As if to say, "This cannot continue!"
(58) . . . vayi tsɔ ebe yi ɖe, vayi si be . . . (he took a knife and went to cut some thatch)		DC	Shows the direction he went
(59) gãa ɖe anyi (big bale of thatch on the ground)		DM	"A *big* bale of thatch."
(60) tsi bea gbɔ (club was lying near the thatch)		K	Koblavi rises from his chair to indicate he went to get the club

Style in Performance

(61) *ekpū! kpū! kpū!*		DM	Imitates Yiyi vigorously pounding the bale of thatch
(62) Agɔsu be, "Avū! Tɔte mava, tɔte mava." (Agɔsu said, "You scoundrels! Wait! I'm coming!")		DC	Shows the direction in which he's going
(63) "Avū, mele wò zɔ. Midzó." ("You fool! I caught you this time. Let's go.")		DM	Agɔsu's emotional outburst
Part Two			
(64) Ko evɔ (Then)		E	Connecting thought
(65) Eye kplɔ Agɔsu ɖo (Yiyi followed Agɔsu)		DC	Indicates direction in which he went
(66) "... mīlɔ̄ ēwɔ̄ mīdzō lā" ("Let's collect the flour and leave")		DM	Exhorts Agɔsu to gather flour and leave
(67) "Gbɔdzi blewu!" ("Be patient!")		DM	Agɔsu's exhortation to be patient
(68) *Mhū!*		N	Implies, "To hell with you!"
(69) "Éwɔ̄ lā vɔ̄ lā!" ("The flour will run out!")		DM	Conveys Yiyi's desperation with which this is said.

(70) ". . . kpoo la." (. . . wait.)		DM	Agɔsu's calmness contrasts strongly with Yiyi's impatience.
(71) Koa elā mawo dzo vɔ keŋ koa (Then these animals left)		K	Neutral gesture indicating motion of animals leaving
(72) . . . vayi tsɔ wɔa lɔ (he went and collected flour)		DC	Shows direction Agɔsu went
(73) Wòzi ɖe eme, zi ɖe eme (He packed it, packed it)		DM	Emphasizes packing motion
(74) di kpo toe, etoe, etoe (he got a club and pounded it, pounded it, pounded it)		DM	Vigorous gestures showing Yiyi pounding the sack of flour to make more room
(75) Ewɔa yɔ vɔ koa (the sack of flour was full)		DM	Shows how full the sack was
(76) . . . yemagba dzodzo gbe o (he was not leaving)		DM	Indicates his resolve not to leave
(77) me' afia dɔ gbe (the mill will not sleep here today)		DM	This is a challenge to the mill as if to an enemy
(78) aƒeme (home)		DC	Shows where he's going to take the mill
(79) Yedzó loo (Agɔsu said he was leaving)		DC	Hand gesture indicates his intention to leave

Style in Performance

(80) Ko Agɔsu dzó le Eye gbɔ (Then Agɔsu left Yiyi there)		I	Neutral gesture accompanying narration
(81) té xedro (he put the mill on his head)		K	Shows how he put the mill on his head
(82) do ha ɗa (he started to sing)		I	Indicates beginning of song
(83) Eye, ne gbugbɔm da ɗio, Eye, ne gbugbɔm da ɗi . . . (Yiyi, put me down, Yiyi, put me down . . .)		R	Interaction with audience, establishes the rhythm by slapping his knees
(84) Agɔsu novi Yiyia, negugbɔm da ɗi (Agɔsu's brother, put me down)		R	Interaction with audience, claps his hands and begins dancing the *agbadza*
(85) *Yoooooooooooo!*		I	Marks the end of the song
(86) tó kè, tó kè (the mill rooted, rooted)		K	Indicates the action of the mill rooting in Yiyi's head
(87) megate' afɔ ɗem o (he could not take a step)		K	Indicates Yiyi's inability to walk
(88) tsɔm da ɗi (put me down)		DM	Mill exhorts Yiyi to put him down

(89) ètéa tíi kpó dze anyigba (the mill jumped to the ground)		K	Illustrates how the mill jumped off
(90) "Avù, le blem!" ("You scoundrel! You must be joking!")		N	Implied threat, "You've got another thing coming. Just you wait!"
(91) Me 'so wòyi ... (I will take you ...)		DC	Shows direction he will go
(92) afianu (tray)		P	Refers to the tray he puts on his head
(93) tso téa kɔ d'anyi (he took the mill from the ground)		K	Shows the action of picking up the mill
(94) keδe keδe keδe		DM	Koblavi's head moves up and down, imitating the movement of the mill
(95) do ha δa (he started to sing)		I	Indicates the start of the mill's song
(96) Yiyi, ne gbugbɔm da δi, Eyiyie, ne gbugbɔm da δi (Agɔsu's brother, Yiyi, put me down, Yiyi, put me down)		R	Audience interaction; Koblavi marks the rhythm by slapping his knees

Style in Performance

(97) Be Agɔsu nɔvi, Yiyie, ne gbugbɔm da ɖi (Agɔsu's brother, Yiyi, put me down)		K	Koblavi claps his hands; audience interjects *kakakaka kaka* as rhythmic markers.
(98) Nye me wɔe ne To . . . (I did it for Buffalo . . .)		R	Audience interaction. Koblavi makes a musical instrument of his body by creating a rhythm slapping his left shoulder with both hands.
(99) tsɔ téa dro yi aƒeme (he took the mill home)		I	Neutral gesture accompanying narration
(100) wotsɔ va aƒeme (he took it home)		DM	Emphasizes action of taking the mill home
(101) ètéa to ke 'ta (the mill rooted in Yiyi's head)		K	Shows how the mill rooted
(102) mete' téa drom o (he couldn't get the the mill off)		DM	Emphasizes the mill's tenacity
(103) *gbli!*		DM	Emphasizes the effort he's making to get the mill off his head
(104) ". . . va, ta gbagba wò . . ." (". . . come you flathead")		DC	Indicates where Funɔ should go. Term is an insult but said with some endearment.
(105) "Me 'so nu gbogbo gbɔ . . ." (I brought you all these things)		I	Neutral gesture

(106) Funɔ va gbɔ (Funɔ came)		I	Neutral gesture
(107) Wókɔkɔe (They raised it)		K	Shows action of trying to lift the mill
(108) Eyi kple téa koe kɔ dzi (Yiyi and the mill rose up)		DM	Emphasizes how firmly rooted the mill was in Yiyi's head
(109) newo wɔe leke, ao . . . (do like this, no . . .)		K	Yiyi instructs Funɔ how to cut off his head
(110) ta nam (cut off my head)		K	Further instructions about how to cut off his head
(111) hetso ne Ye gbé! (she cut off Yiyi's head gbé!)		K	Refers to how Funɔ cut his head
(112) aƒeme (home)		DC	Shows direction Funɔ went
(113) tuna wɔ, blema té, ye ŋutɔ tuna wɔ wólɔna (it ground flour in the olden days by itself; it ground and they collected it)		K	Shows how mill used to grind and how people used to gather the flour

Out of a total of 113 gestures, there were five emblems, eight regulators, and 100 illustrators.[26] These categories are not mutually

---

[26]The breakdown of gestures by type in each of the two narrative parts is as follows:

Style in Performance

exclusive, since there is considerable overlap in the function of a particular gesture at any one time. For example, in Frame 91 "metsɔ wo yi" (I will take you) can be both a deictic motion and an ideograph. On the other hand, the same gestures can serve different functions in different contexts. The following gesture, for example,

can be a pictograph referring to the heap of ground flour (Frame 11), an ideograph narrating Buffalo's arrival (Frame 12), or a demonstrator (Frame 69) emphasizing Yiyi's fear that the flour will run out. For purposes of classification, the significance of each gesture was labeled by its primary context and usage.

The obvious feature of nonverbal patterns in this narrative performance is the predominance of illustrators. The narrative, which has two parts, has slightly more gestures in the first half (63) than in the second half (50). There is a notably higher number of narrators in Part One (10) than Part Two (1), which is significant from a dramatic point of view. Gestures having a narrative function generally tend to add more information than words alone convey and thereby amplify the growing tension in the tale. In addition, there were slightly fewer "demonstrators" in Part Two, which contributed to an overall lack of

	PART 1	PART 2
Emblems	4	1
Regulators	4	4
Illustrators	55	45
Demonstrators	20	15
Ideographs	6	7
Deictic Motion	7	7
Kinetographs	12	13
Pictographs	2	1
Narrators	8	2
TOTAL	63	50

intensity and energy accompanying the gestures in the second half, the exact opposite of the first half.

These disparities led to an interesting observation. Watching the video tape and reading the transcribed narrative, there appeared to be two high points in the narrative: (1) Yiyi's successfully tricking Agɔsu by clubbing the bale of thatch, and (2) the cutting off of Yiyi's head crowned by the firmly ensconced mill. Somewhat surprisingly, Yiyi's beheading was rendered in a calm, undramatic, and restrained fashion. Koblavi portrayed the decapitation itself with a kinetograph devoid of intensity and vigor and was accompanied by no laughter from the audience.

(Frame 111)

Similarly, when Yiyi tried to shake the mill loose,

(Frame 112)

there was a fairly animated gesture, but again the audience did not laugh.

It became apparent, after closely analyzing the video tape, that the climax of the narrative, from the audience's point of view, was Yiyi tricking Agɔsu with the bale of thatch. Leading up to this moment, Koblavi's gestures related to trickery grew steadily in intensity and exaggeration.

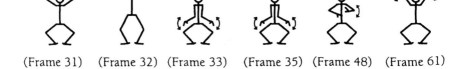

(Frame 31)   (Frame 32)   (Frame 33)   (Frame 35)   (Frame 48)   (Frame 61)

Style in Performance

The final episode in the series, Frame 61, reached a feverish pitch when the audience, in perfect rhythmic harmony with Yiyi, echoed each blow of his thrashing club *ekpū*! with a resounding *gbi*! followed by much laughter.

After that moment, there was a noticeable shift in tone, humor, and level of audience involvement. In the second half of the narrative, attention centered on Yiyi's greedy nature, as Yiyi conveyed his growing concern that the flour would run out and his growing impatience with Agɔsu telling him to be calm.

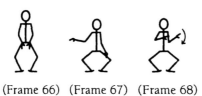

(Frame 66) (Frame 67) (Frame 68)

On the other hand, Frames 73 and 74 highlighted Yiyi's efforts to pack the flour in the sack.

(Frame 73)   (Frame 74)

Apart from these two series of animated images, Koblavi's style of narration in the second half was fairly subdued and evenly paced with no dramatic climaxes. The audience, nonetheless, was intently involved in the unfolding events. The nature of their involvement, however, was different from that in the first part. The key to the audience's mood and reaction to Yiyi's plight was in Frame 86 when Koblavi said, "The mill rooted in Yiyi's head."

(Frame 86)

Instead of laughing or making quips, the audience softly moaned, "Ooooooooooooo." Their reaction was one of sadness and sympathy for Yiyi, not joyful glee at the mill's successful retaliation. In fact, it appeared as if Yiyi's fate of having a mill rooted in his head was tragic, not comic.[27] This would also explain the anticlimactic nature of the gesture in Frame 111:

(Frame 111)

Yiyi's head was cut off because it had to be cut off, and in the audience's mind, there was nothing funny about that. By the same token, the tragedy was not great enough for the audience to feel too sad about the turn of events. Yiyi's beheading was necessary but he did not become a martyr as a result. As an observer remarked, "The narrator did not say Yiyi died." Indeed, Yiyi never really does dies; he always turns up hale and hearty in subsequent adventures.

Audience involvement was also noticeably different in the second half by virtue of the songs. Twice Koblavi sang about the mill telling Yiyi to put him down. The audience members, who in other narratives initiated the songs, in this instance were led in song by Koblavi. It was he who guided the audience, drew them in, and set the tone for the events which followed.

The choice of songs was an important element in this performance, for the accompanying dance was the *agbadza*. Traditionally, *agbadza* is danced in preparation for war or at a funeral. It suggests danger and the menacing approach of the enemy. An ostensibly serious image for a playful trickster narrative, the song sung twice indeed suggested imminent danger. Although the words of the song made no allusion to death and danger, the cultural context of the performed song and dance suggested, on a deeper psychological level, the menacing danger which Yiyi faced. The significance of the *agbadza* song and dance lay in the

---

[27] The tragic character of this scene was suggested by Prof. Amela.

suggestion of death as the enemy. The song was sung from the point of view of the mill, which was highly personified throughout the narrative, and thus there was a subtle dual meaning at play. Removed from the bush, the mill would die in a sense to the natural world. At the same time, Yiyi was warned that he had better prepare himself to do battle with death, suggested by the image of the mill as enemy.

In this fusion of words, song, dance, and gesture, a complex and rich interplay of suggested meanings added a thoughtful dimension to this narrative. The addition of the somber menace of death, suggested nonverbally by the *agbadza*, did not make this narrative any less a trickster narrative. It did, however, point out the expansive limits of the trickster narrative to allow for wide variation in form.

In "Spider Removes the Mill" the emotional and behavioral aspects of meaning were largely conveyed by Koblavi's physical gestures, movements, dance, eye contact, and overall rapport with the audience. These analytically less tangible elements contributed immensely to the energy, vivacity, and appeal of Koblavi's artistry and made his performance compelling. In turn, the audience signalled their approval and appreciation of Koblavi's performance through their spirited laughter and spontaneous singing and dancing.

Interpreting humor and laughter, however, can be very difficult. What appeared to be burlesque comedy in a Western sense in the images associated with the mill rooted in Yiyi's head, the subsequent crashing to the ground and the chopping-off of Yiyi's root-laden head were amusing to the Ewe audience, but did not cause hilarious side-splitting laughter. Quite to the contrary, the images conveyed slightly tragic overtones.[28]

In this particular narrative there were several different sign systems working in complementary relationship to each other. Overlaying the performer's spoken words were nonverbal gestures, tones, and rhythms

---

[28]An example of the differences in cultural perceptions of humor concerns movies shown in Togolese cinemas. When a Togolese audience watched an American movie about an orphan and saw the orphaned child crying, the audience burst into loud laughter. Contrary to appearances, the audience was not insensitive and without feelings. Rather, they wondered what the filmmakers had done to make the child cry!

which signalled a parallel but opposite meaning to that conveyed by words alone. Each system interpreted independently of the other would have led to conclusions quite different from those obtained when interpreted together. Without the benefit of nonverbal signs, this tale could easily have been construed as a simple tale of the comical misadventures of a trickster hero. Missing, however, would be the dramatic and poignant air of tragedy marking the trickster's fate.

This example argues strongly for the necessity to interpret all the sign systems, verbal and nonverbal, in dramatic performance. It is only through an integrated and comprehensive look at the communication system operating in narrative performance that complementary shades of meaning that lay beyond spoken words may be perceived.

Clearly, the intricacies of meaning are deeply layered. It is through the close interaction between listeners and performer that the audience's emotions are stirred and the multiple layers of meaning are evoked and understood.

Stylistically, some performers are better able to arouse emotional responses and create thrilling and highly charged dramatic performances. Koblavi Ahadzi was certainly one of the brightest illustrations of a master artist at work.

CHAPTER SEVEN

Why Trickster?

Viewed across cultures, trickster narratives are readily found in the cultural traditions of many different peoples throughout the world. Some traditions are more replete and elaborated while others are less so. In either case, the trickster phenomenon is extremely widespread. As a result, it is important to understand the larger context of narrative trickster characters, that is, their significance in a symbolic and mythic sense that may shed light and help explain the psychological and cultural needs the trickster fulfills.

There is general agreement among scholars that the trickster plays an important psychological role. It has been understood since Aristotle, for example, that people go to see tragedies on the stage because they vicariously empathize with the protagonist and thereby purge their latent desires.

> That is why Americans go to see gangster films and Japanese go to see puppet actions committing suicide; this is why primitive peoples enjoy their Trickster. It could be stated as a general rule and defended fairly well by ethnographic evidence that the occurrence of Trickster tales is directly proportional to the degree of oppressiveness of socio-religious restrictions. In such situations Trickster is a cathartic way to purge his audience of tensions built up by incest taboos, avoidance restrictions, and similar regulations of conduct in the area of sexual relations. In medieval Europe the Church for all its power had to allow tension-relieving devices like the Boy Bishop, the Feast of Fools, and the Foolish Pope to make religion's interference in life more nearly tolerable. As with nearly everything else in primitive society and culture, these things reach across the ages into our civilization; not many who attend church on Sunday know the altar rail was constructed first to keep the louts from shooting craps on the altar;

not many children who overturn outhouses on Mischief Night or clerks who wear lampshades on their heads at office Christmas parties realize they are reenacting Trickster exploits.[1]

The question then arises whether from an ontological perspective trickster's association with negative elements is unique to Ewe culture or is this a culturally universal trait shared by all trickster figures. In the case of the Ewe trickster, he is primarily associated with an inverted world where social order is disrupted by negative forces and as a result, disharmony prevails.

It may be argued that trickster characters are actually rooted in ritual practices and must therefore be viewed as part of a vast and complex social dynamic. Two important aspects of trickster-like characters observed in rituals as well as in narrative performances are their "marginal" status and their role as mediators. Taking a closer look at ritual practices will help illustrate the important link between ritual practices and trickster narratives.

Victor Turner provided penetrating insights into the study of social order as it relates to ritual practices and the belief systems which rituals and narrative traditions reflect. Although his perspective is primarily anthropological and sociological, Turner's observations have bearing on the cultural processes which trickster narratives mirror.

Turner described the socio-cultural properties of the liminal period in rituals of passage, defined as rites which accompany every change of place, state, social position, and age.[2] These rites of transition are marked by three phases: separation, marginality, and aggregation. Turner used the model proposed by Van Gennep and elaborated the properties of the second phase, the marginal or liminal period, to discuss the symbolism associated with passage rituals.

Typically, trickster flaunts social norms and flies in the face of conventional wisdom. In every culture where he appears he defies the social order. In one sense he is a deviant character. In another, he is a "marginal man," a cultural hybrid whom fate has condemned to live in

---

[1] John Greenway, *Literature Among the Primitives* (Hatboro, Pa.: Folklore Association, 1964), pp. 86–91.
[2] Arnold Van Gennep, *The Rites of Passage*, trans. Monika B. Vizedom and Gabrielle L. Caffee (Chicago: University of Chicago Press, 1960), pp. 1–13.

two societies and in two antagonistic cultures.[3] As a marginal being, he illustrates the socio-cultural properties of the liminal or marginal period, common to all rites of passage.

The marginal state in passage rituals marks the transition between the detachment of the individual or group from a fixed point in a set of cultural conditions to a new stable state. The marginal or liminal state is characterized by confusion in established categories and norms. It is neither this nor that but is a little bit of both. It is "betwixt and between" all recognized points in structural classification. As Turner pointed out, "We are not dealing with structural contradictions when we discuss liminality but with the essentially unstructured."[4]

The liminal period is not uniform in character from culture to culture. Many variations occur depending on the event and the cultural group in which the event is situated. Initiation, for instance, illustrates traits associated with liminality in many African societies. The use of masks, symbols, special languages and formulae, the performance of symbolic acts, and seclusion from the rest of society are characteristics of the liminal phase.

Youngsters in Ewe society, for example, undergoing initation are viewed as neophytes who pass from the state of adolescence to adulthood. Between these two culturally ordered states there is an intervening period of ambiguity and neutrality. Neophytes in the liminal period are considered structurally invisible although physically they are visible. Often secluded, they have physical but no social "reality." In their secluded state, neophytes are taught ethical and social obligations, laws, and kinship rules of their society, as well as the outlines of theogony, cosmogony, and the mythical history of their society. The sacred nature of these teachings is underscored by the formulae, chants, and often secret names used in instruction, as well as the secluded location where initiation rites take place.

Across many African cultures, the liminal period is often marked by the use of polyvalent symbols rich in imagery and connotation. The

---

[3] Everett V. Stonequist, *The Marginal Man* (New York: Charles Scribner's Sons, 1937), p. xv.

[4] Victor Turner, *The Forest of Symbols* (Ithaca: Cornell University Press, 1967), pp. 97–99.

symbols used in rituals illustrate the principles of economy of symbolic reference whereby antithetical processes and ideas are collapsed into a single multivocal symbol. Life and death, for example, may be represented by huts and tunnels, by the moon as it waxes and wanes, by the snake as it sheds its skin and appears to die—only to regrow a new one, and by nakedness that marks a newborn infant as well as a corpse prepared for burial.[5]

In rites of passage such as initiation, a paradox is often created between life and death wherein neophytes are considered symbolically dead, hence invisible, and thus able to cross boundaries and move between the world of the living and the dead without drawing censure or attention to themselves. Likewise, symbolic inversion plays a key role in trickster narratives and is closely associated with liminal or marginal characters such as the trickster.

Symbolic Inversion

Relationships in which trickster participates are primary ones such as those between husband and wife, father and daughter, master and servant, the chief and his subjects. More often than not, the relationships are abnormal and inverted in some way. "Hyena, Goat, and Leopard" (10.2.2.), for example, calls into question the institution of marriage as husband plots against wife, friend against husband, and wife against friend. In this narrative, each of the three characters freely crosses the boundaries between lies and truth and appearance and reality as they stage an elaborate charade. The success of the illusion bespeaks the characters' ability to perform tricks and manipulate reality—ultimately allowing the sanctity of marriage to prevail.

"The Chief and His Two Daughters" (28.2.6.) also discusses marital roles, focusing on Spider's inverted relationships with women. Spider maintains a somewhat aberrant marriage relationship, seeking two new wives while mistreating his first wife. With regard to all three women,

---

[5]Turner, p. 9.

Spider's apparent disrespect for accepted cultural norms reinforces his preoccupation with the desacramentalization of social norms.

Trickster's disregard, even contempt, for sacred institutions such as marriage is further illustrated in "Spider and the Kente Cloth" (51.1.3.). In this narrative, Spider pretends to be someone he is not, betraying his marital vows, and for this he is put to death.

One of the most striking examples of inverted relationships is found in "Spider Commits Incest" (23.1.3.) where Spider violates the most sacred of taboos. By perverting his role as father, he turns his daughter into a surrogate wife, desecrating the institutions of both fatherhood and marriage. Although he himself is not punished, his act leads to the death of his daughter, killed by the very person who gave her life, in an act which ordinarily is intended to create life, not destroy it. Spider is shunned by the townsfolk and his marginal status is underscored as he finds he has to beg the people to bury his daughter.

Another type of symbolic inversion involves stories where traditional customs are inverted and cultural boundaries are violated. In "Spider and the Beans" (51.2.5), Spider pretends to die and asks that yams and other ingredients be buried with him. Paradoxically, the coffin, a symbol of death, contains the ingredients of life, and sustains life underground where death normally reigns. This inverted state of affairs is reinforced by Spider's nightly return to earth to gather more food, leaving a barren farm in his wake. As trickster freely crosses spatial boundaries, he moves between life and death in a pattern frequently repeated in trickster narratives.

Trickster is not limited to ignoring only spatial boundaries; he violates temporal boundaries as well. In both variants of "Spider and the Mill" (5.1.8. and 10.2.1.), Yiyi attempts to turn night into day in order to convince Wawuie that morning has dawned. Metaphorically able to turn night into day, and having power over life and death, Yiyi affirms his role as both a "good" and "bad" character, the creator of order and instigator of disorder. By deftly changing roles, he demonstrates his ability to structure conflict. In a symbolic sense he demonstrates how what appears to be marginal or socially peripheral is, in fact, symbolically central.[6]

Trickster characters skilfully create an on-going dialectic between images. In "Frog and Horse" (9.1.6.), Frog confuses the categories of movement and number as he makes "slow" appear to be "fast" and "one" appear to be "many." In "Spider in the Village of One-armed Men" (21.1.3.), normality and abnormality are blurred as Spider leads his wife to believe that an aberration, a man with only one arm, is a normal condition typical of all men in surrounding villages. The paradox is made all the more tantalizing through disguise, deception, and illusion, underscoring trickster's ability to confound the distinction between illusion and reality.

Trickster further demonstrates his ability to invert social order through his activities as a master trader and negotiator. In "Spider the Trader" (23.2.2.), Spider hatches a clever plot to obtain wives for the chief. As he completes each trade, trickster's bounty grows in value and size, successfully transforming a pfennig into seven women. In "Spider Brings Disharmony into the World" (23.2.3.), Spider again uses his persuasive skills to concoct a ruse where all his invited guests ultimately destroy each other. He accomplishes this by making "deals" with gullible victims where each deal is premised on a false promise naively believed by each of his trading partners.

Finally, Spider's association with trade, market places, and crossroads identifies him with those spaces and activities where clearly defined social statuses and spaces break down and become ambiguous.[7] As is characteristic of most marginal characters, trickster excels in situations of ambiguity which are "betwixt and between."

Interestingly, his perceived marginal status and licentious character belie a symbolic importance that might easily be overlooked. In fact, it is no mere accident that Spider typically lives in web-filled nooks and crannies. Hidden in the rafters or high up on the ceiling he oversees the

---

[6] Barbara Babcock-Abrahams, "Tolerated Margin of Mess: The Trickster and His Tales Reconsidered," *Journal of the Folklore Institute*, I (1974), p. 155.
[7] *Ibid.*

actions of others. He is distant from the center but his presence links the center with the edges through the image of the web he spins.[8]

Trickster as Mediator

Trickster's involvement in contradiction and his proclivity for opposition point out his importance as a mediating figure. Lévi-Strauss observed that all myths, i.e., stories told with words, were logical tools used to resolve apparently irreconcilable contradictions. He cited as examples the conflict between autochthony and biological origins in the "Myth of Asdiwal."[9] In his purview, the permutation of one term by another has as its object finding the term mediating opposites. The world of myth differs from empirical reason and logical proof in the use of symbols. In place of propositions and axioms, heroes, gods, animals and other elements of the natural and cultural world become mediating terms. In the case of the Pueblo Indians, for example, change implies death, but agriculture as the intervening mediating element transforms change into growth. Or, war which is synonymous with death is transformed into life by the activity of hunting. In each case, a mediating term corresponds to each opposition so that a contradiction may logically be resolved.[10]

Trickster figures are among the best known and most effective mediators. In Ewe narratives the most frequent example of mediation occurs as Spider or some other trickster mediates between life and death. In "The Bird with Seven Heads" (1.2.6.), Spider and the monster have a master-servant relationship. Both characters alternately mediate between life and death. In each case, the mediator permits the opposition between life and death to be dissolved or transcended.[11]

---

[8]Robert D. Pelton, *The Trickster in West Africa: Study of Mythic Irony and Sacred Delight* (Berkeley: University of California Press, 1980), p. 59.

[9]Claude Lévi-Strauss, "The Structural Study of Myth," *Structural Anthropology*, trans. Claire Jacobson and Brooke Grundfest Schoepf (New York: Doubleday and Co., 1967), p. 212.

[10]Lévi-Strauss, p. 217.

[11]Paz, p. 36.

Spider first commands the monster to die, then come to life. Ultimately, Spider refuses to revive the monster, but in so doing, the distinction between life and death is blurred. The parasitic monster, who in life deprives Spider of his food, must be killed in order to let Spider live.

In "Spider Refuses the Chief's Daughter" (30.2.2.), the monster commands Spider to swell up and die, then revive, but the process of mediation is similar. Monster lets Spider live, only to deny him food, which will surely kill him. Ambiguity in the images of life and death creates an endless cycle of transformations as life ends in death, and death brings life. By erasing the distinctions between life and death, both Spider and the monster mediate the two opposing terms by dissolving the inherent contradictions they may pose.

Trickster's role as a mediator is central to understanding the ambiguous and seemingly irreconcilable terms inherent in the trickster character. It is precisely the purposeful ambiguity that trickster incarnates that enables him to function as both a narrative and mythic symbol. His position as a mediator is a privileged one. Not only does he express the potential and limits of human existence, but he activates the processes of symbolization where oppositions, permutations, mediation, and new oppositions continually recreate themselves, engendering new contradictions and new solutions, each one slightly different from the one before.[12]

Functional Interpretations of Trickster

Carl G. Jung, an ardent proponent of the psychological origins of trickster, viewed trickster as an "archetypal psychic structure of extreme antiquity . . . a collective shadow figure, an epitome of all the inferior traits of character in individuals."[13] Relegating the trickster to the rudimentary stages of consciousness, Jung perceived humanity as seeking to forget its dark and distant past, and the trickster wavering in

---

[12]Paz, p. 24.

[13]Carl G. Jung, "On the Psychology of the Trickster," trans. R.F.C. Hull, in *The Trickster* by Paul Radin (New York: Schocken Books, 1972), pp. 200–02.

his role as an unconscious buffoon and savior.[14] Jung believed that the trickster character lay dormant in the recesses of the human soul but periodically reconstructed and affirmed itself in a metaphorical fashion. For Jung, the trickster was, in essence, a metaphor for humanity's original and undifferentiated state. In this primal condition the sexes were one, gods and humans were merged, and the human and animal worlds were indistinguishable. Subsequently and in contrast to this primal state, biological and historical evolution, socialization, and acculturation divided the universe into natural and metaphysical spheres inhabited by differentiated beings.

Other theorists held that the trickster demonstrates a poorly socialized personality. His propensity for the violation of taboo, his lack of close and caring relationships, his lack of anxiety and remorse, and his constant use of pretense and trickery are some of the characteristics normally associated, for example, with psychopathic personalities. In fact, it is sometimes argued that schizophrenics use language closely resembling that found in trickster narratives. The problem with interpretations nestled in popular psychological theories, however, points to a fundamental problem of interpretation where trickster narratives are concerned. Regardless of the merits of any particular theory pertaining to trickster tales, there is no single theory that adequately accounts for the "trickster" phenomenon. Monolithic interpretations are as misleading as they are unsatisfactory. Viewed together, however, the various interpretations help elucidate the many functional and symbolic dimensions trickster tales embrace.

Overall, there are six basic functional interpretations of trickster narratives. According to the "steam-valve" theory, ritualized rebellion and licensed aggression are necessary for maintaining the social order. Gluckman observed in his work on Zulu and Swazi societies that ritualized rebellion served to criticize individual and particular authorities, never the fundamental systems of institutions themselves.[15] Accordingly, trickster's inversion of conventional norms and sacred relationships neither jeopardizes nor negates those institutions. Rather,

---

[14]Jung, p. 202.
[15]Max Gluckman, *Rituals of Rebellion in Southeast Africa* (Manchester: University Press, 1954), p. 20.

trickster's cavalier behavior provides a creative outlet for people to express their frustrations with social rules that normally inhibit behavior and prevent them from registering social protest in an acceptable and non-threatening manner. Humor, because it is essentially non-threatening, is an effective vehicle for registering protest as well as for effecting emotional catharsis. Its immediate impact is not to destroy social order but, in fact, to strengthen that order.

Closely related to the "steam-valve" theory is the "evaluative" function attributed to trickster narratives. This argument holds that because trickster narratives allow an attack on social control and permit a questioning of the social order, they lead to the development of a revolutionary consciousness which allows social change to occur.[16] As in many of these arguments, the claims are grandiose but the evidence is slim. In the Ewe context, for example, there is little evidence for this particular line of reasoning.

A third and perhaps more relevant theory concerns the socialization process. This interpretation posits that trickster narratives enable children to master developmental skills such as self-management, autonomy from parental control, and peer group relations. A study by David M. Abrams and Brian Sutton-Smith concluded that children aged five to seven used trickster narratives in a chronological sequence progressing from more infantile forms of tricksterism at younger age levels (clumsiness and moronic self-defeat) to more logical forms at later age levels (e.g., the "successful trickster"). Bugs Bunny, for example, was a popular television program in the U.S. among five to seven year olds. Research indicated that the plots in these cartoons were developmentally beyond what these children generated in their own narratives. It suggested, however, that Bugs Bunny helped model aspects of the next level of children's development. Accordingly, when children were able to generate trickster-like acts themselves (eight to eleven years of age), Bugs Bunny was no longer interesting to this age group.[17] Similarly, in the Ewe context, narratives told by young

---

[16] Babcock-Abrahams, p. 23.

[17] David Abrams and Brian Sutton-Smith, "The Development of the Trickster in Children's Narratives," *Journal of American Folklore*, 90 (October–December 1977), p. 43.

children 5 to 10 years of age often recounted Spider's exploits in a random episodic fashion and were often slapstick in nature. In contrast, older youngsters, 10 years or older, often told finely hewn narratives with well-developed storylines, reflecting their own growth and development.

Abrams and Sutton-Smith's study makes a strong case for viewing trickster narratives as a socialization device for children, but it completely overlooks storytelling as a popular medium for adults. In the Ewe context, in particular, trickster narratives are as popular among adults as they are among children and perhaps even more so.

As discussed earlier, storytelling provides a model for normative behavior through the negation of proper modes of behavior. In this context, it is believed that trickster narratives potentially strengthen the socialization process by sensitizing the audience to the desired values and modes of behavior. Proponents of the "reflective-creative" function of trickster narratives believe that by submitting concepts to wild distortions, the exact opposite will occur and reinforce the learning of that concept. According to this theory, as the trickster character rivets attention on socially significant acts, proper relations between friends, husbands and wives, or parents and children are reaffirmed.

Socialization is also believed to be aided through the investigation of alternatives in a variety of forms. In this respect, trickster activity as a prototype for potentiality is part of a theory of play known as "adaptive potentiation":

> What is implied is that nonsense can simply be nonsense. It may have no other pay-off for other forms of socialization, and it will always have intrinsic emotional satisfaction as a form of play. But it is also potentially a form of novelty that may become meaningful in terms of some future adaptive response. The virtue of this explanation is that it does not deprive play (or trickster) responses of socialization value, but gives them only a potential rather than a necessary relationship to other forms of adaptations. Play can be as exploratory and varied as it is, primarily because it is free of direct adaptive consequence. Without such leeway, it is argued, real variation could not occur.[18]

---

[18]Abrams and Sutton-Smith, p. 46.

This approach posits the belief that when an opposition is asserted, a range of alternatives between two polarities is potentially opened up for the imagination to consider. Without these oppositions, alternatives are inconceivable. Hence, trickster tales provide a means for storytellers and the audience to violate taboos in the guise of humor and thus, explore alternative forms of behavior. As a result, trickster is not only a mode of play and socialization but an instrument of cultural thought process as well.[19]

A final concern is the entertainment value of trickster narratives. Trickster narratives are immensely popular in Ewe culture as they entertain audiences through unabashed humor. Humor is the means par excellence by which people can laugh at their own frailties and character flaws. Certainly performers like Koblavi Ahadzi and Johnny Brofa are among the best comic artists Togo has to offer.

None of the above theories alone adequately explains the functional aspects of trickster narratives. The trickster phenomenon is so deeply rooted in mental and cultural processes that only a carefully detailed cross-disciplinary and multi-faceted approach can begin to discern the complex levels at which these narratives operate. Based on personal observation, in the Ewe context, those theories that address the socialization process and entertainment function appear to be most relevant. However, it is important to remember that these narratives are first and foremost part of an aesthetic dramatic art form. Functional aspects may help elucidate the social context in which trickster narratives are performed, but they are secondary to the aesthetic appreciation and experience of trickster oral narrative performance.

Trickster appears to be a response to all situations of ambivalence and contradiction inherent in social interaction. As a result, trickster-like behavior is evident everywhere we look. Not only Spider, Hare, Tortoise, and Bugs Bunny can claim title as trickster heroes. Brer Rabbit, the "Easy Rider," Butch Cassidy, Robin Hood, Superman, Batman, and the shell game artist on the street are equally adept and familiar trickster characters.

---

[19] *Ibid.*

Batman, and the shell game artist on the street are equally adept and familiar trickster characters.

Rather than view the activities of trickster as an archetype or "regression to the primal undifferentiated unity" in Jungian terms, it may be preferable to view trickster's behavior as commonplace activities. Trickster is not a peripheral being in social organization, a residual "deviant" category lurking in the background. He is central to the social order. Without deviance and marginality there could be no order, classification, or change. Trickster is more than a type of marginal being. Trickster transcends individual characters. Symbolically, he is male and female, young and old, good and bad, timid and bold. Trickster is what Pope describes in his *Essay on Man* as,

> Virtuous and vicious ev'ry man must be,
> Few in th' extreme, but all in the degree;
> The rogue and the fool by fits is fair and wise;
> And ev'n the best, by fits, what they despise.[20]

Trickster is a metaphor for pure possibility. He has the potential for doing anything, at any moment, unfettered by moral structures or social norms.[21] Trickster's connection with reality as reflected in these narratives is such that he influences and transforms the Ewe audience's modes of perception. Through shock, surprise, and humor, audience members are jolted into renewed awareness of social values and imbued with fresh views of contemporary reality at every performed narrative event. By virtue of trickster's charm and magic, audiences in Togo not only tolerate the "margin of mess" that is trickster but warmly and enthusiastically welcome him into their midst.[22]

---

[20]Alexander Pope, *Essay on Man* (Oxford: Clarendon Press, 1884), p. 44, lines 231–34.

[21]Turner, p. 97.

[22]Babcock-Abrahams borrowed the phrase "tolerated margin of mess" from Aldous Huxley.

Appendix

The thirty narratives found in the Appendix were transcribed verbatim and translated with the assistance of Ewe native speakers in Togo and the United States. Ideally, each narrative would appear in the Ewe and translated versions. However, because this would add considerably to the manuscript, all the narratives appear in translation, but only six verbatim Ewe transcriptions are included.

The narratives were transcribed using standard Ewe orthography. Since stylistic variations by the performer are reflected in the Ewe transcriptions, grammatical accuracy may have been sacrificed to a faithful rendering of the spoken word. Audience responses such as laughter and interjections are fully marked, as are performers' pauses and attempts at self-correction. The narratives are numbered according to their location on the original tapes.

1.1.1	RABBIT AND CROCODILE	147
	EWE VERSION	148
1.2.5	LIZARD LOSES HIS TONGUE	149
	EWE VERSION	151
1.2.6	THE BIRD WITH SEVEN HEADS	153
2.1.5	SPIDER PROPELS ANIMALS FROM A TREE	157
5.1.8	SPIDER AND THE MILL	160
	EWE VERSION	167
5.1.10	SPIDER AND THE STONE WITH EYES	172
5.2.1	MOUSE AND THE ADZIGO DRUM	174
6.2.7	SPIDER JUMPS OVER THE PIT	176

7.1.4	MONKEYS AND THE CAPS	179
9.1.6	FROG AND HORSE	180
10.2.1	SPIDER REMOVES THE MILL	183
	EWE VERSION	189
10.2.2	HYENA, GOAT, AND LEOPARD	193
	EWE VERSION	196
10.2.3	SPIDER AND DEATH	199
18.1.1	GOAT IN THE VILLAGE OF ANIMALS	201
	EWE VERSION	212
21.1.3	SPIDER IN THE VILLAGE OF ONE-ARMED MEN	221
21.2.2	MONSTERS EAT WITH THEIR ANUSES	226
21.2.4	MONKEY AND ANTELOPE	229
23.1.3	SPIDER COMMITS INCEST	231
23.2.2	SPIDER THE TRADER	235
23.2.3	SPIDER BRINGS DISHARMONY INTO THE WORLD	240
28.2.6	THE CHIEF AND HIS TWO DAUGHTERS	243
29.1.5	MONSTER FLOGS SPIDER	250
30.1.2	SPIDER DECORATES EGGS	254
30.2.2	SPIDER REFUSES THE CHIEF'S DAUGHTER	259
51.1.3	SPIDER AND THE KENTE CLOTH	262
51.1.5	SPIDER POUNDS FUFU	267
51.2.5	SPIDER AND THE BEANS	269
51.2.7	SHEEP AND GOAT	273
54.1.4	NYANUWUFIA	276
54.1.8	SPIDER AND RAT	284

1.1.1. RABBIT AND CROCODILE

Performer: Yawotse Akapo, 10, school boy
Date: October 12, 1978, 4 P.M.
Place: Bé, Lomé
Audience: 3 adults, 17 children

Listen to a tale. (LET THE TALE COME.)

The tale flew until it fell on Rabbit. (IT FELL ON HIM.) It fell on Crocodile. (IT FELL ON HER.)

Rabbit wanted to cross the river but he didn't know how to swim. He was at the river bank for a long time when Crocodile saw him. Crocodile told him he could come and stay with her so that he could look after her children. Rabbit went to stay with her.

When Crocodile went to the farm, she usually brought back corn for Rabbit to cook. When Rabbit cooked the corn, he would take one of Crocodile's children, put it on the fire, and cook it.

Crocodile came to tell him to bring her the children . . . he should bring the children one by one so she could breastfeed them. Rabbit took the last remaining crocodile, brought it to its mother to be fed again. This he did six times.

Crocodile then told Rabbit to bring all six children together to be breastfed. Rabbit told her that the children and their father had gone to the farm but they should be returning soon.

Crocodile said okay, she would feed them as soon as they returned. The father returned. Oh! The mother asked him where are the children. He said none of the children was with him.

She turned to Rabbit. Rabbit said, "Now that you've already eaten your children, you ask me where they are!"[1] They chased Rabbit into the bush.

That is why Rabbit lives on land and not in the water.

That is what I was deceived with and it is what I deceive you with. (YOU ARE VERY WELCOME.) Indeed![2]

---

[1] This statement is accompanied by vigorous gestures by the performer. Also, his speech is highly nasalized, which adds to the comic effect.

[2] Literally: If you look under your brother, somebody is also looking under you.

T.1.1.1
Yawɔtse Akakpo
Bé, Lomé
10/12/78

Mise gli loo. (GLI NEVAA.)
Egli tso vuu dze Fɔmizi dzi. (WODZE DZI.) Wodze Lɔ dzi. (WODZE DZI.)
Fɔmizi di be yeatso tɔ vɔa menya tsiʃuʃu o. Fifia, élè tɔa to vuu kekekeke ko ye ko Elo kpɔe. Eloa biae be nuka wɔna afia hâa? Wɔbe ... wɔbe yedi be yeatso tɔ vɔa, yemenya tsiʃuʃu o loo. Ye ko Loa be neva nɔ ye gbɔ ne wɔanɔ ye me viwu dzi kpɔ na ye loo. Ko ya ko Fɔmizia yi wole gbɔ afima.
Ne Elo yi agblea, ehena bli gbɔe be Fɔmizia ne ɖa na ye. Ne Fɔmizi ɖa blia, wòakɔ evia ké, evia. ... Elo me vi ɖeka kɔ de blia me aɖa nɛ woadu. Wòdam nɛ wòɖu.
Yeko Lo va gblɔ nɛ be nefɔ ɖeviawo vɛ ... ne nɔ wó fɔm ɖeka ɖeka ne yeana nó wó loo. Fifia, Fɔmizi kɔ ɖeka yi kpɔtɔa, wòkɔe yi wóna noe, wògakɔ ema yi ke, wóga ne, wògakoe yi ke. Wòkoe kaka zi ade.
Fifia, Eloa gatrɔ gblɔ nɛ be nefɔ ɖevi ameaɖe katâ ve de du be ne yeana nó wó loo. Fifia egblɔ nɛ be ɖeviawo kplɔ wó fofo ɖo yi agble, be wo gbɔgbɔ ge fifia loo. Loa be yoo ne wogbɔ koa yeana nó wó loo.
Wóli vuu kekeke Eloa ga gbɔ tso agble. O! Elonɔ biɛ be fikae viwo ɖe hâa? Wòbe ɖevia ɖeke mekplɔ ye ɖo o. Wóbia Fɔmizi. Fɔmizi be gayime mi miame viwo ɖuma. Mimenye o. Eyi miɖuwo vɔa, miva ye biam hâa. Ye ko wóyɔ Fɔmizi ɖe nu Fɔmizi va yi ɖo gbeme.
Ye ŋuti Fɔmizi nye gbemela ɖo, ne menyoa, tɔmelā nye ge wòala loo.
Yewótsɔ matso ble mi loo.
Woezɔ kakakakaka. Yoooooo.

Appendix

1.2.5. LIZARD LOSES HIS TONGUE

Performer: Sieklo Biesi, 9
Date: October 17, 1978, 4:30 P.M.
Place: Kotokou Kɔdzi, Lomé
Audience: 10 adults, 20 children

The chief said there were three girls. The person[1] who learns their names will get the girls. Spider got up, he went ... Spider got up and went to the chief's house where there was a guava tree. Spider got up and went ... he went to climb to the top of the guava tree. He plucked the first fruit and threw it to the ground. The eldest one picked it up. The eldest one's name was Wayawuie.[2] He plucked the second fruit and threw it on the ground. He heard someone say that Nukunukui should go and pick it up. He plucked the third fruit and threw it on the ground. They said Gbamilo should go pick it up. Spider said, "Now I know your names."

Spider went home. At dusk he would go call the girls by their names. By the time dusk fell, however, his jaw was swollen. So he went to tell his plight to his cousin, the Lizard.[3]

Lizard went.[4] ... All the people came and were calling the girls' names until they could call no more. Then Lizard came and struck up a tune:

(Song:)   *Pom, pom, pom!* We are male lizards, yeah!
It is asked, Wayawuie, Nukunukui, Gbamilo,
Who will know their names?

---

[1]Although the narrator uses the word "person," it refers to the animal world as well.

[2]Wayawuie is usually the name given to Spider's brother.

[3]Fovi can refer to a cousin or a younger brother. Poetic license allows the narrator to make Lizard Spider's relative.

[4]Lizard went to the chief's house.

The chief said, "What! What is Spider up to?" He got the girls.[5] He sang the song again:

Pom, pom, pom! We are male lizards, yeah!
It is asked, Wayawuie, Nukunukui, Gbamilo!
Who will know their names?

He sang the song and got all three girls.

Now, by the time Lizard brought back the girls, Spider had recovered. Spider came to Lizard and told him they should share[6] the girls. Lizard said he would not share the girls with Spider.

When the chief falls asleep at eight o'clock tonight, it will be eight o'clock tomorrow morning before he wakes up. Lizard too was asleep. Spider in the meantime went and took . . . he went to pull out a knife from Lizard's pouch. . . . He went to cut out the chief's tongue,[7] then quietly replaced the knife in Lizard's pouch.

When the chief woke up, he went to give an order.[8] . . . He rang the bell calling people to come inspect their knives. The person who had blood on his knife would be the guilty one. Now Lizard . . . everybody[9] displayed his knife until Lizard came. He shouted, "Look at mine, look at mine!" There was blood on Lizard's knife! The people grabbed him and cut out his tongue.

That is why when Lizard is on a wall, even if nobody asks him anything, he says, "*Ekoe, ekoe, ekoe, ekoe*[10] . . . Spider did me so."

That is what I was deceived with and that is what I deceive you with.

Yooooo! Woezɔ kakaka.

---

[5] The narrator says "girl" but means "girls."

[6] Literally: divide the girls between them.

[7] Literally: tongue holder, i.e., cord holding the tongue in the mouth. It is translated here as "tongue."

[8] The chief went to give an order but couldn't because his tongue had been cut out.

[9] The narrator corrects himself.

[10] This is the sound of Lizard knocking his head against the wall, on trees, or on the ground.

T.1.2.5.
Sieklo Biesi
Kotokou Kɔdzi, Lomé
10/17/78

Fifia, fia be yeta . . . be, nyɔnuviaɖe woame etɔ̄ li, be ne ameyi ne nya nyɔnuvia ŋkɔ wòaxɔ nyɔnuvia loo. Fifia Yiyi tso, wòyi ɖe . . . Ayiyi tso wòyiɖe efia me . . . aguatiaɖe le fia ʃeme. Ayiyi tso, woyi, ye wòyia wòvayi de aguatia dzi, wògbe . . . gbātɔ d'anyigba. Amegāxoxotɔ kɔe . . . amegāxoxotɔ ŋkɔe nye . . . ah . . . Wayawuie. Eve . . . wògagbe eve kɔ d'anyigba, wóbe Nukunukui neva kɔe vɛ. Wògagbe etɔ̄ kɔ d'anyigba wóbe Gbamido neva kɔe vɛ. Fifia, Ayiyi be, "Ehē, menya mia ŋkɔ loo."

Ayiyi dzo yi ɖe aʃeme. Fifia, wotrɔme wódza va yɔ mó ɔ̄kɔ. Kaka wòatrɔva wotrɔmea eglā tè nɛ. Wòvatsɔ nyaa gblɔ na efovia, Adoŋlo.

Fifia, ye Adoŋlo yea, amewo katā va ŋkɔ yóm, vuu kekeke, wómete ŋui o. Ye Adoŋlo va yeko wòdo ha ɖa:

> Pɔ̄pɔ̄pɔ̄ miawoe nye Adoŋlo tsuawoee.
> Pɔ̄pɔ̄pɔ̄ miawoe nye Adoŋlo tsuawoee,
> Doŋlotsua ku dzɛ, ku dzɛ, ku dzakalika,
> Doŋlotsua ku dzɛ, ku dzɛ, ku dzakalika,
> Miawoe nye Nukunukui matsɔ amedzro, miawoe
>   nye . . .
> Dzɔgbese ka ɖa Adoŋlo be Agbamido neva.

Efia be, "Nuka? Nuka wɔge Adoŋloa hā?" Wòxɔ nyɔnuvia. Wògado ha ɖa:

> Pɔ̄pɔ̄pɔ̄ miawoe nye Adoŋlo tsuawoee,
> Pɔ̄pɔ̄pɔ̄ miawoe nye Adoŋlo tsuawoee,
> Doŋlotsua ku dzɛ, ku dzɛ, ku dzakalika,
> Doŋlotsua ku dzɛ, ku dzɛ, ku dzakalika,
> Miawoe nye Nukunukui matso amedzro, miawoe
>   nye . . .
> Dzɔgbese ka da Adoŋlo be Nukunukui neva.

Wodzi ha, wò nyɔnuvia etɔ̃ katã.

Fifia, kaka eyi Adoŋlo kɔ nyɔnuvia gbɔea, enua kà ɖe eme na Ayiyi. Fifia Ayiyi va Adoŋlo gbɔ be yeta ne yewonema nyɔnuviawo loo. Adoŋlo be yewomete ŋu nyɔonuviawo ma ge o. Ayiyi be, "Nyawoa?" Wobe, "Ẽ." Fifia Adoŋlo wodzo.

Ne efia dɔ lɔa . . . etsɔ . . . egbe yetrɔ ga enyimea, etsɔ ŋudi ga nyi hafi wò nyɔnyɔge. Ne Adoŋlo hã dɔ̃e nenema, nenema ke wòga nyɔ̃nyɔ̃ ge ema. Fifia yea Adoŋlo dɔ lõa, Ayiyi tso wòva kɔ . . . wòva ɖe hɛ le gɔme na Adoŋlo ko se . . . kɔ va yi sɛ fia m'aɖe aɖeteka, wòkɔ hɛa vade gɔme na Adoŋloa kpoo.

Fifia, efia va nyò, efia va gblò nya . . . wóva ʄo ga be amesiame nava wóakpɔ eʄe hɛ ŋuti. Ameyi ŋuti tɔ evu le koa, wóanya be eyae wɔ nua loo. Fifia, Adoŋlo . . . amewo katã va le fifiam vuu keke Adoŋlo vado koa, ye ko wòdo qli be mikpɔ tɔnye ɖa, mikpɔ tɔnye ɖa. Evɔ ye ko evu le etɔ ŋu, ye ko wóli, wòtso aɖeteka nɛ.

Yena, ne Adoŋlo le gli dzia, ne ameaɖeke mebia nyaa ɖeke oa, ye wònɔa nya tɔm aleke:

Ekɔe, ekɔe, ekɔe, ekɔe, Ayie wɔm alea;
Ekɔe, ekɔe, ekɔe, ekɔe, Ayie wɔm alea.

Te wótsɔ blem metsɔ va ble mi loo. Woezɔ kakakaka.

Appendix

1.2.6. THE BIRD WITH SEVEN HEADS

Performer: Bessā, 10
Date: October 17, 1978, 4:30 P.M.
Place: Kotokou Kɔdzi, Lomé
Audience: 10 adults, 20 children

Listen to a tale. Let the tale come . . . on and on. The tale went until it fell on a bird. (IT FELL ON HIM.) The bird had seven heads. Everybody left their house and went to the chief's house.

When the bird flew and landed on a rooftop, it started to sing:

(Song):   I, a bird, I'm coming,
          I, a bird, I'm coming,
          If somebody sees me, he will know,
          Somebody will know . . . little wings like this.

When it approached, it looked like a cloud descending. When it hovered over a building like this,[1] the building fell. If it saw a person, it killed him. Then it flew away, on and on until . . . on and on. . . .

The chief beat the gongong and said, "Who will kill the bird?" The people answered they would. The *juju* people[2] came but could not kill it. When the bird appeared, people ran away. People came, animals came . . . animals with seven heads came and ran away.

A child came . . . he said his name was Etse. He went to the chief saying he could kill the bird. The chief said to him, "You . . . you . . . old people tried and failed . . . you a little boy, you also want to try?" The child said to find him a spear . . . a dagger . . . find a dagger for him.[3]

They found the things he wanted. They found the things and the child came . . . he came. When the bird started his song, the child too sang a song. This went on until . . . until . . . the child.[4] . . . When he

---

[1] Gesture made to indicate the bird's hovering.
[2] People with strong magical powers, also known as "fetishers" or "diviners."
[3] Frequent pauses are characteristic of this narrator.
[4] Incomplete sentences are another stylistic characteristic of this narrator.

cut the head of the bird, the head fell but regenerated itself again. The child did this many times, cutting off each new head and putting it in his bag until all the heads were in the bag.

The bird died. They burned the bird . . . it burned for seven days. The child went to the chief. The chief distributed his property in three parts, giving two parts to the child.[5] The child became chief and the old chief became his servant.[6]

Now, Spider came and took a ram in one hand and another ram in the other hand and said he was going to his mother's village. He farted in a gourd and carried the gourd with him until he reached a certain spot. There he opened the gourd. When he opened the gourd, a lot of flies swarmed around. He said, "There are too many people[7] in this place." He came to another place, opened the gourd, and this time saw only a few flies. He continued until he came to a datenut tree. There under the tree he opened the gourd containing the fart and no flies came out.

While cooking the ram, a fruit fell. He said, "Let it come . . . let it come . . . let them fall, one, two, three, four. They are my grandfather's. Let them fall one, two, three, four . . . one, two, three, four." (laughter) The fruit fell for a long time until a big bunch fell. As Spider rushed to grab it, it turned out to be a big monster.[8] Spider turned to go but the monster told him to stay put. He said Spider should come and carry him and feed him everything that Spider had.

Spider was feeding the monster, telling him every now and then to look over there at the red bird. While the monster looked at the bird,[9] Spider would take a piece of meat, swallow it, while large tears fell from

---

[5] Intended as the reward the chief offers for killing the bird.

[6] Meant in the sense of a "vassal," not a paid servant. The storyteller, a young boy of 10, seems to end the story here, but without any formal break he starts what appears to be another story. Because of the parallel development of images, these two parts are treated as though they form one narrative.

[7] The presence of flies indicates the presence of people.

[8] A creature miraculously issued from a bunch of dates.

[9] Presumably, there is no bird. Spider uses the idea of a red bird to trick the monster.

his eyes.¹⁰ The monster asked him why he was weeping. He said it was because the monster wasn't eating quickly enough.

This went on until the monster had eaten everything. The monster asked Spider to fetch him some water . . . to go to the spring to fetch some water and pour it into his mouth for him. While Spider was fetching the water, an old woman appeared and asked him why he was fetching so much water. He said there was a monster who was bothering him. The old woman told him that if he says, "Swell up and die," the monster will die. If Spider says, "Come back to life," the thing will come back to life.

Spider saw some people passing by. He continued walking until he met some more people. He went back . . . he went back again.¹¹ The old woman said she had already told him the magic words . . . the old woman . . . the old woman said the magic words to him again. Then the old woman said, this old woman said that if she repeats the words again and he doesn't remember them, she won't tell him again.

She repeated the formula. Spider went until he hit his foot¹² and immediately forgot the magic words. He went back to the old woman a third time. She said that if she tells him and he forgets again, then she won't care what happens to him. He can fetch water forever, she won't care.

He began repeating to himself, "Something should swell up and die, something should come back to life; something should swell up and die, something should come back to life; something should swell up and die, something should come back to life."

He went to the monster and said, "Something should swell up and die." The monster died. He put the water down and said he was going to show him! He took hold of and dragged the monster, who stank heavily *lililililili.* (laughter) (HOHODIOO!) He said, "Something should come back to life," and the monster came to life. He said, "Something should swell up and die," and the monster died. He said he was going to show him now.

---

¹⁰The tears are caused by Spider's gluttony.

¹¹He went back to the old woman to ask her the magic words which he had forgotten.

¹²He hit his foot against a rock and stumbled.

While smelling the monster, Spider's nose got very long until it dragged on the ground. (laughter) He took his nose, heavy and clumsy *lililililililili* ... until he came to the chief. He told the chief that he should make a decree. Everyone should take off his nose and put it down. The one who dives and gets out first will be last, the one who comes last will be first.[13]

Spider said he will blow the whistle for them. All of them put down their noses. Spider blew the whistle *piīa!* All the animals dove. It was finished! Spider was trying on noses *kpatakpatakpata* ... was trying on noses *kpatakpatakpata*.[14] Turkey's nose fit him. Spider left ... never to come back.

When the animals woke up, they shouted, "Spider dives well, Spider dives well, Spider dives well." They said that if Spider liked to dive that much,[15] they were going to leave because they were hungry. The animals went to pick up their noses, one by one. Turkey looked for his nose but couldn't find it. So he took Spider's long one to wear.

This is what I was deceived with and it is what I deceive you with.

Woezɔ kakakakakakakaka.

---

[13]This is a contest Spider invents and for which he makes up his own set of rules.

[14]Ideophone meaning "fast, fast."

[15]Literally: if Spider enjoyed contests so much ...

2.1.5.   SPIDER PROPELS ANIMALS FROM A TREE
Performer: Butyi, 26, fisherman
Date: October 17, 1978; 4:30 P.M.
Place: Bé, Lomé
Audience: 10 adults, 30 children

Listen to this tale. (LET THE TALE COME.)
The tale rose until it fell on Squirrel. (IT FELL ON HIM.) It fell on Partridge. (IT FELL ON HIM.) It fell on Spider. (IT FELL ON HIM.)

Spider and Ðetsuevi[1] were good friends. One day a great famine came and Spider told Ðetsuevi they would go into the bush to search for food. They were walking when Spider saw some spears in the bush.

Spider called Ðetsuevi and they took the spears. Spider told him that they should go under a big tree in the clearing. When any animals passed by, they would trick them into hanging onto a branch. Propelled through the air, they would fall onto the spears. Then Spider and Ðetsuevi would catch the animals, cook them and eat them.

They inserted the spears in the ground. Spider put Ðetsuevi near the spears and said that he himself would stand near the tree to deceive the animals.

Spider was under the tree when Squirrel passed by. Spider said, "Oh my brother, my brother. Where are you going?" Squirrel said he was going to his brother-in-law's field. Spider told him to hang onto the tree so that he could hurl him as far as his father-in-law's field. Squirrel did as he was told and hung onto the tree. (I WAS THERE!)

(Song):   The trip was bad . . .
           The invalid's trip was bad . . .

The tree propelled Squirrel who fell onto the spears. Spider came and took Squirrel, grilled him, and ate him.

Afterwards, Partridge was passing by. Spider said, "Oh my brother, my brother. Where are you going?" Partridge said he was going to his

---

[1] Ðetsuevi is a member of the spider family. It is often the name given to one of Spider's sons.

mother-in-law's field to work. Spider told him to come hang on to the tree. Partridge said, "Tree, tree, propel me." *Gblo!* Partridge fell onto the spears. When Partridge had fallen, Ɖetsuevi went to relieve himself and returned. He took Partridge and put him in his bag.

Spider went back under the tree. A while later, Cow was passing by. Spider told her to come and hang onto the tree so the tree could transport her quickly to where she was going. Cow hung to the tree and said, "Tree, tree, propel me." Spider was running ahead, saying, "As far as the spear, as far as the spear. . . ." *Gblo!* Cow fell onto the spear. Because Cow was so big, Ɖetsuevi could not carry her alone. He ran and told Spider to come and help him carry her. They carried Cow and hid her under some grass, after which Ɖetsuevi returned to the spear. Spider also returned to his place under the tree.

A while later, Pigeon was passing by. Spider called to him and asked him where he was going. Pigeon said he was going to the riverside to drink. Spider told him to hang onto the tree and to say, "Tree, tree, propel me." The tree would propel him to the riverside. But Pigeon was clever. He went under the tree and said, "My brother, my brother, how shall I do this?" Spider said, "Do like this." Pigeon said, "Shall I do like this?" Spider said, "No, do like this."[2]

They continued like that until Spider was fed up and Pigeon told Spider to do it himself so he could see. Spider was angry but he had to do something.

Spider mulled over the situation and said to Pigeon, "My brother, my brother. Please go there. You'll see some spears. Extract them for me." Pigeon said he did not know who had planted the spears there, but he had watched Spider plant the spears. Spider pleaded in vain, but Pigeon refused.

Finally, Pigeon asked Spider to tell him why the extraction of the spears was important to him. Then he would extract them. Spider said he did not know who had put the spears there, but if the tree propelled him, he would fall onto the spears and hurt himself. Therefore he begged Pigeon to extract them for him.

---

[2]This statement is accompanied by vigorous speech by the performer. Also, Spider's speech is highly nasalized, which adds to the comic effect.

Pigeon was clever, so he accepted. He went over to the spears, returned, and said to Spider, "My brother, my brother, I've extracted the spears." He showed him two sticks, saying they were the spears.

Spider said, "Ah, oh . . . do I have to do this? I'll say 't . . . tr . . . tree . . . p . . . pro . . . prope . . . propel me.'" The Pigeon ran ahead, saying, "As far as the spear . . . as far as the spear. . . ." *Gblo!* Spider fell onto the spear and exploded. He was scattered all over the place!

Pigeon gathered Spider and put him in a basket. A while later, Ɖetsuevi appeared and said, "Oh, what animal is this impaled on the spear like this?" Pigeon went over to him and said, "Oh my brother, my bother, what are you doing here?" Ɖetsuevi said, as he was passing by, he had seen some meat scattered about and wanted to collect it. Pigeon told him to come and they would leave together. Ɖetsuevi showed him the meat he had gathered. They took home all the meat and shared it . . . without Spider.

That is why the ancestors have a saying: "If you seek to do harm to someone, harm will also find you."[3]

This is what I was deceived with and this is what I have brought to deceive you with.

Yooooooooo.

---

[3] Literally: If you look under your brother, somebody is also looking under you.

5.1.8. SPIDER AND THE MILL

Performer: Koblavi Ahadzi, 45, washerman
Date: December 7, 1978, 5:30 P.M.
Place: Amoutive, Lomé, Chief Adjalle's house
Audience: 8 adults, 15 children

Listen to a tale. (LET THE TALE COME.)

The tale went until it fell on Funɔ; it fell on Spider; it fell on Agɔsu.[1]

In the olden days, the mill . . . the mill we used to grind with, was not in the house. It was in the bush. The mill made flour by itself. All you needed to do was collect it, prepare it, and eat it. We don't know, nobody knows how or why.[2]

There was a great famine. Spider, his brother Wayawuie, and Agɔsu went to the bush to search for food. They were there three weeks, but didn't find any food. At the end of the third week, they left, leaving Agɔsu alone in the bush. He said he couldn't go home to find his children weeping. In the bush he heard *gli! gli! gli!* (HM!) He was going to see if it would kill him. There was an old mill grinding by itself *gli!*[3] There was a lot of flour. Oh! Thank God!

He went to hide. A little while later, Buffalo arrived carrying a big sack. As soon as he arrived, he gathered the flour in his sack. He packed it and packed it until the sack was full. Then he left.

Agɔsu was there watching when soon after, a very big pig arrived, dragging a sack on the ground. Pig filled his sack and left.

Agɔsu stayed there hiding and watching, his hand placed behind his ear.[4] Soon, a big bull arrived. He collected the flour . . . collected it . . . collected it and he too left. Agɔsu watched for a while and saw that nobody else was coming, so he too went to the mill. He gathered flour

---

[1] Agɔsu is Spider's relative.
[2] Nobody knows how the mill made flour by itself.
[3] The traditional mill consists of a big flat stone tablet on which food was placed and ground by a small smooth cylindrical stone.
[4] The narrator makes a gesture here indicating that Agɔsu was listening to hear if anyone was coming.

Appendix

until his sack was full, then left. He left and prepared *akplē*[5] for his children and wife. They were very happy.

Spider arrived and knocked *kɔ̄kɔ̄kɔ̄*.[6] "Come in," said Agɔsu. "I'm not looking for anyone in particular . . . Oh! My brother, how could you do me this way?" Agɔsu and his family had eaten all the food and thrown away the rest!

At night a heavy rain fell. The flood carried all the remaining *akplē* to the dunghill. Spider and his children went to eat.

Spider went and begged his brother to lead him to where he had found the food. Agɔsu agreed. As soon as it was daybreak, they would go. But for the time being, Agɔsu wanted to sleep. It was about eleven o'clock. Again, Spider arrived and knocked *kɔ̄kɔ̄kɔ̄*. "Agɔsu, it's day." Agɔsu said, "No, the cock should crow first. The cock hasn't crowed yet." "Is that so?" said Spider. "Okay, I've heard. I'm going to sleep a little."

As soon as Spider left, *pāpāpāpāpā kɔkɔliakœɛɛ kɔkɔliakœɛɛ pāpāpāpāpā kɔkɔliakœɛɛ!*[7] "Agɔsu, Agɔsu, it's day, it's day. Let's go!" Agɔsu said, "No, it's not day yet. The sky should get light first." Spider thought to himself, "Is that what he wants? Okay."

Spider ran and went to remove the thatch from his roof, then lit it at the dunghill. The sky became very light. "Agɔsu, Agɔsu, it's day! Look at the sky!" Agɔsu said, "No. I have not had enough sleep yet. Go sleep a bit, then return." "What!" exclaimed Spider, "Is that so? Okay. I'll go sleep a bit and come back."

Spider went to sleep but he overslept. By the time Spider awoke, Agɔsu had gotten up and left. Spider woke up.[8] (HIS EFFORTS OF THE NIGHT BEFORE LEFT HIM EXHAUSTED.) (laughter) He hadn't slept at all. (I WAS THERE!) Let's hear it. (I WAS THERE!) Let's hear it.

---

[5]*Akplē* is a cooked dough made from cassava and is eaten with soup or stew.

[6]This ideophone indicates someone knocking.

[7]Spider imitates a rooster crowing. *Pāpāpāpāpā* suggests the flapping wings of a rooster.

[8]The redundancy in this performer's narration is very characteristic of his style.

(Song):   Tete will beat Agɔsu,
           Agɔsu says he's his mother's son,
           Tete will beat Agɔsu,
           Agɔsu says he's his mother's son. Tiiiii!

Agɔsu left. Spider didn't see him. This annoyed Spider very much. Agɔsu came back and prepared more *akplẽ* and sent a little to Spider. Spider said, "Tomorrow only you and I will go." Agɔsu told him not to worry.

It was night . . . about one o'clock. Spider went and called Agɔsu to tell him they should leave. Agɔsu said it was not day yet. Spider said, "Okay. I'll just stay and watch Agɔsu's flour sack. If I see the sack I'll know he's not gone." Spider went and hid in the house. As soon as Agɔsu went to sleep, Spider went and collected some ash, some fine ash, and poured it in the sack to the brim. Then he punched a hole in the bottom and went to bed. He went to sleep and overslept again!

When Agɔsu woke up, he took the sack and hung it around his neck. The ash fell to the ground leaving a trail from about here to Ametɔyikpenu. . . .[9] Suddenly he turned around to look and said, "The wily spider has done this to me?" Agɔsu emptied the sack. He shook it well, slung it around his neck, and left.

When Spider got up, he started after the trail of ashes . . . went until he reached the spot where the ashes had been emptied. Oh! Agɔsu did this? He thought, what could he do to get Agɔsu to come . . . to hear him? Spider took out his machete, went and cut a large bale of thatch, and tied it *fine!*[10] He then cut a big club, thought it over, and started hitting the thatch *kpù!* Spider lamented, "*Oobobobobobobobob!* I am dead! Agɔsu, I am dead!" (Audience joins Spider, crying, "AGƆSU, I AM DEAD!") *Ekpù!* "Agɔsu, a wild animal has caught me!" he cried.

Agɔsu arrived. "Spider, what's going on here?" he asked. Spider said, "You fool![11] I've caught you. I've caught you, you fool! I've caught you. You ran away from me! I've caught you. See? Shouldn't I also eat

---

[9]This is a place name in Togo.

[10]This performer is originally from Ghana, hence the interjection of English words.

[11]Literally, You dog!

what you're eating? Let's go!" (I WAS THERE!) Okay. Let's hear it. (laughter)[12]

(Song): A wild ram shall meet me in the fields,
A wild ram, wild ram shall meet a calf,
A wild goat shall meet me in the fields,
A wild ram shall meet an ox in the fields,
Wild ram, wild ram shall meet a calf, tiiiii!
Wild goat shall meet a calf, tiiii!

Agɔsu took Spider and away they went. Agɔsu told him when they got there, he should remain still. They will see strange things. He shouldn't talk. "What can possibly be there that would stop me from saying what I see? We'll see," said Spider. They went and hid. Oh! A mill grinding by itself!

"Let's take the flour and leave," said Spider. "Be patient," said Agɔsu, "you're such a fool! That's why your children don't have enough *akplẽ*." "I'm going to collect a bundle," promised Spider. (laughter) "Just be patient," admonished Agɔsu.

A little later, Buffalo arrived. As Buffalo collected the flour, Spider said, "Oh! you're going to take it all! Take a little and leave some for us!" Agɔsu said, "Just be calm." "Okay, I've heard ... I've heard ... Mmmmmmm. Good, he's finished." Buffalo left. "Let's go get it!" exclaimed Spider.

Agɔsu said, "Ssshhh! Something is coming." "What! To collect again? What'll be left for us?" Spider worried aloud. "Be patient," said Agɔsu. Pig arrived. "What! Pig is going to collect before us?" "Be patient, just be calm," said Agɔsu. "Okay, I've heard," said Spider. Pig collected his portion and finally left. Spider said, "Now, let's go." "Be still," said Agɔsu.

Soon Cow came, collected the flour and left. "Now let's go and collect," said Spider. Agɔsu admonished, "Be patient."

After a while, Spider and Agɔsu walked to the mill. Spider said Agɔsu should collect first. Since the mill ground continuously, if Agɔsu

---

[12] The audience is clearly pleased with this performance.

went first, there would be plenty for Spider. So Agɔsu gathered flour until his sack was full. "Spider, collect your flour," said Agɔsu. Spider collected and was packing it in . . . in heaps! He stomped his foot on it *gbì gbì gbì gbì gbì*! (HE SURE LIKES HIS SACK FULL!)

Agɔsu said they should go. Spider said, "What! Leave the mill here and have to come back again? No, I'm taking the mill home!" (WHAT?!) Agɔsu said, "You can carry the mill home?" "Yes," answered Spider. Agɔsu said he was going home and left. (IT ROOTED IN HIS HEAD!)[13] Agɔsu said he was leaving. (I WAS THERE. I, KƆSI AGBAGBLANYA.)

(Song): The horse tail flew into the bush,
So, so, so, the horse tail flew into the bush,
The horse tail flew into the bush.
So, so, so, the horse tail flew into the bush.
Tìiii!

Agɔsu left. Spider went to make a pad for his head and put the mill on his head. "I'll go home and make some flour for me and my children . . . Funɔ and my children will eat!" The hand mill that people used in the olden days.[14]

Spider took one step and the mill grew a root into his head. When he took a second step, the mill grew another root in his head. By the time he went three meters, the mill was rooted all the way into the ground.[15]

Spider couldn't move. The mill struck up a tune:

---

[13]One audience member is ahead of the performer. The rest of the audience does not appreciate his jumping ahead of the story.

[14]This comment is in response to the audience member's request for a description of the mill.

[15]The roots apparently passed all the way through Spider's head, his body, and into the ground.

(Song):   Let Yiyi take me back,
          Let Yiyi take me back,
          Brother of Agɔsu, let him take me back.
          I helped Buffalo,
          Buffalo ate and left.
          Brother of Agɔsu, let him take me back.
          I helped Pig,
          Pig ate and left.
          I helped Cow,
          Cow ate and left.
          Brother of Agɔsu, let him take me back.

Spider asked, "Should I take you back?" The mill answered that he should. As soon as Spider turned, the mill's roots slipped out from under his foot. Spider walked until he reached the mill's usual location. There the mill jumped off *di!* Then Spider said, "You must be joking! You're going back to my house! (laughter) Funɔ and the children will eat flour at home. No longer will you stay in the bush." "Is that so?" said the mill. "Yes!" answered Spider.

Spider went and took something and made a tray.[16] He put the mill on his head and carried it. The mill sang again:

(Song):   Let Yiyi take me back,
          Let Yiyi take me back,
          Brother of Agɔsu, let him take me back.
          I helped Buffalo,
          Buffalo ate and left.
          Brother of Agɔsu, let him take me back.
          I helped Pig,
          Pig ate and left.
          I helped Cow,
          Cow ate and left.
          Brother of Agɔsu, let him take me back. Tiiii!

---

[16] He put the tray on his head to try to prevent the mill's roots from penetrating

Spider said, "You're joking! You will go home today. Funɔ will see me and be pleased. You will make flour which Funɔ will prepare for me to eat." Spider kept on like that until he finally arrived home with the mill. The mill in the meantime had actually sprouted.... [17]Funɔ (SPIDER'S WIFE ... SPIDER'S WIFE ...) Spider's wife is Funɔ. (THE WOMAN ... THE WOMAN'S NAME IS. ...)[18] He said if the mill goes to the house, she'll cook for him.

Meanwhile, the mill grew roots but the tray was strong. The roots couldn't go through Spider's head before he got home.[19] As he arrived home ... you know that the roots were in Spider's head!

Spider said, "Help me unload." Whenever they tried to lift the mill, Spider rose up with the mill. (OH OH!) "Funɔ, Funɔ, just hold me tight!" He rose with the mill![20] "Now, the only thing left to do is to cut off my head ... (WHAT?!) ... If you cut off my head and I die, you'll have enough to eat until the day you die." (REALLY!)

They took hold of Spider's head and cut it off té! The mill fell down di!

An old man at Agrimenti in Bé[21] a few Sundays ago deceived me with this.... He said, the mill ... the old mill, when it made flour in the old days, you did not have to put corn in it. It would grind by itself and made flour for people to collect and prepare for eating. It is Spider who brought the mill home. From that day on, you have to put grain on the millstone in order for it to make flour.

You good listeners, you!

Woezɔ kakakaka, woezɔ, woezɔ!

---

[17]An audience member makes a vulgar remark which displeases some in the audience. They react by muttering inaudibly.

[18]An audience member momentarily tries to change the direction of the performance with this digression about Spider's wife, while the performer skilfully acknowledges the comment but refuses to be sidetracked.

[19]Spider thought the roots could not go through the tray to his head but obviously did.

[20]Here an audience member offers another digression: "Woman is not satisfied with only one penis?" he asks. The performer as well as other audience members largely ignore this comment.

[21]This is the old section of Lomé, the capital of Togo.

Appendix 167

T.5.1.8.
Koblavi Ahadzi
Amoutive, Lomé
12/7/78

Mise gli loo! (GLI NEVA!) Egli tso vuuu dze Funɔ dzi, dze Yiyi dzi, dze Agɔsu dzi.
Eblema mea, èté, blematé yi mituna, mele aʃeme o, gbeme wònɔna. Ne eyi va ke ɗe eŋuti go ye ŋutɔ tuna wɔ, ne eyi kɔ alɔ ava ɗa aɗu. Mímenya o, ameaɗeke menya o, dɔ gāa aɗe va tó.
Eyiyi, nɔvia Wayawuie kpakple Agɔsu wótso, wóɗo gbe, wóyi nuɗuɗu di gbe. Wónɔ gbeme kɔsiɗa woame etɔ̃ wómekpɔ nuɗeke o. Kɔsida etɔ̃ ʃe nuwuwua, wótrɔ gbɔ wòkpɔtɔ Agɔsu ɗeka ɗe gbea me, be ye mi afia ... afea? Nuka? Yebe viwo afa avi. Agɔsu yi dzè gbè viɗe kaka koa yi ko wòva se gli gli gli gli. Yeayi ne yeakpɔe yeaku. Agɔsu va yi do ɗo koa, èté, nyagāté koe nɔa eɗokui tu gli. Ewɔ yɔ té kolɔa zā! Agɔsu be, "Ao! Mawu meda akpe na wo."
Wòdzó bè. Wòli sɛɛ koa, elā ɗe wóyɔ be Etò. Tò kɔe va dò, kplà golo gāa ɗe. Tò va ɗo ko wòlɔ wɔ de, golo me, lɔe kɔ de lɔe kɔe de me kaka goloa yɔ vɔ koa. Eva dzó.
Agɔsu le afima le ekpɔm, le fima sɛ koa. Ehatsu gāa ɗe koe va do, kplà golo anyigba tɔm. Hatsu lɔ wɔ kɔ ɗe golo kaka goloa yɔ. Wòdzo.
Agɔsu le fima, bè, le ekpɔm, kɔ asi ɗo to nu aleke. Sɛɛ koa, Nyitsu gāa ɗe va. Yí va lɔ wɔa do eme, kòdo eme kaka koa, ye hā dzó. Ko Agɔsu le fima sɛɛ. Ameaɗeke me le vavam o. Ko ye hā yi. Eyi tea gbɔ vayi lɔ wɔa kaka koa ebe goloa yɔ. Ah, wòdzo. Wòdzo va aʃeme vaɗa akplē. Via kple srɔ̃ wóɗu wókpɔ dzidzɔ.
Ayiyi va do ɗe afima, "Kɔ̃kɔ̃kɔ̃," be "Agoo. Nye me ameaɗeke dim o; ao ʃofonye nyò ewɔ alekea?" Ao, wóɗu nua keŋ 'so kpɔtɔea ʃu gbe. Ezāme tsi gāa ɗe dza, tsi kplɔ akplē yiwo susɔ kaka vayi kɔ ɗe aɗukpo dzi. Eyiyi kple viawo vayi fɔ heɗu.
Eyiyi va kuku ɗe na efoa Agɔsu be yi ɗe kuku nɛ afi wòva kpɔ nu yia le. Ne kplɔ ye yie. Agɔsu be, yoo! Ne ŋu ke koa yewoayi, ne va mlɔ anyi. Eʃo zā be ga wuiɗeke. Ye ko Ayiyi va do, "Kɔ̃kɔ̃kɔ̃," be, "Agɔsu, eŋu ke." Agɔsu be, "Ao, koklo neɗè gbè gbɔ, koklo meɗe gbe haɗeke o." "Nyawoa? Enyo mèsi, mèyi mamlɔ anyi viɗe."

Eyiyi yi koa, "Pāpāpāpāpā kɔkɔliakɔɛɛ!" Evu du kɔ yi afie, "Pāpāpāpāpā kɔkɔliakɔɛɛ!" Etrɔ yi afi, "Kɔkɔliakɔɛɛ!" "Agɔsu, Agɔsu, eŋu kè! Eŋu kè, mídzo mídzo!" Agɔsu be, "Ao, eŋu meke o, xexeame nakɔ vɔ." Eyiyi be yɔ, nenem wɔ gbe wòle mā? Enyo. Eyiyi va vudu vaðè bè le eʃe xɔdzi keŋ, va tɔ dzo ðe kɔkɔli dzi tìii! Xexeme kɔ nyɛɛ. "Agɔsu, Agɔsu eŋu kè, eŋu kè, kpɔ xexeame kɔ ða." Agɔsu be, "Ao, alɔ̄ mesum o. Vayi mlɔ anyi viðe na va. "Yɔ! Enyāwō! Enyo, mamlɔ anyi vie mava."

Ko Yiyi va xe anyi mlɔ, kè èmlɔ anyia, édɔ dɔtra. Ye be ke Agɔsu fɔ̄ dzo koa, Ayiyia gba nyɔ. (EDƆ KE EVA WƆ ZĀMEA, EDƆA LOLO WUIE.) Medɔ alɔ kaka na ga ma me o. (MEKPƆ ETEƒE.) Tsɔe ʃo miase. (MEKPƆ ETEƒE LOO.) Tsɔe ʃo miase lòo.

Tètè lagbà Agɔsu yee,
Agɔsu be yi nye yi nɔ tɔ yee,
Nuka ŋuti, Tètè lagbà Agɔsu yee,
Agɔsu be yi nye yi nɔ tɔ yee. Tìiii!

Agɔsu va dzo yi. Yiyi mekpɔe o. Enua ðe ʃu na Yiyi ŋutɔ! Agɔsu yi kaka gbɔ, va ða akplē, ka vi ðe ðo ða Yiyi. Yiyi be esɔa mi kpakple wò koe ayi. Agɔsu be ya megavɔ̄ o. Yewoayi.

Eʃo abe ga zā ga abe ga ðeka ene. Yiyi va yi yɔ Agɔsu be yewoadzo. Agɔsu be ŋu meke o. Eyi be, yō, mé goloa éŋoa wɔ fo de eme, mano efia manɔ kpom. Sɛ makpo, ne goloa koa, menya be m'dzo o. Ebe yoo, Yiyi dzo bè ðe aʃeame. Agɔsu vayi mlɔ anyi koa, Yiyi va yi ku afí (DOME FIA, DOME NUYIA) kɔ ðe kpetia me, kpètia yɔ. Tsɔ gɔme ŋɔ nɛ, to vayi mlɔ anyi, ðɔ lɔ̄, gba dzo dɔ dɔtra. Ye be kaka Agɔsu fɔ̄, Agɔsu fɔ̄ koa wòtso kpètea tsɔ kpla, kpètea 'sɔ kpla, afía kɔkɔ d'anyigba kplɔe ðo nene kakakaka egogo abe afia kple Ametɔiyikpenu ene. Wòva geðe etea gbɔ, ye ko wònye kɔ kpɔ megbedome be, "Ah! Yiyi fuflu wɔ nuyia kplema?" Wòtsɔ afia ðɔli ko nenema he vuvu kpètea keŋ he kplà m'dzo yi.

Eyiyi fɔ̄ koa, ye ko Eyi dze afí ma dzi nene kekeke va ke ðe woðoli afia kɔði. Ah! Agɔsu wɔ numa. Ye ko wòbe, "Nuka mawɔ fifia tututu ne Agɔsu na va asè ŋkɔ nye?" Yiyi ðe ébe adeyia toe, va yi si bè gāa ðe blɛ nuiðo, "Fine!" Va tsɔ kpo gāa ðe tsò, bu tame kaka tsɔ kpo va fu bèa dzi

Appendix

kpũ! "Oobobobobobobo i! Meku loo! Agɔsu, meku loo! Agɔsu, meku loo, ekpù! Agɔsu, lã lem loo!"

Ko evɔ, Agɔsu va do. "Yiyi nukae dzɔ?" Wóbe, "Avũ mēlē wō āvũ mēlē wō, nēsī lē gbɔ̄nyē mēlē woē, yɔ̄ wō ɖēkā nũa dũm kō nyā mē dūgēā? Zō midzō!" (MEKPƆ TEƑE SƐƐ.) Ƒo mísè. (MEKPƆ TEƑE.) Ƒo mísè.

Agbo wɔada de lakpɔm le 'zogbe,
'Gbo wɔoada 'gbo akpɔ ye dzɛɛ,
'Gbosu wɔada lakpɔ ye le 'zogbe.
'Gbo wɔada 'gbo akpo ye le 'zogbe. (Tĩiii!)
'Gbo wɔada kpe nyi le 'zogbe,
'Gbo wɔada 'gbo akpɔ ye dzɛɛ. (Tĩiiii!)
Meda 'kpe.

Ye Agɔsu tsɔ Yi hekplɔ wóyi. Agɔsu be ne yewoyia ɖe, ne wòanɔ anyi kpoo élè nuwo gbe megaʃo nuʃo o. "Tso enyē, nukae wɔ nyea, nye. Ye wóyi koa, wòva yi bè, "Oo!" Eté ɖokui tum alekea!

Mílɔ wɔ mídzo la!" Agɔsu be, "Blewu." Wòbe O! woa ne flu akpa, numa tae akple mélè viwowó sum o ɖo nyea mele elɔ gbe zā." Wòbe, "Yoo, woa gbɔ dzi ɖi la."

Ko, sɛɛ koa Eto va do. Eto le wɔa lom ko ebe, "O! wò ɖeka alɔ wɔ katā? Lɔ vina kpɔtɔ ɖe na mí." Agɔsu be, "Nɔ anyi kpoo la." "Enyo mèsi." Sɛɛ ko woabe, "'Mesi.' Mm! Elɔe édzo milɔe." Etoa dzo vɔ. Ebé, "Va míyi." Agɔsu be, "Nɔ anyi kpoo amebu ga gbɔnɔ." "Agbava lɔe kea? Eka lɔgbe milè?" Ebé, "Gbɔ dzi."

Ye ko evɔ, Eha va do. Tso! Eha tsya nua lɔ gbe hafi mia lɔ nua? Agɔsu be, "Nɔ anyi kpoo la, Yiyi, nɔ anyi kpoo." Ebe, "Yoo mèsi." Ko Eha va lɔ nua kaka koa, Eha dzo. Ebe, "Evɔ mídzo mí yí." Ebè, "Nɔtè."

Sɛɛ ko Enyi hā va. Enyi va tsɔ wɔa lɔ dzo. Sɛɛ koa, "Milɔ la!" Agɔsu be, "Gbɔ dzi."

Wóli sɛɛ koa, wó kple Agɔsu wózɔ yi ɖe téa gbɔ. Ayiyi be Agɔsu ne lɔe gbā, 'labe etéa le wɔ tum, ne eva lɔe, ne eva tsyi vɔa, ava sugbɔ le egbɔ. Agɔsu lɔ woa kaka eʃe goloa yɔ. Eyi lɔ woa. Eyi lɔe le zizi de edzi asɔ ezi ɖe . . . azi afɔ ɖe edzi gbì gbì gbì gbì. (NUGĀ DZƆNA DZI ƉE.) Wɔa zi ɖe edzi azi ɖe edzi azi ɖe. Ao! Kakaka, kpetea va yɔ vɔ.

Agɔsu be yewoadzo. Ayiyi be, "Enye madzo le té yea gbɔ mayi aƒeme gbava va afia kea? Etéa ɖeko madroe yi aƒeme." (YO!) Agɔsu be, "Ao, adro téa yi aƒeme?" Wòbe, "Ḕ." Agɔsu be yedzo loo. (EVA TO ÐE TAME NE.)

Agɔsu be yedzo loo. (MEKPƆ ETEƑE. NYE KƆSI AGBAGBLANYA:)

> Awuza zo ɖe gbe,
> Nanana awuza zo ɖe gbe.
> Awuza zo ɖe gbe,
> Nanana awuza ɖe gbe. . . . Tiii!

Agɔsu dzo le Yiyi gbɔ. Eyi va tsɔ tsihe he, tsɔ téa drom eta. "Mela yi aƒeme atu wɔ ne mia kple vinye. . . . Funɔ kple vinyewo miaɖu." Asite yia, blema te mi tuna. Ne Eyi ɖe afɔ ɖeka, ètéa to ke ɖeka ɖe tame nɛ. Ne eɖe efɔ evea, ètéa to ke ɖe tame nɛ. Kaka ne ezɔ zigbe "meta" etɔ̃ ene, ko evo ètéa to ke kaka la anyigba. Eyi mete ŋu tɔtrɔm o. Ko ètéa do ha ɖa:

> Yi ne gbugbɔm da ɖi lo,
> Eyi ne gbugbɔm da ɖi Ye,
> Be Agɔsunɔvi Ye, ne gbugbɔm da ɖi;
> Nye mawɔe na To,
> Eto ɖu, To dzo;
> Agɔsunɔvi Ye, ne gbugbɔm da ɖi;
> Ne mawɔe na Ha,
> Ha ɖu, Ha dzo;
> Agɔsunɔvi Ye, ne gbugbɔm da ɖi;
> Nye mawɔe na Nyi,
> Nyi ɖu, Nyi dzo;
> Agɔsunɔvi Ye, ne gbugbɔm da ɖi loo.

"Matrɔ mayi da wo ɖia?" Etè be, "Ḕ." Eyi trɔ koa, evɔ tea ƒe ke katā koe dogo le afɔ gɔme ne. Yiyi zɔ kakakaka ɖo tea ƒe noƒe koa, ètéa koe ti kpo va dze eteƒe dì! Eyie ma, "O! le blem! Ayi aƒeme. Efunɔ kple viawo aɖu wɔ le aƒeme. Magba gbeme nɔgbe o!" "Nyawoa?" Wobe, "Ḕ."

Eyi va tsɔ nude . . . afianu (agbɔnu) he kpa kɔ tea kɔ da ɖe edzi hedro. Ko téa ga doe ake:

Appendix

Yi ne gbugbɔm da ɖi lo,
Eyi ne gbugbɔm da ɖi Ye,
Be Agɔsunɔvi Ye, ne gbugbɔm di ɖa;
Nye mawve na To,
Eto ɖu, To dzo;
Agɔsunɔvi Ye, ne gbugbɔm da ɖi;
Nye mawɔe na Ha,
Ha du, Ha dzo;
Agɔsunɔvi Ye, ne gbubgɔm da ɖi;
Nye mawɔe na Nyi,
Nyi ɖu, Nyi dzo;
Agɔsunɔvi Ye, ne gbugbɔm da ɖi loo. Tìiiiii!

Eyi be, "Neble nyea, ayi aʃeme egbea. Eʃunɔ la kpɔm ado dzidɔ ɖe ŋuti nye, atu wɔ Funɔ aɖa du." Yiyi le dzi nene kakakaka va ɖo aʃeme kple téa. Nyawo etó ge . . . (FUNƆ, YI BE SRƆ́ . . . YIYI BE SRƆ́ ENYE. . . .) Yiyi srɔ̃e enye Funɔa (NYƆNUA . . . NYƆNUA . . . NYƆNUA NYIKOE TƆ. . . .) Ebe ne eyi aʃeme koa na tsɔ aɖa nɛ.

Ko ètéa eto kea, afianua sɛɛ, ekea megate ŋu ɖo lāme na Yiyi hafi Yiyi va ɖo aʃeme o. Ko eʃe afeme ɖoɖoa mia ŋutɔ m'be, ekèviwo le ta na Yiyi.

Yiyi be, "Midro nam." Ne wokɔ tea koa, Yiyi kpakple té wótso. O! (O! EFUNƆ MILEM SESIÊ LA.) Wó kpli wótso. (AVA ÐEKA ME SUA NYANU O.) Be, "Fifia ɖe fifia nuyi miawɔ koe nye be misò ta nam." (YƆ!)

Ye (wo)lé ta tso na Yiyi té! Etéa dzo va nɔ anyi dì!

Ye amegā xoxoa ɖe la Be ʃe Agrimenti xe blem nyitsɔ k̯wasida gbe ɖé ɖèa va yia, be téa, blèmatéa ne tuna wɔa, le blema mea, wómekòna bli dzi hafi wòtuna o. Ye ŋutɔ koe tuna ɖokui wólɔna wɔa nɔa ɖaɖa ɖu. Eyié va na téa va tsi aʃeme, ne metsɔ bli kɔ le edzi o la mate atu wɔ aɖa ɖu o loooooo.

Adrotseto globui mi loo!
Woezɔ kakakaka, woezɔ, woezɔ.

5.1.10. SPIDER AND THE STONE WITH EYES

Performer: Koblavi Ahadzi, 45, washerman
Date: December 7, 1978; 5:30 P.M.
Place: Chief Adjalle's house, Amoutive, Lomé
Audience: 4 adults, 20 children

Listen to the folk tale. (LET THE FOLK TALE COME.)
Folk tale fell on Spider. It fell on Squirrel; it fell on all the animals.

Spider was a great hunter. His kind is not to be found in Togo today. One day Spider went to hunt. He roamed all night long but got nothing. On his way home, he came across a large stone, a stone with eyes. Spider cried, "Hey! What's this? A stone with eyes?" Then and there, Spider fell into a dead swoon. Lying there, the stone commanded, "Come back to life." Spider stood up and said, "Oh! I've got a treasure. Stone, may I take you to a clearing by the side of the road?" Spider carried the stone and placed it at the junction of three roads.

When any large animal passed by, Spider came out and cried, "Oh, oh welcome. Where are you going?" The animal replied, "I am going to visit the town." Then Spider would point to the stone and say, "What is that?" The animal would say, "Stone with eyes." (OH OH! HE IS DEAD!) Immediately the animal fell dead. Spider dragged the dead animal away, then returned to the side of the road.

After waiting there a while, Antelope came. Spider said "Antelope, what is that?" Antelope said, "Stone with eyes." He fell dead and Spider carried him away.

The Bull came. "Papa Bull, what is that?" Bull bellowed, "Stone with eyes." He fell with a loud noise. Spider cried, "Oh, it's all over!" (ANIMALS CERTAINLY CAN FOOL ONE ANOTHER!)

All that time Squirrel was in a tree watching silently. Three days passed and no animals came. Spider lamented his plight. Then Squirrel appeared. When Squirrel came to the spot, Spider cried, "Oh Squirrel, welcome, welcome." Squirrel said, "Thank you. What's the matter?" Spider asked, "What is that?" Squirrel asked, "What's what?" Spider said, "Man, you are really stupid! Don't you know the name of that thing? What is that?" Squirrel answered, "What's what?"

Spider persisted, "What's that? Say, 'that, stone....'" Squirrel repeated, "Say 'that stone'..." then pointed at his eyes. Spider said, "You fool!" Spider continued, "Call it 'stone with e ... e ... e....'" Pointing to his eye, Spider said, "Call this thing 'stone.'" Squirrel said, "Call this thing 'stone.'"

Spider said, "You are so stupid! Say 'does a stone also....'" Squirrel said, "Does a stone also...."

"Squirrel, you are really dumb! People who came here and named the thing have long since gone home. Squirrel, say 'Does a stone also have e ... e ... e....'" Squirrel said, "Does a stone also have e ... e ... e...."

Spider said, "So many people have come and left. You are giving me trouble." (THE CHILDREN OF TODAY ARE VERY CLEVER!) "Say, 'that stone with e ... e ... ey....'" Squirrel repeated, "Stone with e ... e ... ey...." Spider said, "Stone with e ... e ... ey...." Squirrel said, "Stone with e ... e ... ey.... Spider, just say the name and let us depart!" Spider finally blurted out, "Does the stone have eyes?"

Immediately Spider fell with a thud! Spider fell! Squirrel said, "Aha! He who lays a trap for his neighbor often falls in it himself!"

Yoooooooooo.

5.2.1. MOUSE AND THE ADZIGO DRUM

Performer: Koblavi Ahadzi, 45, washerman
Date: December 7, 1978; 5:30 P.M.
Place: Chief Adjalle's house, Amoutive, Lomé
Audience: 8 adults, 15 children

Listen to a tale. (LET THE TALE COME.)

Long ago all the animals made drums for dancing, as today. There was a big dance. Leopard, Lion, all the big animals participated, but Mouse was the master of the dance drum. They were going to play at the funeral of Mouse's mother-in-law.

They were all guests in the house of Mouse's dead mother-in-law. A goat was killed for food. When the food was ready, Mouse said he was very shy and did not want to eat. He said he had eaten not too long ago and did not want to eat again.

When they began to play, Mouse became hungry and felt dizzy. What to do? Mouse said he must go to the house and gnaw at bits of porridge left in the pot. Mouse left, saying he was going to urinate. Instead, he went into the kitchen, jumped into the cooking pot, and started gnawing at the porridge, bit by bit, *klí klí klí klí*.

When he heard someone approach, he would jump out and hide under the pot. When the person left, he would come out and jump into the pot again. He did this three times.

The third time, the pot turned over and fell on him, covering him. He didn't know what to do.

The others were waiting for Mouse, for without Mouse there was no one to lead the dancing and singing. Mouse was stuck under the pot, singing.

Get ready to sing, *hoδoδio, hoδoδio:*

(Song): *'Kpaku, 'kpaku,*[1] corn-making pot,
I am trapped, I am trapped.
I wanted to do this,
I wanted to do that,

---

[1] *Akpaku* is a kind of calabash.

> I am trapped.
> I wanted to do this,
> I wanted to do that,
> I am trapped.
>
> Come, lift up the heavy pot,
> I am trapped, I am trapped.
> The heavy pot covered me,
> My *adzigo* drum mates will beat me today,
> I am trapped!

When his friends heard the song, they rushed to the house but saw no one. They could not imagine where Mouse was until they heard the song again. They ran into the kitchen, but by that time, Mouse was exhausted and his voice had changed. Very feebly he sang,

(Song):
> *'Kpaku, 'kpaku*, corn-making pot,
> I am trapped, I am trapped.
> I wanted to do this,
> I wanted to do that,
> I am trapped, I am trapped.
>
> Come, lift up the heavy pot,
> I am trapped.
> The heavy pot covered me,
> My *adzigo* drum mates will beat me today.
> I am trapped.

He was totally exhausted by the time his friends arrived. Where was Mouse? Someone said, "Let us lift up the heavy pot and look." Barely had they lifted the pot when Mouse jumped out . . . he escaped. He was gone!

In the old days Mouse lived among people. He did not live in the bush. But because he ate the food of his mother-in-law, Mouse had to go live in the bush.

This is what I was deceived with and this is what I want to deceive you with.

Yoooooooo.

6.2.7. SPIDER JUMPS OVER THE PIT

Performer: Koblavi Ahadzi, 45, washerman
Date: December 15, 1978; 6:15 P.M.
Place: Amoutive, Lomé
Audience: 9 adults, 15 children

Listen to a tale. (LET THE TALE COME.)

The tale fell on Spider. (OH! SPIDER AGAIN?) Yes. The tale fell on him and it fell on his mother-in-law.

Spider's mother-in-law asked Spider to help her work the field. Spider sent for his brothers and sisters to do the work. While they were in the field working, the mother-in-law was in the kitchen preparing yams for sixteen people. (WAS SPIDER AMONG THEM?) Yes. If you count Spider, they were sixteen.

When she finished cooking the food, she called Spider and said, "My son-in-law, come! Here are the yams I've prepared them for you." Spider announced he did not like yams and asked her to prepare *fufu* instead. She obliged and pounded *fufu*, rolling it *goro goro* into sixteen balls. (COULD HE EAT IT NOW?) Then she left to fetch some water. Before she returned, Spider had devoured the *fufu*—all of it! (OH!) Then he returned to the field.

A while later, he said to the workers, "Attention! Attention! It's time to go eat. We have been called to eat." He led them back to the house, but there was no food! Spider said, "Mother-in-law, where is the food?" The woman stared in disbelief and said, "What do you mean, where is the food? Did I not leave you here with the food I prepared?" Spider said, "No, not me! Never! Never! Never!" (HE HAD ALREADY EATEN ALL THE *FUFU*!)

"Who has stolen the food?" the woman asked. She could not understand what had happened. She knew she had prepared the food, so how could it disappear like that? The mystery must be solved by jumping over the pit. (HM! MY HEART IS ALREADY BEATING FOR SPIDER!)

The people were very hungry, but they would take part. They set a trap in a big pit. (HM!) Everybody would jump over the pit. The one who had eaten the *fufu* would fall in. The trap will catch the culprit.

(WILL SPIDER BE ABLE TO JUMP OVER THE PIT?) The people got ready. Everyone had to sing as they jumped. (WHAT IS THE SONG?)

(Song): It was a field we went to,
Mother-in-law's field we went to,
It was a field we went to,
And *fufu* balls disappeared.

It was a field we went to,
If I've eaten them,
It was a field we went to,
I must fall in the hole.

It was a field we went to,
The trap must catch me,
It was a field we went to,
May my leg stay in the trap.
It was a field we went tooooooooooo. *Dzrà!*

One animal jumped over the pit, *dzrà!* Another animal jumped over the pit, *dzrà!* Everyone jumped until only Spider remained.

He said, "As for me, I am the one who organized the work in the field. Therefore, it's not right that I have to jump." (LIE! LIE! IT WILL NEVER HAPPEN. HE MUST JUMP! SPIDER MUST JUMP!) "Comrades, wait! I'll tell you something . . . the other day we went to my mother-in-law's field. We were asked to fell palm trees. I alone felled all of them. My chest hurts and I can't jump."

The mother-in-law said, "My son, I beg you, do this thing. Jump quickly and let's get it over with so we can go back home and prepare more food." Spider said it's not possible. She told him he must do it. Spider asked, "You mean I really must do it?" "Yes!" they all exclaimed. Everyone raised their machetes threatening Spider that if he did not jump, they would cut him to pieces.

Spider said, "I'll stand over there, I'll sing and I'll jump. They agreed. (HE CAN SING AT AGOME, HE CAN SING AT TSEVIE. . . .)[1] Spider thought that if he stood far enough away and took a running leap, he could clear the pit. He struck up the song, "It was a field we went to. . . ." He ran, he ran, he lept . . . *klatsà*! (THEY GOT HIM!)[2]

"Oooooooooooh, it's not I!!!!" They told him to tell the truth and confess. "It's not I!!!!" "Tell the truth," they said. This continued until the trap caught Spider by the leg, by the arm, by the neck. . . . His face wore a strange expression![3]

The onlookers said, "Confess . . . confess!" Spider said, "I say . . . I say . . . I say it is Spider . . . that has taken the f . . . f . . . f . . . food to eat!" (OOOOOOH!) They told him to say it again. His voice changed. "If I do, will I not die? Okay, okay, I'll say it." (HE MUST SAY IT!) "It is Spider who ate the *fufu*!" (OOOOOOOOH!) A shout went up.

Spider was ashamed and ran away to hide in the clefts of the walls. That is why if you look in the clefts of walls, you will see Spider there. (YES!)

That is what I was deceived with and this is what I deceive you with.

Yoooooooo!

---

[1] Meaning "He can sing all he wants to, it won't help."
[2] Spider fell into the pit.
[3] Presumably, he was gasping for breath in the throes of great pain.

7.1.4. MONKEYS AND THE CAPS

Performer: Koblavi Ahadzi, 45, washerman
Date: December 15, 1978; 6:15 P.M.
Place: Amoutive, Lomé
Audience: 9 adults, 15 children

Listen to a tale. (LET THE TALE COME.)

The tale went and fell on a man. The man was a tailor who made caps and then went to sell them in villages. (OH! HE WAS A HAUSAMAN![1])

One day he made one cap in great numbers. These were caps like the ones the Hausa people wear. (OH! HE WAS GOING TO MEET THE MONKEYS!) His load was heavy and he was tired, so he put down his load in order to rest. (HMMMMM! HE HIT A TREE WITH HIS FOOT!) As he sat there, a large troop of monkeys came, took the caps, and tried them on one by one.

When the man came back, he noticed that the monkeys were in the trees wearing the caps. The man thought a long while but did not know what to do. When he shouted at the monkeys, they shouted back at him. Whatever he did, they did likewise. So the man took off the cap that was on his head and put it on the ground. The monkeys did likewise. They all took off their caps and put them on the ground. The man quickly bent down, collected all his caps, and left.

That's what I wanted to deceive you with.

Yooooooooo! Hausaman, welcome!

---

[1] The Hausa are a large ethnic group in West Africa, concentrated in Nigeria and Niger, and are known for their skill as traders. There are small pockets of Hausa people throughout the rest of West Africa, including Togo.

9.1.6. FROG AND HORSE

Performer: Minyanu Amuzushi, early 20s, fisherman
Date: January 10, 1979, 6 P.M.
Place: Kodzovia Kofe
Audience: 4 adults, 8 children

Listen to a tale! (LET THE TALE COME.)

The tale flew until it fell on Frog. (IT FELL ON HIM. FROG HIMSELF?) Yes, Frog. The tale went until it fell on HORSE. (IT FELL ON HIM—LAMB'S RELATIVE WITH A BIG BROAD FACE?) (laughter) The one that carries people. (YES!) That is Horse.

They were always challenging each other and others as well. One said he can run faster than his brother. Another said he can run even faster. The chief came to see what the fuss was all about. Frog came and said he can run faster than all of them! (THE FROG WE ALL KNOW?) Yes! Faster than the rest of the animals, Antelope and ... eh ... Monkey ... Rabbit. ... All said, since Horse is in the race, they would not run. (BECAUSE HORSE IS THE ONLY REAL RUNNER.) Horse is the only great runner. He will be able to pass all his friends.

Horse thought about it. Is there not one animal who will run the race? Everyone refused. Frog alone said he and Horse will run the race. (FROG? RUNNING IS NOT HIS STRONG SUIT!) Yes!

His friends looked at him for some time, saying, "How is Frog going to race Horse?" The chief said, "No, I cannot agree to this." They should stop this. Everyone else has refused. Frog will not race Horse. Frog said, "Do I not know what I can do?" They should give him a chance to show that he can run and come back.[1] ... He will show them all ... especially Horse!

Money ... and a golden staff were offered as prizes. The one who comes in first will get the golden staff ... and money. Horse said, "Frog, God is the only one who could win against me!" Horse teased and teased, saying, "Is Frog not going to kill himself? I don't understand this. Is it *juju*?" (THIS THING IS VERY PUZZLING!)

---

[1] That he can finish the race.

Appendix

Then they announced the distance and set the time. Everybody said, "This contest . . . this challenge rests between two people, Horse and Frog."[2]

Frog came and gave his name. He entered his name. The distance was like that from here to Atakpame.[3] They should run to Atakpame and back to get the "winnings," ē, the "winnings."[4]

Early in the morning people gathered and started the race. You see, before the race started, Frog tried . . .[5] in the first lap when they reach Tsevie . . . they will call the names of the contestants. When they arrive at Ŋotse, they will call their names. When they reach Ra, they will call their names. When they reach Atakpame, they will call their names to announce who arrived first. They posted officials in all four places.

Frog went to find three of his brothers.[6] He placed one brother at Tsevie, one at Ŋotse, one at Ra, and one at Atakpame. (giggles) Well, well . . . they ordered that . . . the race began. Horse started. If you saw him you would not believe it.[7] Only dust along the way! (laughter) Meanwhile Frog went *gblógbó gblógbó gblógbó* . . . and disappeared. The people kept laughing, saying, "Are we hallucinating? Horse alone is going to run the race." (laughter)

When they got to Tsevie . . . they called Horse. They called Frog. The runners were nearing Tsevie. The people were about to greet Horse when Frog jumped out and said, "*Nyē nyē nyē nyē* . . . I alone am here!"[8] (uproarious laughter) Horse said, "What trick is this?" He wondered whether he was seeing things and started to run again.

Whey they reached Ŋotse, Oh! Frog again leapt out, "*Nyē nyē nyē nyē*. . . . Horse thought he was seeing things. He turned the corner . . . he turned the corner[9] . . . he kept running until he got to Ra. But Frog

---

[2] This particular performer has a very repetitive style of narration.

[3] A distance of approximately 150 miles.

[4] The performer uses the word "gagnea," which is a bastardization of the French verb *gagner*, which means "to win."

[5] The performer corrects himself.

[6] The narrator actually means "four."

[7] Horses's speed was astonishing.

[8] "Nye" literally means "me." This is said in a sing-song comical fashion.

[9] Meaning, he kept running.

was already there in front of him, jumping up and down, saying, "*Nyē nyē nyē nyē nyē!* I have won!"

Horse didn't see anyone. He ran to Tsevie. Oh! Frog was there . . . approaching the elders, who were waving them on saying, "Here comes Frog!" Horse looked at the back of Frog's head. Why he's not even running, he . . . he passed him! (laughter) People were laughing so hard they fell down!

Horse started to run again. Tsevie . . . he approached Lomé. He ran toward the elders . . . if you saw him you would feel pity for him.

Horse ran, heading for the finish line, while on-lookers cleared the road.[10] He wanted to stop but stumbled. (HE DIED!) He and Frog were both there! It was Frog who got there first. (AH!) They exclaimed, "Frog has won! Frog has won!" Horse was not even alive to see it. He had run too hard. He was dead *yìtsìi*.[11] The people were shocked . . . they could not understand.

Actually Frog was not the only one on the road.[12] Frog and all his brothers were in the race.

That is why, if you use trickery in the world, you can win. Everyone feared Horse and withdrew from the race. Did not Frog use trickery to defeat him?

If you use trickery . . . if you use trickery in whatever you wish to accomplish . . . strength alone will not always help you.

That's what I was deceived with and what I want to deceive you with also.

Yooooooooo.

---

[10] So that the runners could cross the finish line.

[11] Meaning "dead as a stone!"

[12] The ruse consisted of placing many frogs along the route, creating the illusion that only one frog was running in the race.

10.2.1. SPIDER REMOVES THE MILL

Performer: Koblavi Ahadzi, 45, washerman
Date: January 22, 1979, 3 P.M.
Place: Amoutive, Lomé
Audience: 3 children, 6 adults

Listen to the tale. (LET THE TALE COME.)

The tale flew *vuduvudu vuduvudu* and landed on Yiyi *kpàm*! There is a man by the store watching us.[1] (IT FELL ON HIM.)[2] It fell on him. Spider was there. There was great famine. (THAT'S RIGHT!) There was no food in the village. Spider and his children . . . Spider and his children were starving to death. One of Spider's brothers named Wawuie took . . . took a gun one day and went to hunt for food in the bush. As he entered the bush, he went for eleven days. (IT WAS REALLY FIVE DAYS!) That's true. (THAT'S IT!) That's exactly right . . . they're laughing. It was eleven days.[3]

He went and came across a mill. The mill was grinding all by itself *egli! egli! egli!* (THE MILL ASKED WHERE. . . .) Wawuie said, yes, his name is Agɔsu. Yes, the mill said his name is Agɔsu.[4] (THE STORY IS GETTING HOT!)

Agɔsu stood there and watched the mill until the mill had ground a heap of flour. As Agɔsu watched, Buffalo came, gathered some flour, and left. Agɔsu stood there quietly waiting. After a while, Pig came and

---

[1]This is a reference to the owner of the bar next door who had given permission to use the electric current from his shop in order to videotape the performance. He is standing outside the immediate circle of listeners and by drawing attention to this fact, Koblavi draws him into the group.

[2]An audience member draws Koblavi back to the story.

[3]Koblavi acknowledges his concern for "narrative order," those unstated rules and conventions that shape the narrative tradition. Even if, as the audience points out, it took only five days for Wawuie to find food in the bush, the story calls for eleven days. Koblavi's comment "they're laughing" acknowledges the audience's playful complicity and participation in Koblavi's creation of comic illusion.

[4]Throughout the rest of the narrative Koblavi confuses Wawuie and Agɔsu. For the sake of consistency and clarity, I have taken the liberty to use "Agɔsu" whenever reference is made to Yiyi's other spider friend.

gathered some flour. Agɔsu again waited quietly. After Pig left, no one else came.

After a while, Agɔsu came to collect the flour in a big bag *ti*! He took it home, cooked all the flour, and ate it. (AS IF YOU SAW THE WHOLE THING!) Early in the morning, Agɔsu took the remaining porridge and threw it on the ground. Spider watched him, saying, "*Obobobobobobobobobobobo*! This isn't right! Agɔsu got all these things from the bush. Where can I get some too?" If any of you were there, you should introduce songs! (THAT'S RIGHT!)

Agɔsu went to Yiyi . . . Yiyi went to Agɔsu and asked him where he had gotten the flour. "Don't worry," Agɔsu said. At dawn they would go.

Dawn approached. It was about eleven o'clock at night. Spider went to Agɔsu. "Agɔsu, *kɔ̃kɔ̃kɔ̃kɔ̃kɔ̃*,"[5] he said. "It's day. Let's go." Agɔsu said, "No, it's not day yet. The sky isn't clear yet."

Yiyi left and went to set his house on fire. The whole sky was lit up! He said, "Agɔsu, *kɔ̃kɔ̃kɔ̃*. It's day, it's day. Let's go." Oh! Agɔsu said, "No, it's not day yet. The cock has to crow first."

Yiyi left. "*Kɔkɔliakɔɛɛɛ*." (JUST LIKE COCK CROWING!) "*Kɔkɔliakɔɛɛɛ*." Agɔsu said, "No, the sky should be clear first. Hey! What's that fellow Spider doing?"

Yiyi left and went to sleep. It was four o'clock in the morning. Agɔsu left while Spider was still asleep. Agɔsu left him there. When Spider woke up in the morning he didn't see Agɔsu. Not so?

Soon after, Agɔsu returned and brought with him more flour. Spider said, "You deceived me again!" but Agɔsu told him not to worry, saying tomorrow they would go.

Agɔsu cooked and ate his flour, throwing the rest on the ground. Spider collected the remaining flour and ate it.

When it was dawn, Yiyi said, "Tonight I will sleep by the entrance of Agɔsu's house. (laughter) Spider slept at the entrance of the house. Spider slept at the entrance of the house until daybreak. Agɔsu woke

---

[5]This is the sound of someone announcing his arrival. Since traditional houses do not have wooden doors, people usually clap their hands together to announce their arrival.

Whenever Yiyi speaks in this narrative, his voice is nasalized.

up and said, "It's not daybreak yet. Oh no you don't! You're trying to fool me!" (SPIDER HIMSELF HAS SIX FEET.) No, It's only four![6] (laughter)

Yiyi took Agɔsu's sack, punched a hole in it, and filled it with ashes, (MHŪ!) and then went to sleep.

Soon after, when he awoke again, he found that Agɔsu had left! Yiyi followed Agɔsu's trail. The ashes were spilling out of the sack. Spider followed it *kakakaka* until they came to a clearing. There Agɔsu discovered the hole in his sack and said, "Yɔ yɔ yɔ! See how Yiyi has tricked me!" He took the ashes and emptied the sack on the ground. He shook the sack clean and went on his way.

Yiyi in the meantime was following the trail of ashes a long way *kakakakakakakakaka*. (laughter) (OOOOOOOOOOOOO! BROTHER KOMLĀ IS REALLY GOING TO DECEIVE US TODAY!) Oh no! I would never deceive you! (laughter) Yiyi came across the trail of ashes. The trail suddenly stopped. The ashes had been dumped on the ground. Oh! He was finished! "I've been deceived!" he said.

Yiyi went and cut a big bale of thatch and took a large club lying near the thatch. *Ekpū! (GBI!* "THEY'RE KILLING ME!) *Ekpū! (GBI!* "THEY'RE KILLING ME!) Agɔsu said, "Scoundrels! Wait, wait, I'm coming!" He came running to see what the commotion was all about. "What's going on here?" he asked.

Yiyi said, "You fool! I caught you this time! Come on. Let's go!" (laughter) (YOU'RE REALLY FOOLING US NOW!) Oh no! I wouldn't do a thing like that!

Yiyi followed Agɔsu. They came to the mill. The mill was grinding flour. Yiyi said, "Agɔsu, let's get the flour and leave." Agɔsu told him to be patient. *Mhū!* Yiyi said they didn't do things like that in his village.[7] (HUNGER IS KILLING HIM, BUT HE SHOULD WAIT.)

---

[6]The meaning of this expression is, that despite Yiyi's excessive zeal and determination, he is not a superhero. He is an ordinary mortal being just like the rest of us.

[7]Yiyi means that where he comes from, if one is hungry, one takes the food. Waiting out of politeness or deference is not something he is familiar with or wants any part of.

Yiyi waited patiently for a moment. Buffalo came. He collected the flour and left. Pig came and did the same. "The flour will run out!" said Yiyi. Agɔsu replied, "Sit down and take it easy." (*YOOO!*)

When the animals finally left, Agɔsu went to gather flour. Yiyi said, "I'll go first." Agɔsu told him to go gather some. He gathered and gathered until his sack was full. He packed it, packed it . . . he got a club and pounded it, pounded it, pounded it . . . (HE PACKED IT *OBOBOBOBOBOBOBOBOBOBOI!*) . . . until it was full. (laughter)

Agɔsu gathered the flour and said his sack was full, so he was going to leave. But Yiyi said he was not leaving. "The mill will not sleep here today! (HEY!) I'll take it home with me so that it will grind flour for me when I cook," he said.

Agɔsu said he was leaving. Agɔsu left Yiyi there. (WHEN THE THIEF SEES A GOAT HE RUNS AWAY.[8] . . .) When Agɔsu left, Yiyi lifted the mill and put it on his head. He started to carry the mill. He took two steps when the mill began to sing:

(Song:)   Yiyi, put me down, Yiyi, put me down.
                Agɔsu's brother, Yiyi, put me down.
                I made flour for Buffalo; Buffalo ate and left.
                Agɔsu's brother, Yiyi, put me down.
                I made flour for Pig; Pig ate and left.
                Agɔsu's brother, Yiyi, put me down.
                Yooooooo! (laughter)[9]

The mill rooted . . . rooted itself into Yiyi's head.[10] (OOOOOOO!) Yiyi could not take a step. Yiyi said, "O! (IT'S ALL OVER!) What am I going to do?"

The mill said, "Put me down!" Yiyi took the mill and as he carried it, the mill jumped off and fell to the ground. Yiyi said, "Fool, you won't get away! I will take you home by whatever means it takes!"

---

[8]This is a proverb that means, when a thief on the prowl sees the shadow of something, even a goat, the thief will take off in fright.

[9]Koblavi dances the *agbadza* to this song.

[10]The roots of the mill pass through Yiyi's head.

Then Yiyi took ... went to get a tray which our ancestors called *agbɔnu*. He carved a big tray, took the mill from the ground and put it on his head when the mill *keδe keδe keδe* began to sing:

> (Song:)   Yiyi, put me down, Yiyi put me down.
> Agɔsu's brother, Yiyi, put me down.
> I made flour for Buffalo; Buffalo ate and left.
> Agɔsu's brother, Yiyi, put me down.
> I made flour for Cow; Cow ate and left.
> Agɔsu's brother, Yiyi, put me down.
> Yiyi, put me down, Yiyi, put me down.
> *Tii! Kaa!*[11]

Yiyi carried the mill home. The mill had again rooted itself in Yiyi's head.[12] He couldn't get the mill off! They struggled until both Yiyi and the mill fell down with a crash *gbli!* O!

Yiyi said, "Funɔ,[13] Funɔ, you flat-head, come! Since I brought you all these things, come at least and eat! Come help me!"[14]

Funɔ came. They got up. Yiyi and the mill had gotten up. "Do like this," Yiyi said to Funɔ. "Cut off my head!" Funɔ cut off Spider's head! (IT'S ALL OVER! YIYI WILL REMAIN LIKE THAT FOREVER.) It was from that moment on that the mill remained at the house.

In the past, the mill was in the bush. When you went into the bush the mill would grind by itself ... the mill of olden times would grind flour by itself for the people to come and gather. Today ... today because Yiyi took the mill from the bush and brought it home, you

---

[11] In singing this song, Koblavi makes a musical instrument of his body by rhythmically hitting both hands over the left side of his chest and shoulders.

[12] The tray is useless in protecting Yiyi's head, as the mill's roots pass through the tray and into Yiyi's head.

[13] Funɔ, the name of Yiyi's wife, means "pregnant woman."

[14] The literal meaning of this expression is "come share my song with me." It highlights the importance of the song in Ewe culture, for all events of importance are ritualized and commemorated in song. The expression is a metaphor for the people's communal traditions, history, joys, and sufferings. By asking his wife to share his song, Yiyi asks for her help and alerts her that he is going to tell her something important.

must first put corn in the mill for it to grind it into flour and make food.

That's what I deceived you with in front of the fire! Woezɔ kakakaka. Yoooooo!

The yam is cooking in the fire. Bring it so we can peel it and eat it. Woezɔ looooo! Yooooo!

T.10.2.1.
Koblavi Ahadzi
Amoutive, Lomé,
1/22/79

Mise gli loo. (GLI NEVAA.)
Egli tso vùdùvùdù, vùdùvùdù va dze Ye dzi kpàm! Ŋutsua ɖe va le fiase tame le mia kpóm.(EDZE DZI.) Edze dzi.
Eyi lia sia. (MHŨ.) Edo gāa ɖe va tó. (YEMA.) Nuɖuɖu megale dua me o. Ye kple viawo, do su wókple viawo be wóaku. Eyi nɔvi ɖeka wóyɔna be Wawuie, tsɔ àdè . . . tsɔ tu gbeɖeka ɖo gbe. Egbe wòɖó koa . . . eyina kakakaka exɔ ŋkeke wuiɖeka (VOA ŊKEKE AME ATƆ̃E LOO!) . . . nenema wógblɔnɛ ema. (YAA. YEMA. YEKOE MA.) Ê, yewosɔkɔna. Ŋkeke wuiɖeke sia.
Ye ko wòyi kaka ko vayi ke ɖe èté ŋti. Eté le eɖokui tu eglì! eglì! eglì! (ETE BIAE BE FIKA. . . .) Wawuie be, Ê! yiŋko tɔ Agɔsu. Ê! Etè be ŋkoe, ebe yiŋko tɔ Agɔsu. (EDZA KPA KUA ABƆ VƆ.)
Ye koa, Wawuie tsɔ tɔ tè le afima, le tea kpɔm sɛɛ kɔa, ètéa koe tu wɔ gɔròɔ. Ko be yèakpo, ko Eto koe va, lɔ wɔa xedzoe. Wawuie zikpí le afima. Wawuie le sɛɛ koa evɔ. Ha va, va lɔ wɔa. Wawuie zikpí. Ko Ha dzo koa ameaɖeke mégava o.
Sɛɛ koa, Wawuie va lɔ wɔa lɔ, goloe gāa ɖe tì! Kɔ va aƒeme, va ɖa ɖu kakakakakaka. . . . (L'EKPƆ ETEƒE!) Koa, eŋu ke ŋdi ka' wòlɔ akplē kpɔtoe ʃu gbe. Eyi le kpɔm be, "Oboboboboboi!" Nya ɖe dzɔ! Wawuie yi kpɔ nu nyuie tso gbedzi gbɔa? Fika mato akpɔ nuyia. . . ?" Ne ameaɖe kpɔ teƒe ne eha ɖe le, ne nɔ dòdò loo! (YE KOE MA!)
Koa, Wawuie vayi Eye gbɔ be . . . Eye vayi ɖe Agɔsu gbɔ bena ɖe fika wòkpɔ wɔa tsoea, ne yewoayi. Megavɔ o. Fɔʃɔme yewóaʃɔ adzo lòo.
Fɔʃɔme ɖo vɔa, eʃo zā abe ga wuiɖeke. Eyi va do ɖe Agɔsu gbɔ. "Agɔsu, kɔ̃kɔ̃kɔ̃kɔ̃kɔ̃, ŋu ke, midzo." Be, "O, ŋu meke haɖe o. Xexeme mekɔ o."
Wawuie dzó. Eyi dzo va tɔ dzò yi be xɔ. Xexeme katā kɔ nɛɛ! Ebe, "Agɔsu, Agɔsu, kɔ̃kɔ̃kɔ̃, eŋu ke, ŋu ke, midzo." O! Ebe, "Ŋu meke o. Ne koklo neku atɔ gbò."
Wòdzo. Kɔkɔliakɔɛɛɛ! (KOKLOE KU ATƆ!) Kɔkɔliakɔɛɛɛ! Wawuie be, "Ao, xexeme nekɔ gbɔ. YƆ! Nuka ŋutsu wɔ kpli ye leke hā?"

Eyi dzó va mlɔ anyi. Ga me ko eʃo ga fɔfɔme ga ene. Ne Agɔsu dzoa, Eyi dɔ alɔ̃. Wòdzo le egbɔ. Wòfo ŋdia kaka me kpɔe o. Me yia? Wòle sɛɛ koa, Agɔsu ga tsɔ wɔa gbɔe. "Yɔɔ, le blem!" Wobe, "M'gba vɔ̃ o. Etsɔ mia yi."

Wògbɔ va ɖa ɖu, Kpɔtɔa tsí wò tsɔ ʃu gbe. Ye gba lɔ ɖu ke. Fɔfɔme ɖo koa Ye be, "Egbēā mā̀ɖɔ̃ kpɔ̃... dɔ̃ nū kōkōkōkōkōkō aʃēmē mɔ̄nū madɔ̃." Eyi dɔ m'aʃeme mɔnu. Ke Yi dɔ aʃeme mɔnu kaka fɔfɔme. Wawuie fɔ vakpɔ ɖa be, O. Wòkpɔ Eyi ko wòbe, "O, ŋu meke o." Eyi be, "Le blem." (EYIA ŊUTƆ AFƆKA ADE LE ESIE? OHO! AFƆ WOAME ENE MA KOE!)

Ye sia, koa, Yiyi tso vayi tsɔ Agɔsu ʃe goloea he ŋo, tsɔ afí ku kɔɖe eme (MHŪ)! Ko dzo yi mlɔ anyi.

Sɛɛ ku, evɔ wògafɔ ko Agɔsu dzo! Eye dze Agɔsu yome. Afía ɖuɖu le mɔdzi wòdze eyome kakakaka va yi ɖo dzogbe ɖe dzi ko evɔ. Agɔsu va kpɔ ... be, "Yɔ yɔ yɔ, kpɔ Yiyi flum ɖa!" Tsɔ afía helɔ trɔ kɔ ɖe anyigba, tsɔ kpeteame vúvú kakaka ko evɔ edze mɔ.

Ko dzo yi afía fɔ do nenea kakakakakakakakaka (OOOOOOO- OOOOOO! EFO KƆMLÃ MIA BLE GE' GBE!) O la, nye me' mia ble ge o la. Ko ɖe, wòva yi ke ɖe gbɔ koa, afía vayi se. Wótsɔ afía kpɔtɔa lɔ kɔ anyi. O! Ye dɔ̃. "Eblem."

Eyie vayi tsɔ ebe yí ɖe, va yi se bè blɛ gāa da anyi. Be dí kpɔ gāa ɖe tsi bea gbɔ, ekpû! (GBI! WÓ WUM LOO!) Ekpû! (GBI! WÓ WUM LOO!) Wawuie be ... Agɔsu be, "Avū! Tɔte mava, tɔte mava." Agɔsu va do, "Nukae dzɔ? Ebe, "Avū, mele wò zɔ, midzó." (LE ADZE ÐAM ÐE!) Tsoo, me nye adze ɖam mele o.

Ko evɔ, Eye kplɔ Agɔsu ɖo. Wova yi ɖo tea gbɔ koa, ètéa wɔ tum. Eye be, "Agɔsu, mīlɔ̃ ēwɔ̃ mīdzō lā." Ebe, "Gbodzi blewu." Mhū! Oh! Mia miewɔ mia de nenema o. (A, DƆ LE WUI MADZO TƆTE GBƆA!)

Wògbò dzi sɛɛ ko evɔ, Eto va dò. To lɔ wɔa, xedzo. Eha va lɔe, xedzo. Yi be, "Ewɔ̃ lā vɔ̃ lā!" Agɔsu be, "Nɔ anyi kpoo là." (YO!)

Koa elā mawo dzo vɔ keŋ koa, Agɔsu vayi tsɔ wɔa lɔ. Eyi be, "Nyea ma lɔe gbã." Agɔsu be, "Ah! lɔe." Wòlɔe kaka yibe goloa yɔ. Wòzi ɖe eme zi ɖe eme, di kpo toe etoe etoe kaka (EZI KAKA ÐE ... OBOBOBOBOBOBOBOBOBOBOI!) ... ebe yɔ.

Appendix

Agɔsu le étɔa lɔ keŋ. Ewɔa yɔ vɔ koa, be yewòadzo koa. Yi be yemagba dzodzo gbe o. "Etéa me' afia dɔ gbe egbea o." (YƆ!) "Mako yi aʃeme ne wòatu wɔ na nya ŋtɔ, nye ɖeka manɔ ɖàɖà." (OH HOO!)

Agɔsu be yea yedzó loo. Ko Agɔsu dzó le Eye gbɔ. (FIAFI KPƆ GBƆ FI.) Agɔsu dzó. Koa Eyi tsɔ té xedrɔ. Etéa Eye dro koa, éɖè afɔ, éɖè, eve koa èté koa do ha ɖa, be:

> Eye, ne gbugbɔm da ɖio,
> Eye, ne gbugbɔm da ɖi,
> Agɔsu nɔvi Yiyia, negbugbɔm da ɖi.
> Ne me wɔe ne To, To ɖu, To dzo,
> Agɔsu nɔvvi Yiyia, negbugbɔm da ɖi.
> Nye me wɔe ne Ha, Eha ɖu, Ha dzo,
> Agɔsu nɔvi Yiyi, negbugbɔm da ɖi. Yoooooo!

Ko vò ètéa tó kè . . . tó kè ta na Yeye. (OOOOOOO!) Yeye megate' aʃo ɖem o. Yeye be, "O! (ENYA GBLE!) Leke wɔgbe mele?" Etéa be, "Tsɔm da ɖi." Ye tsɔ tea kaka va ɖo téa gbɔ, ètéa tí kpó dze anyigba dì! Eyi be, "Avū, le blem. Me 'so wòyi gbe aʃeme kòkòkò!" Koa Eyi gba tsɔ . . . vayi di afianu alo eyi mi yɔ miade be, "Agboɔnu." Afianu gāa ɖe kpa, tsɔ téa kɔ d'anyi, xedro . . . keɖe keɖe keɖe ètéa do ha ɖa:

> Yiyie, ne gbugbɔm, Eyiyie, ne gbugbɔm da ɖi,
> Be Agɔsu nɔvi Yiyie, ne gbugbɔm da ɖi.
> Nye me wɔe ne To, To ɖu, To dzo,
> Be Agɔsu nɔvi Yiyie, ne gbugbɔm da ɖi.
> Enye me wɔe ne Nyi, Nyi ɖu, Nyi dzo,
> Be Agɔsu nɔvi Yiyie, ne gbugbɔm da ɖi.
> Nye me wɔe ne Ha, Ha ɖu, Ha dzo,
> Agɔsu nɔvi Yiyie, ne gbugbɔm da ɖie.
> Eyiyia, ne gbugbɔm da ɖi.
> Eyiyia, ne gbugbɔm da ɖi.
> Be Agɔsu nɔvi Yiyie ne gbugbɔm da ɖie.
> Tii! Kaa!

Mea, koa me ya Yiyi tsɔ téa dro yi aʃeme. Eté yi wotsɔ va aʃemea, ètéa to ke, 'ta na Yeye. Mete' téa drom o. Ne wó wɔ kaka ko evɔ ètéa kple Yeye dze anyi gblì! O!

Eye be, "Efunɔ, Efunɔ, va, ta gbagba wò. Me 'so nu gbogbo gbɔ, mava ɖu nua! Va xɔ . . . va le."

Funɔ va gbɔ. Wókɔkɔe. Eyi kple téa koe kɔ dzi, newo wɔe leke, ao! Eyi be, "Mitso ta nam!" Funɔ tsɔ ta hetso ne Ye gbé! (EVƆ! EYI TSI NENEA.) Etéa dzo tsi aʃeme.

Le blema mea, ètéa gbeme wònɔna. Ne eyi ye ŋutɔ tuna wɔ, blema té, ye ŋutɔ tuna wɔ wólɔna. Fifia, fifia Eyi va na be èté va le aʃeme, ne mekò bli 'dzi oa, mate' atu wɔ aɖa la ɖu o loo.

> Ye mehe blemi le dzotikpuia nu sia.
> Woezɔ kakakaka. Yooooooo.
> Etè bi zoa me. Va tsɔ tè ve n'aʃlɛ miaɖu.
> Woezɔ looooo. Yooooo.

10.2.2. HYENA, GOAT, AND LEOPARD

Performer: Wofo Govina Otto, 33, carpenter
Date: January 22, 1979, 3 P.M.
Place: Lomé, Koblavi's house
Audience: 7 adults, 3 children

Listen to the tale. (LET THE TALE COME.)

The tale flew until it fell on Goat. (THE ONE WHO SAYS BĔĔĔĔĔ!) It fell on Hyena. It fell on Leopard. (THAT'S RIGHT!) They were there, they were there until one day Goat married Leopard. (MHŪ!) Goat came and took Leopard in marriage.

When Goat married Leopard, it was Goat who would go to the market to do the trading. When she returned from the market, she usually brought back things for her husband.

Meanwhile, a friend craved Goat. Leopard's friend is Hyena. Hyena craved Goat and wanted to kill her. In spite of Hyena's craving for Goat meat, Hyena never could find a way to get any. Hyena thought a while and wondered how he was going to get Goat.

He went out, came back, and told Leopard he had seen Goat's excrement some place. Goat's excrement was very tasty. He wondered aloud . . . how could he take . . . how could he take Goat's excrement from her stomach? Leopard asked, "Really?" Hyena said, "Yes!" Leopard said he was lying. Hyena said it was true, he saw it himself. Goat's excrement is very tasty. Why did he doubt him? (HYENA HAS ALREADY TRICKED LEOPARD!) That's right!

Hyena went out and returned . . . went out and returned after buying tiger nuts . . . (THAT'S IT!) the black nuts. He brought the black tiger nuts and gave them to Leopard to eat. (TO EAT AND SEE FOR HIMSELF.) Leopard ate the nuts and discovered how good they tasted. Leopard said, "Ooooooooo! Did I have these things here all this time and not know it? Well, okay, we'll see." (LEOPARD ATE THE TIGER NUTS THINKING HE WAS EATING GOAT'S EXCREMENT!) Leopard said he was ready to eat Goat's excrement.[1] (LEOPARD ATE THE TIGER NUTS.) Leopard ate the tiger nuts.

---

[1] The performer says Hyena but means Leopard.

Now then, soon afterwards, Hyena returned to Leopard, asking him what they could do to get more nuts. Leopard asked, what did he usually do to make the excrement so tasty? Hyena told him to get a club . . . a big club . . . a very big club. The first nut he hits will not be tasty. The second one won't be tasty either. It's the third one that will be tasty . . . and the fourth one . . . (THE THIRD ONE WILL KILL HER!) Yes, that's the tasty one. So, Leopard went to carve a club . . . he went to carve a club. He carved a hardwood club; he carved it very well with a good handle on it.

In the meantime, while Goat was at the market, her children overheard Hyena and Leopard conversing. Goat's children were in the house (LISTENING . . .) listening to the conversation. They heard what was being said. (WELL, IS IT NOT FROM CHILDREN THAT WE NORMALLY HEAR NEWS?) It's from children alright. (RIGHT!)

The children got up, left their father in a hurry *prrrr!* and went to tell their mother at the market (GOAT . . .) Goat, who was at the market. Goat asked whether indeed, this was all true. Oh! Goat headed back but stopped to buy honey . . . buy honey. . . . She poured it in a calabash, put the calabash on her head, and returned home.

When she arrived, her husband greeted her, saying "*Agoo!*" (HE WELCOMED HER.) He welcomed her and she responded, "*Yooooo.*"[2]

She asked him to help her remove the load from her head. Her husband, Leopard, helped her lift off the heavy load, but while he was helping her, the woman shook the container and poured the contents on him . . . all over him. He asked what was it that she poured on him? She told him not to worry. It was something very good. She told him to lick it and see. He licked it and found it very tasty. He asked what it was. She said it was Hyena's urine. (OH! IT'S ALL OVER!) (laughter) (HE'S GOING TO KILL HYENA NOW!)

Yes indeed! (OH!) She said it was Hyena's urine. He asked whether it was true that it was Hyena's urine? She said, "Yes indeed! Isn't it sweet?" She said she bought it on her way home from the market. He said, "Oh well, if Hyena's urine tastes this good, all is well."

---

[2]Traditional greeting and response meaning "Hello, I acknowledge your presence."

Hyena hadn't arrived yet. He had gone home to prepare for (FOR GOAT . . .) for Goat herself. Leopard said to Goat, "Have you heard what Hyena said about you?" He brought her some of the tiger nuts, that is, what remained of them. (THAT WAS GOAT'S EXCREMENT!) Yes, her excrement! And if he hit her, more excrement would come out! She said, "Is that so? You know that Hyena's urine is sweeter than my excrement." Goat and Leopard then conspired against Hyena. (THEY WERE CONSPIRING AGAINST HYENA *U-U-U-U-U*!)

They were talking when Hyena arrived. Hyena sat down and chatted for a while. Leopard went behind Hyena . . .[3] and then *vudi*! (Ai!) They started to beat Hyena. Goat lashed at him . . . she lashed at him! Urine was running from out his bottom while Leopard licked it, saying, "It's not sweet!" Goat said, "Just continue. It'll get sweet." Goat said it was not enough yet. They beat Hyena until he was dead *kranananananananana*!

Finally, Hyena was dead. They took Hyena, singed his hair, cooked him, and ate him.

That is why they say, in this world (DON'T SEEK EVIL FOR YOUR BROTHER . . .) don't seek evil for your brother. For if you wish evil on your friend, you will meet his end.[4]

Woezɔ kakakakakaka! Woezɔ looooooo!

---

[3] Narrator makes a gesture.

[4] Literally: Don't seek evil for your brother; you too just keep on your own little way and keep on at it and be watching the world. If you wish to seek evil for your friend, you will meet your friend's death.

T. 10.2.2.
Govina Otto
Amoutive, Lomé
1/22/79

Mise gli loo! (EGLI NEVAA!)
Gli zɔ̀ kaka dze Egbɔ̃ dzi. (EGBƆ̃ ATOKUI KATONI . . . BḖḖḖḖḖ!) Edze Agbètè dzi, dze Kpɔ̃ dzi. (YUIEE!) Eh, ke wóli kaka wóli koa, ke gbeδeka gbe vaδo, ke Gbɔ̃ ye va δè Ekpɔ̃. (MHṺ!) Egbɔ̃ va tsɔ Kpɔ̃ va δè.
Ye Gbɔ̃ δè Kpɔ̃a, Egbɔa eyina asime, étsànà asi. Ye be yi asigbe me, ne eyi asigbe me kaka gbɔ va, eʃlena nuwo gbɔna na esrɔ̃a. Vɔa Gbɔ̃a dzó nɔna exɔlɔ̃a. . . . Ekpɔ̃ xɔlɔ enye Gbètè . . . edzo nɔna Gbètè dzrɔm, be ne yawui. Be yima la dziona Gbètè be yeaδu, vɔa Gbeti mete ŋu kpɔna mɔ le eŋuti o. Fima mea, Gbeti va bu tame kaka be leke tutu ye le nu yia wɔ gbe fià hā?
Eyi kaka gbɔ va koa va to na Ekpɔ̃ be ye kpɔ Gbɔ̃ be mi gbale afiδea, Egbɔ̃ be mia, evivi ŋuto. Ya ebe, leke yeawɔ̃ kaka ne . . . leke yeawɔ kaka te wɔ numa . . . aga teŋ δe Egbɔ̃ be mia le dɔme nɛ hā? Ye ko Ekpɔ̃ be, "Nyawoa?" Wòbe, "Ḗ." Ebe adze δa èbéle. Ebe nyawo la, ye ŋutɔ ye kpɔe be yeto nɛ be Gbɔ̃ be mi vivi na lò, wòbe nuka hā? Ne adzea, ne yi yi xɔlɔ̃ yike gbɔ yikpɔ ma δoa, ne yi kaka gbɔ va yeadi gbɔ nɛ woakpɔ. (KPƆ DZE SƆ GBETE SƆ KPA VƆ). Yema!
Ye ko wòyi kaka gbɔ va koa . . . yi kaka gbɔ va ʃle fio-kuyibɔa (YEMA!) tsɔ gbɔe . . . Efio-kuyibɔa tsɔ gbɔe koa, ye ko wòtsɔe va na Ekpɔ̃ be ne xɔ δu. (WOAĐU AKPƆ.) Ekpɔ̃ xɔ efio kuyibɔ ma tsɔ δu kpɔ koa evɔ enua vivi na Kpɔ̃ kakakaka. Ekpɔ̃ be, "Oooooo! enuyia le yigbɔ tsā leke kafi yemenya kpɔ o hā? O, enyo, ke yewoakpɔe δa." (AKPƆ̃ ĐU BE YIĐU EGBƆ̃ BE MI!) Agbete be yea yeδe Egbɔ̃ be mi vɔ. (AKPƆ̃ ĐU FIO!) Eδu fio xoxo.
Evɔ Gbeti li zāa δe koa. Ye ko wòva trɔ va Kpɔ̃ gbɔ be leke, nya yia wógblɔ δe ate dza wɔ̀nya nuti dɔ hā? Yeko wòbe leke wòwɔna hafi emia vivi na hā? Ebe O, ne eyi 'so kpɔ . . . be kpò ga lokpò wókpana, be lòlòna nyui δe. Ko né légbé 'sɔe, né le dui ni tutu gbā, yibe dona koa mevivina o. Eyi ne gba dui ni zi evelia, eyi ne doa goa mevivina o. Etɔ̃liae vivina. Etɔ̃lia ku enelia 'so yi dzia. . . . (ETŌLIA EWUGBE!) Ehē,

Appendix

ye vivina! Koa, wótso va yi kpa kpò ... wóva yi kpa kpò enuyi. ...
Wótsɔ xé kpo ŋutɔ wókpe nyui ɖe adóduímetɔ wókpa leʃe ne nyui ɖe.
Ko ne Egbɔ̄ nya dzo yi asime koa, Egbɔ̄ me viwo, ke wóle asema
kama. Egbɔ̄ be viwo dzo lè aʃeme ... (NYA SEM. ...) sɔ nya sɔ se. Nya
be nene yi wógblɔ le yewonɔ ŋuti ema. (KO AƑE BE NUGBEGBLEA ÐE
MENE ÐEVIWONU WOSENA ÐO OA?) Ɖeviwonu wósenɛ ɖo. (Ẽ!)

Ye ko wótso ko ɖe ... enuyi koe 'so ... deviwo 'so prrrr! le wotɔ
gbɔ kɔ ɖe wódzo dza tsɔ nya va 'sɔ gblɔ na (EGBɔ̃!). Egbɔ̄ le asime.
Egbɔ̄ be nyawo hã? O! Egbɔ̄ dza yeagbɔ koa, Egbɔ̄ koe va dze anyitsi
keŋ ... tsɔ dze ... nyitsi keŋ koa, 'sɔ kɔ ɖe ètré me 'sɔ ɖo agba dzi kéɖé
koa dzo gbɔvɔ.

Koa ... yi ko wòva ɖɔ aʃeme ko yi ko wòbe ... va ɖo afima yi ko
srɑ̄a tsɔ ago do nɛ ... (WOTSO WOEZƆ DO NE) ... woezɔ do nɛ, koa
wòbe, yooo.

Yiko wobe ne dro ye. Ye ko srɑ̄a zɔ ... Kpɔ̄ zɔ kaka ko va 'sɔe dro
ko, yi dro gbe ko nyɔnu nye keviwo, nua kɔ ɖe edzi ... yiko nua kɔ ɖe
edzi. Wòbe O, nuka wòtsɔ kɔɖe yi ŋuti hã? Yiko wòbe, o la, be nu
nyuiɖe ŋutɔe. Be ne ɖuɖɔe kpɔ. Yi ko wòɖú ɖɔe nyuiɖe kpɔ koa, wòvivi
nu kaka. Wòbe, nukae yia hã? Wòbe o, be Gbete be aɖùɖoe ma.
(OOOO! EVƆ! WODZA WU AGBETE ZƆ. FIFIA EFIA ÐUI SƆ ƑLE
ADZETƆ EMA.)

Yema! (OO!) Ebe Agbeti be aɖùɖoe ma. Ebe, "Nyawoa Agbeti be
aɖùɖoea?" Wobe, "Ẽ." Oh! Ye vivina nene hã? Wòbe evivina ŋutɔ. Be ye
yi asinu fia ko wolesɑ̄ le asiame yi ko yifli gbɔe. Wòbe, "Oo, ne Gbete
be aɖùɖɔ le lekea, ke ela nyo ŋutɔ.

Gàma Gbeti m'kpɔ va haɖe o. Eyi aʃeme dza trɔ va le dzra ɖo le. ...
(EGBƆ̄ ŊUTI!) Egbɔ̄ ŋuti vɔ. Yeko wòbe Ā, be ekpɔ nuyi Gbeti gblɔ 'so
eŋuti hã? Be etsɔ nuyia va fia yi la ... etsɔ nua ɖe kpɔtɔ 'sɔ fiɛ ... efioa
ɖe kpɔtɔ wòtsɔ fiɛ bena be ekpɔ étsɔ nuyia va fia bena de (EGBƆ̄ BE
MIE MA!), Ẽ. Yibe mie. Be ne yewofoe koa be mia adogo. Wòbe,
"Nyawoa?!" Wòbe, "Ooooo ... aɖùɖɔ ŋutɔ boŋ ema be aɖùɖɔ vivina
ŋutɔ." Fyi gblɔm molea, o ɖɛ Ɛgbɔɔ kple Ekpɔ wòdzo bla ɖe Gbeti ŋuti
(WOBLA SE LE GBETI ŊUTI DA ÐI ... UUUUUU!)

Wódzo le afima le asem ka ko Gbeti va ɖo. Gbeti be ɖoɖo kple
maɖomaɖo ko yi ko wóva asem ka zɑ̄aɖe koa evɔ. Ekpɔ koe ... be yeato
megbe dɔme na Gbeti alé koa de, vudi! (AI!) Yi ko wò ɖe Gbeti dzi.

Egbɔ̃ tsya ye ɖe edzi wó ya edzi. Aɖùɖɔ dodo le gɔme nɛ. Ekpɔ̃ le eha nɔ ɖúɖɔm be me vìvím o. Be o, ega kpɔtɔ . . . be nɛ yi dzi. (HOOOO.) Meka be . . . ne do, ne guda. Koa, ebe mékpɔ su hade o wóle fo, wole Gbeti fo nene kakakaka ko evɔ Gbeti koe ku kranananananananana.

Fima ye Gbeti dzo ku vɔ koa. Wótso Gbeti le keŋ, tsɔe me keŋ, tsɔe dza, tsɔe ɖu.

Fima wógblɔ bena ɖe ne ebé xexemea ɖe (MEGBA DI VƆ̃ NA NƆVI O) . . . megba di vɔ̃e na nɔviwo o, wo tsya wo ŋutɔ tɔwo vi tukuia dzi elea ɖe, nɔ dzi na nɔ yiyi na nɔ xexeme kpɔ loo. Ko me lebe yeanɔ vɔ̃e di na nɔviwoa ɖe wo ŋutɔ la xʋ nɔviwo kua sɔ ku loo.

Woezɔ kakakakakaka. Woezɔ looooooo.

10.2.3. SPIDER AND DEATH

Performer: Otto Govina, 33, carpenter
Date: January 22, 1979, 3 P.M.
Place: Amoutive, Lomé
Audience: 7 adults, 3 children

Listen to this tale. (LET THE TALE COME.)
The tale rose and fell on Death, Azangidigo.[1] (IT FELL ON HIM.) It fell on wild animals. (IT FELL ON THEM.) It fell on Spider.

One day famine came into the village. The question of food became a problem. Spider thought about going to see Azangidigo to ask him for food. But if Death gave someone food, he always set a date when he would come and take that person away.

Spider decided that he would go to Death anyway. He went and saw Death and told him his needs. He told Death he needed yams and cassava. (SPIDER NEVER HAS ENOUGH FOOD!) Death led Spider to the field and Spider dug up as much cassava and yams as he needed, then packed the things in a basket. He began to sing:

(Song:) Death wants to eat,
Ẽ, Ẽ, Death wants to eat,
But Death will never eat me.

While Spider was going back home, he met many wild animals on the way who asked him where he had found food. He told them he had found a big farm and it was there he had gotten the food.

When Spider arrived home, he went to see Efui[2] and told her they would become friends. Efui could come stay with him and he would give her food. But at night, a friend of Spider's will come, so Efui should open the door for him.

Efui agreed and came to stay with Spider. They ate until they were satisfied. When night fell, they went to bed and after a few hours, they heard knocking at the door. Spider called Efui and told her to go open

---

[1] Nickname for Death.
[2] It is not clear what kind of animal is Efui. It may be a kind of antelope.

the door. As soon as she opened the door, Death knocked her down with a heavy piece of wood and she died. Death went away thinking it was Spider he had knocked down.

When Death had gone, Spider smiled and took the dead Efui, cooked her and ate her.

Then Squirrel came and asked Spider to help him find something to eat. Spider said he would help him. Spider prepared food and they ate. But when it was night Spider told Squirrel to sleep near him. Squirrel answered that he had some important work to do and could not stay.

Spider went back to Death's field to get more food. Seeing him, Death was astonished and asked him if he was not dead. Spider answered that he had not died when Death tried to kill him. Death gave Spider more food and Spider went home.

Another animal came and asked Spider to give her food to eat. Spider agreed. She ate and he did to her the same thing he had done to Efui. Spider managed to set a trap for many animals and they all died.

One day Mole came to ask Spider for some food. Spider told Mole what he had to do if he wanted food. Mole accepted gladly and went back home. He dug a hole all the way from his house to Spider's room. When it was night, Mole joined Spider and they ate and went to bed. After a few hours, there was a knock at the door and Spider told Mole to open the door. He called Mole many times but Mole did not answer. Mole had gone home through the underground tunnel. Spider himself had to get up and open the door. Quietly, Death raised his log and hit Spider on the head. Spider fell down and died.

I've told you this story to teach you that there is more than one clever person in a village.

My voice has fallen down.[3]

---

[3] I have finished.

18.1.1. GOAT IN THE VILLAGE OF ANIMALS

Performer: Kɔdzo Gadagboe, 44, farmer
Date: March 27, 1979, 5 P.M.
Place: Kpalime
Audience: 5 adults

It's Kɔdzo Gadagboe . . . again telling you a story and those people listening at the entrance . . . they will hear . . . as will those who read it in the newspaper . . . they too will hear.[1] Now, for what I am going to tell you it's appropriate that I begin with the following.

Listen to a tale. (LET THE TALE COME. LET THE TALE COME.)

Mhhhhhh.[2] The tale fell *ziŋŋ* and fell on Goat. It fell on Hyena. It fell on Lion. It fell on Leopard. It fell on all the animals *pɛtɛpɛtɛpɛtɛpɛtɛpɛtɛpɛtɛ*[3] in the forest. (THEY WERE ALL THERE.) Is it not said in a story that tapped wine will spoil? What happens to the stomach cannot happen to the shinbone. If it happens to the skin, the bone will be exposed.[4]

So there we all were. In the olden days the wild animals all lived in one place. They were in a village, a big village, they all lived there. One day . . . oh . . . they left and went to work on the farm. They always left someone to guard the house because they did not want to lose their things. That's right . . . there were thieves in the village.

One day they asked, "Who is going to guard the village?" Hyena said he was strong. If anyone showed up and he knocked the intruder on the head *ti*, he (the intruder) would die. So he'll guard the village. All agreed. They were sure Hyena would be able to do the job.

---

[1] This performer has a rather unique style of narration and chooses an original type of introduction.

[2] The implied meaning is "exactly."

[3] This ideophone emphasizes the idea that *all* the animals were involved.

[4] These are two proverbs. The first one means that well-tapped wine ordinarily will not spoil, but in a story where anything can happen, even well-tapped wine can spoil. The second proverb also refers to the extraordinary events that can happen in narratives. The stomach can absorb blows which the shinbone cannot. The stomach, therefore, is likened to the narrative universe where things can occur which could not occur in ordinary real life. The shinbone is fragile and could not withstand the blows.

Brothers and sisters, isn't that so? (YES!) *Ehē*. So Hyena guarded the village while they went to the bush. Everybody went to his own farm.

Soon after, there was a knock, *agoo*. "*Ame.*"[5] A man came in. He did not . . . he did not equal Hyena in strength. He came to the house. He said, "Oh my friend, Hyena, won't you give me the meat that's on the fire? I'm very hungry. That's why I came." Hyena went and brought him a leg.[6] He said it wasn't enough for him. He should give him all the meat.

Hyena saw he was a thief so he refused. An argument ensued. Hyena thought himself strong so he wanted to fall on the Short Man and grab him. Hyena excreted around the whole village.[7] Ah! Is this an easy case? He finally had to beg the little man . . . he begged him . . . not to return tomorrow . . . not to do it again. He took the meat from the fire and packed it up for the small round man *kpaŋ kpaŋ*! The Short Man took it and left.

In the evening when the animals returned from the farm there was no meat to eat soup with. They questioned Hyena but Hyena couldn't open his mouth. All around were footprints and a lot of excrement. They asked how come Hyena, whom they left to guard the village . . . how come all of a sudden things turned out so badly for them?

It wasn't an easy matter, not easy to all. So they kept quiet and waited for tomorrow.

The next day they said they were leaving again. Who would be able to do the "strong man's job" and guard the village for them? Leopard said he would . . . he would guard the village so that if anyone dared to come, they would find a dead body when they returned. The animals went to the farm. Leopard was left alone in the village.

Again, there was a knock. The Short Man came, the one who had beaten Hyena to a pulp, was here again. This time he came to meet

---

[5]These are standard greetings. Because village houses often do not have wooden doors, people clap their hands to announce their arrival and say "agoo." In response, the person in the house acknowledges the visitor's presence by saying "ame" ('person').

[6]Literally: he brought him an arm.

[7]He excreted, presumably, to scare the short man off with the bad smell.

Leopard. Leopard trembled saying, "How come. . . . ?"[8] How did he dare? Wasn't he the one who was here yesterday? "Yes, of course," the man answered. Hadn't he asked Hyena? Leopard said they have nothing to talk about. His business was with Hyena. . . . [9]

The man asked him whether he didn't have a taboo?[10] Leopard told him to take this one. The Short Man caught Leopard's tail and started whipping him, *ao*! Leopard didn't dare . . . he couldn't open his mouth! Just as I was saying this, Leopard excreted over the entire village. His paws had clawed the ground all over . . . his screams . . . his screams. . . . Finally, he gave up. He begged the Short Man for mercy. Leopard went and cut palm branches, made a basket, took the meat, put it in the basket and put the basket on the creature's head so he would leave.

The big animals returned in the evening. Oh no! There was no meat! "Leopard, you who are a hunting animal, we had more confidence in you than Hyena. What happened?" Leopard showed his disgust *nts*. He couldn't talk, it pained him too much. Oh! "What are we going to do?" asked the animals.

It was another day. Another animal guarded the village. Lion . . . he too was not up to the task. Elephant took his turn. . . . Since they had all failed to guard the village, they decided to move. Isn't that right? They made a plan to move and all agreed. They moved, all of them *pɛtɛpɛtɛpɛtɛpɛtɛ* . . . all the animals left and went to start over in a new village.

The following day they wondered, what are they going to do? They said, today they would make special food to eat in the evening on their return.[11] They decided they would all go into the forest and bring back an animal before they built another shelter. They finished preparing

---

[8]Literally: "How is it?"

[9]Literally: There is no case between them. It was between him and Hyena.

[10]Whatever is a "taboo" is considered to be sacred and may not be touched or uttered without risking one's safety and well-being.

[11]Literally: They will make slices to eat.

their food. They wanted to grind pepper to eat with their food, but their grinding stone was left in the other village.[12] *Ao!*

Who would go and bring back the grinding stone? Everyone remained quiet. They all remembered what had happened to them in the other village. It was a big problem. It wasn't easy. It was a very big problem. They thought for a while. They wanted to send someone who was strong, who could run and get back quickly. They thought . . . they thought . . . they chose Dog because he could really run. Eh! "Your father is Kɔsi; your mother is Kɔsi." Yes, he said, that was his name . . . he who runs and doesn't sweat. He could run and get back before a word is uttered . . . and he wouldn't sweat. "Is that so?" He said yes.

They said, "*Axe*,[13] go and bring back the grinding stone." Axe agreed. He tucked his tail between his legs tightly *go go*. (laughter) You know him already, don't you? (OH, WE KNOW HIM ALRIGHT!)

When he took off,[14] it didn't even take him six minutes to get there. Before you knew it, he was back again.[15] When he returned, he opened his mouth, stuck out his tongue, panting *xaxaxaxaxaxaxa*, but he wasn't sweating at all. He wasn't sweating at all. They praised him, not knowing about the Short Man.

The Short Man had gone to the first village looking for the animals but in vain. He saw no one but did find the grinding stone. In our Ewe language we have a thing we call a *sɔsi*.[16] He took the *sɔsi* and hit the grinding stone. Lo and behold, the stone split in two, *klpà!* He entered the stone and the stone closed. He sat there calmly *kpóo*.

The dog came and took the stone. (OBOBOBOBOBOBOI!) (laughter) *Ehē!* It wasn't easy. He took the stone to the new village. Unwittingly, he brought the Short Man to the animals' new village. He showed him their house!

The animals were grinding pepper. As they were grinding . . . the Short Man was lying in the stone very still, *kpi*. They finished grinding

---

[12]Literally: Just as they finished making their main course, they found they didn't have the stone with which to grind the pepper.

[13]Nickname for a dog.

[14]Literally: He fired, meaning he took off like a bullet.

[15]Literally: Just as I was saying this, he was back already.

[16]Literally: a horsetail wisk.

the pepper and prepared to eat. They made a circle. One of them bragged he would call the Short Man and insult him. Another bragged he would call him and insult him . . . everybody should insult him because if you didn't insult him, others would think you were conspiring with the Short Man and the *compagnie*[17] would look at you with suspicion. Yes, the people would look at you with suspicion *pɛpɛpɛpɛpɛpɛ*.[18]

Another said he would insult him by saying that he was plump and bothersome . . . and if he dared come again, he would stomp him . . . they would all stomp him. (THE BAD PERSON?) Yes, the bad person *pɛpɛpɛpɛpɛpɛpɛpɛpɛ*. So it went. They all bragged and said anything they felt like saying.

Just as they were about to eat, the stone opened up and someone said "*Agoo.*" (*TSALÉLÉLÉLÉ.*)[19] Everybody simply . . . everybody stopped in midair. (laughter) (IT'S BAD NEWS. MAN AND SON HAVE ARRIVED.)[20] I swear, it was no joke. Yes, *Agawu Kakrakas*[21] has arrived. When they saw him . . . nobody who saw him needed to be told what to do.[22] (laughter) This had happened to them before—in the other village. Here it was happening again. They took off as if they were in a race. They scattered *pɛtɛtɛtɛ*. No one remained.

They again formed a group and settled in a third village. There they lived in peace. They left the grinding stone, they left everything behind. No one asked that it be brought to the new village. (laughter) If they needed a grinding stone, they would look for a new one. (laughter) (ARE THEY EVER COWARDS!) No one—but no one—should go and bring back anything. They agreed . . . so they decided among themselves.

---

[17]The performer uses the French word *compagnie* but an audience member corrects him, giving the Ewe word *fufofea*.

[18]Meaning "exactly."

[19]This expression indicates surprise, fright, and shock.

[20]Suggesting that the worst or the impossible has happened.

[21]This reference is not clear.

[22]Literally: Just after his emergence, when they saw him, everybody whose eyes came across him, when you saw him, nobody wanted to be told by his brother to look, get up and start, find some place to go.

In the new village they saw that Goat was not strong at all. Moreover, he had no claws with which to hunt. In the evening when everyone returned from the bush, they all brought back game. That was what they ate. Goat couldn't kill anything. So their big man . . . that big man Lion—five fingers four legs—you've heard of him, he said, "From now on, from this day forward, anyone who does not bring back game, will not eat with the others. Moreover, anyone who does not comply with the new decree, will be sorry." He told everyone to go and bring back game from the bush. Anyone who doesn't bring back any . . . the animals will grab him and eat him. (GOOD GRIEF!) Yes, the law is strong!

Goat did not have any claws. He had nothing to hunt with. He ate only grass and the meat the animals prepared. What was he going to do? All the animals went in turn and returned with game until it was Goat's turn. They told Goat it was his day to go. He should go to the bush. Goat said, "Is that right?" Goat went to the bush. He went to bring back some meat. But how was he going to manage to kill game?

He came across an old . . . an old *kɔdzokpui*.[23] He started to butt her, thinking if he butt her long and hard enough, he would butt her to death and take her home. But she asked him why he was bothering her like that. He said he was obeying a law made in the village and therefore, when he saw her he wanted to butt her. She said she would show him some *juju*. If he used the *juju* he would be able to kill any animal in the bush from then on. But if he saw her, he should not kill her. Goat agreed.

The grandmother *kɔdzokpui* picked some leaves. She rubbed them in her palm like this[24] and asked him to turn his anus toward her. Goat did so. She squeezed the juice of the leaves into his anus and inserted the squeezed leaves as well—like you put suppositories in people. Then she told him that what she has done, from now on if he meets any animals, he should tell them to inspect his anus . . . that there's a swelling there. As the animal turns his face, Goat should fart *ti*. A bullet will shoot out and kill the animal, which he can then take home. (IS THAT RIGHT?) But he should never get wet. Goat agreed. Do you see

---

[23]This may be a nickname for the leopard.
[24]The performer makes a gesture rubbing his palm.

why this is a difficult matter? (IT'S DIFFICULT ALRIGHT!) Goat said, "Okay." (GOAT? OH NO!)

Goat left and soon after, he met an old grandmother Hyena. He said, "Oh, Grandma Hyena, I have a boil. I've tried but I cannot see it. It's in a place where I can't see it." He begged her to come take a look to see if it was "ready."[25] He turned his anus toward her. As she bent to check it . . . (HE HIT HER!) He hit her and she fell down flat. (WHAT!) Goat used his horns, put them beneath Grandmother Hyena, and rolled her back to the village.

When Goat arrived, the animals looked at him in disbelief. They told Hyena to go burn[26] Grandmother Hyena. While he did so, he wept. It was his grandmother who had been killed. He wept. . . . They asked him what was wrong. He said the smoke was bothering him. Oh! They finished preparing the animal, cut it up, put it on a curing rack,[27] and smoked it. They cooked it and ate. Hyena said he had a headache, he didn't want to eat, he didn't feel well enough to eat. Grandmother Hyena . . . he couldn't eat his own grandmother!

The next day the animals wondered how Goat was able to kill Hyena and bring her home. They decided they would make him go into the bush again. Goat roamed all over until he came across a lion. He told Lion he had a boil so he should come and check it. Before Lion could bend over . . . (OH NO! MAN!) The gun fired! (HE LET HIM HAVE IT!) Lion rolled over. (IS THAT SO?) (laughter) He dragged Lion until he got him home. The other animals found it hard to believe. They puzzled and puzzled over it but couldn't imagine how Goat was managing to kill these animals.

While the animal burned, Lion wept. "What's the mattter?" the animals asked. Lion said the smoke was bothering him. The animals wondered how Goat had killed the animals he brought home. Who could find out?

Squirrel said he could. Since he could hide in the grass, he could do the job. Someone pointed out, if Squirrel found groundnuts, he

---

[25]Literally: He begged her to come see if the boil was ready to burst.
[26]The animal was to be burned in order to remove the hair and fur.
[27]This is the way meat and fish are cured and preserved in the traditional manner.

would forget about Goat . . . and they wouldn't be able to trick Goat. Another said, only Cat could do it. Cat said he would go *pɛpɛpɛpɛpɛ* and spy on Goat, then come back and tell them, because he thrives on cunning and patience. So they sent Cat after Goat.

When Goat left the village, Cat followed, tracking him stealthily . . . patiently . . . tracking him until he got to the bush. Just then, a leopard passed. Quietly Goat watched. He knew the Leopard's immense strength. He wasn't going to kill any small weak animal. From now on, he would hunt only big animals, hunters themselves. That way there would be a challenge.

Leopard passed by. Goat saw Leopard and called him. He told him to come and see whether the boil was ready.[28] As soon as Leopard showed his face, Goat pulled the trigger. (HE FELL!) Leopard fell while Cat watched. Is this how it is? (HE HAD *JUJU*!) Goat certainly had something. . . . Cat ran away. (laughter) He raced through the grass *tsrà tsrà tsrà tsrà*.

Cat told the animals what he had seen.[29] "This is how it is," Cat reported. "If tonight Goat lies next to someone, if he turns his anus toward that person, that person will die!" (laughter) Hey, it's true! It's no joke! (laughter) (ISN'T THAT SERIOUS?)[30] It's a serious matter. Well, would you let someone turn his anus toward you?(NEVER . . . NOT ON YOUR LIFE!) This is what Cat told the animals.

When it was evening, Goat returned, dragging the dead Leopard home. Oh! Everyone was frightened . . . even Elephant was afraid. They started to cook the elder Leopard. Young Leopard himself wept. "What's wrong?" asked the animals. Leopard said the smoke was bothering him. Every time game was brought, someone among the animals was asked to cook the meat. (HIS MOTHER!) That was the rule. (THAT HE SHOULD COOK HIS RELATIVE!) He should go and cook his relative. (laughter) While doing that, the animal would weep and say smoke was bothering him. They stared at Goat with great apprehension.

---

[28] Literally: whether the boil in his anus was ready to burst.
[29] Cat snitched on Goat.
[30] Meaning, "the matter is dangerous."

Appendix

At night while Goat slept, everyone would shift to one side *wuii* (laughter) to sleep. (HE BECAME THE CHIEF OF THE HOUSE!) Goat slept for a while—as people do when they toss and turn. As soon as Goat turned ... (uproar) (HIS FRIENDS MOVED TO THE OTHER SIDE ... HE BECAME THE CHIEF IN THE HOUSE!) Right! (laughter) Yes! Who told you?[31] Goat was all powerful. He became the chief. When Goat lay down and moved a little, everyone was alert. *Ehē!* (laughter) (THEY COULDN'T SLEEP ... THERE WAS NO SLEEPING!) There was no sleeping. When they lay down and Goat moved a little, everyone was alert. (laughter)

Daylight came. It was day. They worried about Goat's ability to remain in the house. Goat troubled them. Finally they said Goat should not go to the bush. He should become the chief in the village. He should not go to the bush anymore. They tested him for three or four days and found that Goat was strong, no doubt about it. It was someone else's turn to go to the bush. Whatever was brought back, they wouldn't refuse ... they'd eat it.

Meanwhile Goat remained at home. At night when Goat slept and turned his anus toward them, the other animals moved to the other side. (laughter) This went on all night long. If Goat turned like this,[32] there was general pandemonium. (laughter) (THEY WOULD TURN TO HIS FRONT.) Exactly! (IT WAS NO JOKE!) So Goat became the chief in the village. He who had never been strong became the chief.

They then decided to make some plans. They had had enough. Why was Goat bullying them so? Was it because of the bullets in his anus? He asked why they were asking such a thing. A big argument broke out between Goat and the other animals. They wanted to beat Goat to death. If they didn't kill him, there would be a long and bitter feud in the bush ... never to be reconciled. So that day, they decided they would kill Goat. Everyone was of one mind—they would beat Goat to death.

As soon as Goat turned ... turned his anus toward them, he "hit his gun." Whenever Goat turned, the person fell over. (THE PERSON

---

[31] The performer is joking with an audience member, reproaching him in a jocular manner.

[32] The performer gestures showing how the Goat turned around.

DIED!) Goat finished them off like that, one by one. HE WORKED HIS JUJU ON THEM! There was general pandemonium. They wanted to run away. The animals said they were no longer brave enough to withstand what was happening. They should run away, so they dispersed.

Goat alone remained. The number of animals he had killed, however, was large. (SOUP!)[33] You see, my brothers, when you take a gun into the forest and kill that many animals, you can get tired of eating the same thing. (THAT'S TRUE!) Yes. Goat was tired of the game he killed; he couldn't eat it any longer. When night . . . Goat was the only living creature among all the dead animals. Goat said, the way things are, he too should leave and go some place else.

Goat started running . . . it hadn't started to rain yet. It was dark and cloudy. Rain clouds covered the sky . . . it was dark but it wasn't raining yet. Goat kept going. Remember the wind that blew last time? That kind of wind started blowing now. You see, the Twi say that rain is always preceded by wind.[34] (TRUE! WIND PRECEDES RAIN.) The wind started blowing. Goat started running . . . running . . . running . . . until the wind subsided a bit. Heavy rain began to fall. Goat was being rained on. He was bleating *bē! bē!* (GOAT'S *JUJU* IS DEAD!) *bē! bē!*[35] He ran like that in the rain until *tòliò!*[36] He arrived in a town like Tove.[37] Quickly, he crossed the tarred road and approached a building. He went to hide under the house there. He was very wet, however, and cold. He didn't see anyone in the house . . . so he remained there. He slept there until daybreak when he crept along the wall of the house and entered. (OH!)

The owner saw an animal! He called him and asked him what his name was. Goat identified himself. "What's the matter?" the owner asked. Goat told him the whole story . . . what had happened in the

---

[33] Literally: He made soup of all the animals.

[34] This is a Twi proverb. The Twi are Akan-speaking people who live in Ghana.

[35] This is the bleating sound made by the goat as he runs.

[36] This is an ideophone which in this context marks surprise at seeing the town.

[37] Tove is a town near Kpalime where the performance takes place.

forest, how he escaped, the rain that fell . . . fell on him until he came to the building. When he got there, he said the house was quiet. Everyone was in bed. That's why he didn't knock on the door but remained outside by the wall instead. He waited for daybreak before entering the house.

The owner asked him what was on his mind. Goat said when he escaped from the bush, he was left all alone. All the animals had scattered. He did not know where they had gone. So he came here to live with him. "Is that so?" said the owner. "Yes," answered Goat. That's how Goat entered the human community. That's how Goat became a domestic animal. He no longer . . . none of his kind lives in the bush anymore. Any animal called Goat no longer lives in the bush. From that day on, Goat became a domestic animal.

Furthermore . . . the rain that fell, the big rain that fell on him . . . turned Goat's bullets into excrement. That's why when Goat excretes, his excrement looks like bullets . . . like ball bearings. Goat's excrement became like ball bearings. From that day on Goat became a domestic animal and no longer has "bullets" in his stomach. His bullets turned into excrement.

This my grandfather heard a long time ago and never forgot, and I still remember it until today. So those of you at the gathering here, you also should hear. People who read it in a book should hear how this happened a long time ago.

I stop here. Good night.

Yooooooooo. Woezɔ kakakakakakakaka.

T.18.1.1.
Kɔdzo Gadagboe
Kpalime
3/27/79

Enyo Kɔdzo Gadagboe. Ke sigbe alesi mínɔ se vayi ene ... wó dzim le Kpalime, yaa me xɔ fe blaenevɔene. Menye agbledala. Nyee ga le nutinya viaðe gblɔ na me gbe egbea na ameyiwo xe le todzi le mɔnua, wóase, ya ameyiwo xe nava xlɛ le "paper" me alo "newspaper" gbalɛ me tse yewó tsye, yewó tsye wóaganɔ se.

Azɔ nya yi xe gblɔ gbe megbɔ egbea, ewɔ nam be ma gblɔ na mi be, "Mise gli loo ye migblɔ nam be, egli neva (EGLI NEVA ... EGLI NEVA). Mhmmmm. Egli tso zíŋŋ, va dze Egbɔ dzi, wòdze Gbete dzi, dze Adzata dzi, dze Kpɔ̃ dzi, dze lāwo pɛtɛpɛtɛpɛtɛpɛtɛ dzi le gbeme. Wóli wóli wómegblɔe gli me o. Egli kpa aha, aha ya. Enui wɔ dome mewɔ akpatigbe o, ne ewɔ akpatigbe eʃua na dze.

Yaa ... miawoe yi kakaka koa, eh ... egbemelāwoa, wo keŋ keŋ teʃe ðela wónɔa tsā. Ye wóle koʃe ... wótso koʃe gāa ðe wó ʃete le kɔʃea me. Gbeðeka ... oh ... wódzo yi agble dɔwɔʃe. Ne wóyie ðe agblea, ame nɔ aʃea me dzɔ kokoko, elabe wóbe nuwoa, wómedi be ni bú o. Ah, yewo tsye le nenea, fiafitɔ le wó de.

Ye wóle kaka koa wóbe meka ... egbe meka na dzɔ afea? Gbete be yi ŋu ŋuse le ne enua va ne yi xlā ekɔ ni le tì! Enà ku, ne ame ... ta eyia na dzɔ aʃea. Wóbe yoo, yewoka ðe edzi be ate ŋu awɔ nenem dɔ na yewo, ta ne dzɔ fea. Nɔviwo menye nene oa? (NENE.) Ehē. Ya Gbeti le afeɛ dzɔ kakakakaka wóyi egbeɛ dzi, amesiame yi be agble.

Zāaðe koka, medidi kura o ... eh ... ðeko wòse, agoo. Wóbe, "Ame." Ðekadzevi lotolotoea ðe koa va gbɔ. Mede gbe ... mede gbeti be kɔ nɔnɔnlɔa nu tsye o, ye va feɛ me. Wóbe, "Oh xɔ̃nye Gbeti." Wòtɔ. "Elā yi xe le dzoi ðe matsɔ nam maðu oa? Eðo koe le wunye ta meva." Ya gbeti va yi tsɔ lā ðeka le dzui be abɔ tsɔ nɛ. Ebe, O, mesu na yi o ðe mitsɔ wo ʃete na yi. Gbeti be le fi gbe loo?

Yi kpɔ be fiafi wònye ta yimalɔ̃ ðe edzi o. Wòzu dzre ðe wó kpli gbeti dome. Oh! Gbete susu be ŋuse le yi ŋu yeadze dzi yeali. Enuvi lotolotoe mia ʃo gbeti kakakaka emi koe gbɔ ŋu (GBƆ LE EŊU.) Gbeti nye mi ʃo xla kɔʃea kekeŋ kpe ðo. Ah! Enya yi na bɔbɔa? Ðeko wòva dze

Appendix 213

ta na enuvi lotolotoea mia, be yi ɖe kuku ... yitɔ me ... yiɖe kuku yimagawɔ tsɔ o ... yi ɖe kuku yimega wɔ o. Elāwo ʃeteʃete ɖe elɔe le ekpɔo dzi blɛ ɖe agbe me na ... Gbetee ... enuvi lotolotoe kpaŋkpaŋ, wòtsɔ dzo.

Wógbɔ, tso agble fiɛa elā ɖeke meli wóatsɔ ʃo detsi o. Wóbia Gbete sea, Gbete mete ŋu ke nu o, me míwo ko wókpɔ ma afɔ tefewo kpaŋkpaŋkpaŋkpaŋ le kɔʃea. Ya wóbe o, leke wó ya Gbeti dzi xe yewo ɖo na dzɔ kɔʃe yi le koa, enu na ga gble le yiwo ŋu lea? Eh ... enya mele bɔbɔe ɖe o, menya gblɔe kura o. Ya wozi kpi do dzi sɛsɛ ɖe eŋu ke.

Eŋu ke vɔ ɖe, wóbe egbe yewo gale dzodzo gbe. Eme tututue na do dzi xe awɔ me ŋuse dɔ xe adzɔ kɔʃeɛ na yiwo ɖa? Ya wóle kaka koa, Ekpɔ be eyie na dzɔ kɔfee gbe ... eyie na dzɔ kɔʃea gbe ta ne nye be nane va tso mɔ sia mɔ nu ne wóva wóakpɔ be kukua le kɔʃea. Wódzo. Wóyi agble. Ekpɔ le kɔʃee. Wóga ... elā yi wógatsɔ ɖo dzo nua, elā le dzoɔ nu. Kakaka ko agòo koe ga ɖi. Enuvi yi xe va ... ameyi xe va nyà Gbete tsa amea ga va, ga va tu Kpɔ, tsɔ gbe do ni.

Kpɔ lɔ be fifia leke? Ekpɔ be ezo mebli o, yae va kɔʃea tsɔ hā? Wòbe, ah yie va, mebia Gbeti o ɖa? Eya yi xe le fi gbea, nya ɖeke mele yiwo kpli dome o, wokpli Gbeti be akɔntae ma ... kemi ɖeɖi na te ŋu. Wòbe, eh, ékà atabu na yi lo. Nene hāa? Ekpɔ ne xɔe se ɖa. Xe wòle kpɔ me ble xe le nu tu ɖia, ao. Zo meble Kpɔ kura o. Mete ŋu ke nu o. Kaka, se eyi gblɔ mele, Ekpɔ nye mi ʃo xla kɔʃea. Be fewo dze nyigba keŋkeŋ, be yli yli, be yli, ko enu te ŋu vɔ Ekpɔ be yi ɖe kuku. Kpɔ ŋutɔ va yi tso abaya, ʃo kle keŋkeŋ, lɔ alāwo "packi" ɖe eme ni tsɔe dro. Wòdzo.

Amegawo gbɔ tso agble fiɛsi. Ao, elā ɖeke meli o. Ekpɔ, ewo xi nye lālénu wò boŋ yiwo ka ɖo gatsɔwu Gbeti, nuka nyae dzɔ? "Nts." Ekpɔ de hūu mete ŋu gblɔe kura o été ɖe edzi ŋutɔ. Wóbe, "Yoo, enyo." Fifia ele sea, leke yewole enuyi wɔ gbe fia?

Eŋu bubu ke, elā bubu dzɔ kɔʃea nene. Adzata dzɔe, mekpae o. ... Atiglinyi dzɔe ... wóbe leke tutu ... kemi fifiɛ yiwo dzɔ kɔʃee do kpoa, yiwoayu. Enenea? Wóɖó aɖaŋu bo yewoawua, amesiame da asi ɖe edzi. Wovu le fima keke hòò. Lāwo pɛtɛpɛtɛpɛtɛpɛtɛ dzo vayi tso kɔʃe bubu.

Yaa wóle fimi kakakaka. Eh, le gbema ... tso ŋdi kaka na fiɛ. Eŋu ke evea gbe wóbe fifia leke yewoawɔ? Wóbe egbe ya ɖe yewoaɖa nukɔ viade ŋdi yi le xé aɖu koa kaʃi akaka fiɛ ɖe ... ezu kɔʃe yiye. Be yewoyi gbedzi xe gbɔ, amesiame be lā yi wòkpɔ xe wua, ne tsɔ gbɔ kaʃi yewoagado agbaɖo bubu. Wóbe, "Yoo." Eŋu ke, woɖa nukɔ la vɔ pɛtɛɛ, atadi yi xe woatu xe aɖu ɖe nukɔ ŋua ataditukpe via etsi kɔʃe xoxoa me. Wóbe, "Ao!"

Meka tututue nate ŋu ayi kɔʃe xoxoa me ava atsɔ ataditukpea vɛ hā? Amesiame wɔɖíí, elabe enuyi ke tu wó le fima kpɔa wóle ŋku ɖo edzi. Ameyi xe nagayi kɔʃe xoxoa me avayi tsɔ ekpea atsɔ gbɔ va fia, ezu agba. Sìgbè ɖe enya ene. Mele bɔbɔe ɖe o. Enua zu agba. Wóle tame bu vuu. Wódi be yewoate ɖe elā ɖe xe yiwokpɔ be ŋuse le ŋu, xe asi du yi xi agagbɔ kaba. Wóbu tame vuu avu dzi ko wóva dae ɖo. Be avu koe etea siɛ du. Eh! "Axe . . . etɔ tsye Kɔsi, enɔ tsye Kɔsi." Ebe yi ŋkoe kemi . . . yi, vudumadzade. Ne yi ʃu du le fifia, yia de fime agbɔ fifi dzē, nya ɖeka ma ɖi o, afifia tsye mato yi o. Enene ɖa? Wóbe, "Ē."

Wóbe, "Axe." Wòtɔ be, "Agoo." Ekemi yi navatsɔ ataditukpeɛ vɛ. Axe be, yoo. Wòle blè de atame goŋgoŋ, mia ŋtɔ minyɛ tsā xoxo. Alo mimenya oa? (OH, MINYAE.) Xe wò "fire" le fia, mexɔ "minti" ade kaʃi wòde fimiɛ o. Eyi tsye gblɔ me le, egbɔe xo. Wogbɔa, nume ko wòke dó aɖe ɖe xexe be xaxaxaxa, ko medze afifia kura o.

Fifia metoe koŋ o. Wókafui kaka be . . . sisio, enukpekpe yi xe va nɔ wónya le fima ɖe, eva kɔʃea me, va di wo do kpo megakpɔ meɖeke o, wòkpɔ ataditukpea. Miyɔ nane be sɔsi le miabe evegbeɛ me, ya wòtsɔ xɔsia tsɔ ʃu ataditukpevia ko ataditukpevia koe ma ɖe eve kplà! Wòyi ɖe eme ko ataditukpevia tu. Wòli fima kpóo.

Avū va dro wo kple ataditukpevia keŋkeŋ (OBOBOBOBOBOBOI!) Ehē! Mele bɔbɔe ɖe o. Gava yi kɔ dɔ kɔʃe yiyia me, gava yi kɔ fia fi xe wótsɔ afea ɖo zi evelia. Wógava fia fima tsye ɖi!

Yaa, wóle atadi tu. Gayi me wótu atadia kakaka . . . ele kpea me wótsɔ le atadie tu wòzi kpíí! Wótu atadia kaka tui vɔ keŋ, xe wóle nua ɖu gbe vɔ zɔ ɖe wóda to godoo, ameyi na yɔe adzui kpɔ, ameyi tsye ne yɔe adzui kpɔ elabe amesiame nadzui . . . ne wò . . . ne ameɖe . . . ne wò ameɖe medzui oa, wóava susu be ewoé wɔ ɖɔɖɔ kpli, yata wòle vava kemi "compagnie" aɖe ŋku tɔ wo ya (ʃUʃOʃEA). Eh, ʃuʃoʃea, na ɖe ŋku tɔ wo. Pɛpɛpɛpɛpɛpɛ eɖo ŋku dzi, ʃuʃoʃea (VEGBEA NU) aɖe ŋku tɔ wò.

Meyi yɔe, wodzui be wòle lotolotoe ɖe koa va nɔ fu ɖe na yewo le kɔʃea kaka ne dzi ble wògava yewo be fia, afɔ xe yewoadugu . . . ya yewoadugu de edzi. (AMEGBEGBLA?) Mhū! Amegbegblɛ ma.

Appendix

Pɛpɛpɛpɛpɛpɛpɛpɛpɛ. Amebubu, nene . . . amebubu eyi, enya yi xe dze ameasi koa, egblɔ ɖe eŋu. Wogblɔe ʃo xla keŋ kpeɖo.

Enua ɖu gbe wógbɔ, xe nya dze enua ɖuɖu gɔme le koa, ekpevia koe vu le kpla ko be, "Agoo." (TSALÉLÉLÉLÉLÉ.) Amesiame ko eva . . . amesiame be asi koe tsi yame. (ENYA GBLƐ . . . AME KPLE VIA DO.) Meɖe kuku nawo, mele bɔbɔe ɖe o. Mhū, Agawu Kakrakasi, eva dze. Sɛɛ ko ɖe me dodo kple madomado xe wo nya kpɔe, ameasiame me ŋku yi xe kpɔe le koa ameɖeke megablɔ na nɔvia be kpɔɖa tso ne na dze . . . di afiɖe to o. Elabe enua tu wo keŋkeŋ kpɔ le kɔʃe xoxoa me, vɔ amea tutue gava ɖo fi 'fia. Ta ne wo tsye enya tso koa ehe (EDE ASI AŊLƆ ME. . . .) Meɖe kuku nawo. Etsè ka . . . tsè ka sìgbè du nene. Wókaka le fima tsye! Ameɖeke mekpɔtɔ li o. Ya wo pɛtɛtɛtɛtɛ gavayi wɔ "compagnie" va yi tso kɔʃe bubu.

Xe wósi nene vayi tso kɔʃe bububu—si nye kɔʃe etɔlia ɖe—efimi ya wóva le zɔ, ɖe ŋu ɖe anyi. Ataditukpe ma . . . wódzo le nua ɖesiaɖe gbɔ zɔ. Ɖeke megava bia naneke ta be de wónigava yi tsɔ vɛ o. Kemi na woagava di nanea, ezu nu yiye bubu woadi (VƆ̄VƆ̄NƆTƆWOEA?) Eh, ameɖeke magayi kɔʃe me gava yi tsɔ naneke vɛ o. Ya wobe, "Yoo." Ɖoɖo ma le wo dome.

Wóle kakaka koa . . . wókpo be Egbɔa, ŋuse ɖeke mele eŋu o. Azɔ efe mele esi woleɛ nu tsye o. Gake ne wonya yi egbea me xe nya gbɔ fiɛ ko amesiame wuna lā vana. Ya ko ɖu wónɔ (DUM WONA) le aʃe me. Egbɔ me . . . mete ŋu le naneke wu o. Koa, wobe amegā . . . sígbe amegā Dzanta Biɖibi, asi atɔ̄ afɔ ene, mia ŋutɔ mise ŋkɔ, minyae ɖa tsye xo, wòva ko gblɔ be. Fifia tso gbe dzi . . . tso gbe yile dzi ɖe ne ameɖe ke mete ŋu wū naneke tso vɛ o koa magaɖu nu le yiwo dome o. Vɔ ese yi xe yea . . . yea do fifia, ne ameɖe gbe mewɔ ɖe edzi oa, kema amea ɖe, baba ni. Amesiame nava wu la le gbeme atsɔ vɛ. Ne ameɖe mekpɔ wu ve woa kemi wóale eya ŋto tsɔ̄ ɖa du. O! Eséa, eséa sɛsɛ wu yewo, ena nya wɔa?

Evɔ Gbɔ efe mele esi o, naneke mele esi wòtsɔ lea nu o, egbe ko wò ɖū, vɔ ya tsye le lāa ɖu gàmā me. Leke yewɔlę nuyi wɔ gbo? Wúlu ŋltelu ɖɛ kakakaka elawo le yiyi enenɛɛ le gbɔgbɔ vuu wòva ɖo egbɔ dzi. Wóva to na Egbɔ be egbe enye ŋkeke, ya hā na yi gbeme. Egbɔ be nyateʃe hā? Egbɔ tso ɖo gbeme. Eyi elā di gbe atsɔ vɛ. Leke wòwɔ kaʃi wuna lā?

Egbɔ vayi ke ɖe kɔdzokpui tsitsi xoxo ɖe ŋu . . . nye kɔdzokpuinɔ tsitsi xoxo ɖe, wodze dzo tu dí, dze dzo tu ɖí kple susu be ne yele dzo tu ɖí koa, yeaʃoe wu, akɔ agbɔ. Ya kɔdzokpui va biaeɛ se be nuka koŋkoŋ wòle fu ɖe na yi nene hā? Wòbe ā, ese yi xe wówɔ na yewo le yewo be nɔfeɛ kemi, eyata yi va fifia yi kpɔe le yibe yeatu dzo ɖí. Ya wòbe, OOO, menya nene wòawo kaʃi awu yi o. Yeafie amatsi ɖe, ne yi sa dzo ni ɖe, enate ŋu awu lā sia lā le gbeme zɔ. Gakea, ne ekpɔ yi ya, ne megawu ye o loo. Wòbe yoo, yilɔ̄ ɖe edzi.

Ya kɔdzokpui mama ma va wɔ gbé, wòxitsi egbeɛ le asi le keŋ be Gbɔ ni tro ŋlɔme doɖa. Egbɔ trɔ ŋlɔme doɖa wofiɛ gbeɛ ɖe be ŋlɔme, tsɔ atiketsa tsɔ ɖe aŋlɔme ni sìgbè ale xe wodoɔ nu na ame ene. Ya wòtó ni be enuyi xe yi wɔ ni fie tso egbe dzi ne eya xe ke ɖe lā sia lā ŋu, ne to na elā be ɖe, ne kpɔ yibe aŋlɔme ɖa, nane dé tsi ɖe efi, ne nua be yeado ŋkume ɖa koa, ne enye ŋo le tì! Etúkpé nado go awu lā ko wòatsɔ yi dzi. NENEA? Gake tso gbe dzi xe yile enu yi wɔ nia, etsi ni megaʃoe le afi ɖeke gbeɖegbeɖe o loo. Egbɔ be, "Yoo." Mikpɔ be enya sɛsɛ ŋutɔa? (ENYA SẼSẼ ŊUTƆ!) Egbɔ be, "Yoo." (EGBƆA? O-O-O-O.)

Ya Gbɔ tso. Egbɔ tso yia ko sɛɛ ko ɖe ɖeko wòvayi ke ɖe Gbetinɔ xoxo de ŋu. Ya wobe, "O! Gbeti màma." Wòtɔ, nene koe tè yi ɖe, yidze agbagba yi mete ŋu kpɔe tsye o. Elè fi xe yimate ŋu kpɔ le o. Fima nua te na yi eyata yiɖe kuku, ne niva kpɔ ɖa be ɖe enua de tsi hā. Wòtrɔ ŋlɔme do de egbɔ. Kaka Gbetinɔ la be . . . mama be yeakpɔ ɖa, tsia. (EXLƐ NI!) Exlɛ ni ya, ɖeko wodze nɛ. (Ẽ!) Nyataʃe, Egbɔ le edzò . . . ta de gɔme le mli ɖoɖoɖo kaka tsɔ va kɔʃea me.

Gbemagbe la wóva, elā ɖesiaɖe kpɔ wónɔe be ŋkume. Wóbe Gbeti va yi mè o, wòle lā me Gbeti le avi fa. Egɔme nye be màma wóvayi le vɛ. Ele avi fa. Wóbe nuka le ewɔ hā? Ebe, o, adzudzɔ koe le yi yɔ. Be, yoo. Wótsɔe me pɛtɛɛ. Ekoe, tsɔ ɖo agba dzi le dzo do ɖe ŋu. Fiɛ ɖo, wóɖae amesiame ɖu. Ebé egbea ta mele . . . eta le yi ɖu, ébé nuɖuɖu medzro yi o. Yibe lāme mekɔ yɛadunu o. Gbeti mama . . . Gbeti lo . . . mete ŋu du mama be lā o.

Eŋu ke ɖe, elāwo wɔ susu kakakaka be leke wɔ kakaka Egbɔ te ŋu vayi wu Gbeti tsɔ vɛ hā? Yewóagana negayi egbeme egbe. (MENYE WOE DƆEA?) Wógana Egbɔ gayi gbeme. Wòyi ɖe, Gbɔ le tsatsa kaka koa, ekpɔ Dzata le gbeme. Wòto ni be élé aɖi te yié yì neva kpɔ ɖa. Kaka Dzata be yeado ŋkume ɖa, o suìa, ŋutsu! Efo asi etuo be aʋa me (ETSƆE

Appendix

NI). Dzata mli. (ENENE HÃ?) Edze agbagba te Dzata kaka tso yi. Wókpɔ Dzata kuku yi xe Egbɔ tsɔ vea, esɛsɛ ŋutɔ. Wóbu tame kaka womenya leke tututu Egbɔ wɔ kaʃi le elã wu o. Wógatsɔ eya tsye le memea, Dzata le avi fa. Nya kae dzɔ? Ebe 0–0, adudzɔe le yi yɔ.

Wógatsɔ eya tsye wɔ. Wóbe fifia leke yewaowɔ Egbɔ kakaka anya eleyi tututu wòwɔ hafi le lã . . . té le lã wu tsɔ le yewo dome va hã? Ameyi be . . . wóbe meka na te ŋu abiɛ tututu?

Adɔ be yie. Yìa, ne wókpɔ, egbe gɔme ko yi tónà. Yeate wɔ dɔ me pɛpɛpɛpɛpɛ akpɔe keŋkeŋ. Ameɖe li kakakaka be Adɔ . . . Adɔ neva yi ke ɖe ameɖe be azi ŋu fia, ena ŋlɔ gbɔ be. Magate ŋu abie tutututu o. Kemi yiwomate ŋu adze aye na Gbɔ o. Ya ameɖe be Adadi koe na yi. Dadi be yeayi pɛpɛpɛpɛpɛ, yeavayi kpɔ agbɔ va gblɔ na wó elabe yia aye dzi yenɔna, ya yigawɔna blewu hã ta yeate yi. Ye wótsɔ Dadi tsɔ ɖe ɖé Egbɔ ŋu.

Adadi le Gbɔ . . . eyi Gbɔ nya tso le aʃeme ko Adadi le eyome le ɖia le wɔwɔ blewu li ɖia kakaka wóvayi ɖɔ egbeame le afi ɖe. Yeakpɔ ko ɖe Ekpɔ̃ ɖe va yina. Ɖɔɖɔɖɔɖɔ, wò kpɔe . . . elabe eya tsye nya be ŋuse yi xe yi xɔa, yimagawũ lã vi ɖeke si ŋuse mele o. Eyiwo xe nye tìtrìa xe lea nu ɖe yewo ko yia ya nɔ wuwu zɔ. Ne wóninya be nya ɖe le.

Ekpɔ̃ va yina, Egbɔ kpɔ Ekpɔ̃ kaka yɔe ɖa, wòtɔ, wòbe niva kpɔ aɖia na yi be edetsi hã. Kaka Kpɔ̃ be yeado ŋkume ɖa. Egbɔ ʃo asi etua ma aʋa me (EDZE ŊƐ). Ekpɔ̃ dze ŋɛ, Edadi kpɔe kakakaka. Elé nya le yia? (EDZI LE ESI.) Adadi . . . Egbɔ nya ɖe le esi. Adadia si . . . wòsi tsrà tsrà tsrà tsrà vaɖo aʃeme.

Esa sakpli le Egbɔ ŋu xoxo, be nya yi le ɖe yae dzɔe ke. Ele Gbɔ le eyi, ta ne egbo va ʃeme egbea ne emlɔ ameɖe gbɔ . . . ne yiwomlɔ anyi ne etrɔ ŋlɔme do ɖe ameɖe gbɔ ko amea ku loo. Hmm. Mélè bɔbɔe ɖe o. (NYA SƐSƐ MA!) Ẽ! Mesɛsɛ ŋutɔa? (NYA SƐSƐ MA.) O . . . na . . . wò na lɔ̃ be amea netrɔ ŋlɔme do ɖe yigbɔa? (GBEÐE GBEÐE YA!) Yaa wòva sa sakpli ma.

Fiɛ ɖoa kaka negbo . . . Egbɔ dze agbagba hè Ekpɔ̃ kuku tsɔ va aʃeme. Atiglinyi dzi, amesiame keŋkeŋ le aʃeme võvɔ̃ le. Wóbe yoo. Wótsɔ kpɔ̃ me Ekpɔ̃ le avi fa. Nya kae dzɔ hã? Ebe adzudzo pɛ le yi yɔ yata . . . ne elã ɖe va ko ewò ameyi . . . elã xe wówu vɛa, wótóna na . . . be ne vayi mè . . . ema (AME NƆ). Ese yi xe le wósi ema. (BE NI ME

NƆVIA.) Eya ŋutɔ niva yi mè. Ne evayi le eme le avi fa wóbe nya kae dzɔ, ebe adzudzɔe le yiyɔ. Koa, wókpɔ Gbɔ dūū.
    Eza doa ne Egbɔ mla anyi, ameɖe . . . amesiame la tra ɖe fi wùìi, avayi mla fimi. (EZU FIA LE KPƆAME.) Ne Egbɔ mlo anyi kakakaka . . . ele xe wónɔ alɔ̃me kakaka xe muna alɔ̃ ko gatrɔna, ne kaka Egbɔ be yeatrɔ. (XƆLƆ̃WO VA YI AKPA EVELIA . . . EZU FIA LE KPƆAME!) Ehē! Ê! Mekae gblɔe nawò . . . Egbɔ kpa tsye. Egbɔ ɖu fia. Ne Egbɔ nya mla anyi yeava vide koa amesiame le ŋudzo. Ehē! (MAGADƆ ALƆ̃ O, ALƆ̃ ÐƆÐƆ MEGALI O.) Alɔ̃ ɖɔɖɔ meli o. Ne wómlɔ anyi kaka ne Gbɔ be yeava viɖe ko amesiame le ŋudzɔ.
    Alebe eŋu ke. Wóva bu tame le Egbɔ be aʃeame nɔnɔ ŋua, évayi ɖe fu. Ne ezā nya do wóle dza . . . kaka wóva gblɔe be Egbɔ magayi gbeme o, ya ni zu amegā le aʃeme. Egbɔ mega yia gbeme o elabe wódoe kpɔ sìgbe ŋkeke etō ŋkeke ene, wónya be gbɔ ŋuse le ŋu kukuko, koa wóva kpɔe dze si ko ɖe wóbe egbea ŋkekea dze ame bubu dzi. Ame ma dzo yi gbeme. Enuyi xe eva kpɔ tso vɛa, wómegbe o, ya . . . ya ŋudɔ wóawo.
    Ya Egbɔ le aʃeme. Eza doa, ne Egbɔ mla anyi xe trɔ ŋlɔme do ɖe fia, amewo na nye zi le fi hoooo ava yi fi. Ne wóle dzi kakaka ne wódɔ alō, zātsitsi me Egbɔ le vāvā kaka, nye alɔ̃me, mu alɔ̃ kakaka ne egabe yeatrɔ alea, kemi ezi ga tɔ le fi. (KE AMEWO GATRƆ VA YI EBE ŊGƆGBE.) Ah! (MELE BƆBƆE ÐE O!) Alebe Egbɔ zu amegā le aʃea me. Ya ameyi si ŋuse ɖeke mele o, zu amegā.
    Ko wòva va eme be wóneva wɔ susu. Ne ewɔ ko . . . ameyi tsye . . . kaka ko eva glò, wóva to ni gbeɖeka be o nukata wòle yewonu ɖia ale hā? Alo tukpea xe le ebe ŋlɔmea ya ŋu . . . ya ko wòle dzadzra nene hā? Yako wòbe yo, nukata wógblɔ na yi nene hā? Wòzu dzre de wó kple elāwo kekeŋ dome, wóbe yewoafoe wu.
    Ne ameyi tso be yeadze dzi le fi, ne Gbɔ nya wɔ . . . ne enya do . . . eh (TRƆ VIDE) trɔ viaɖe ko, ne enya trɔ ŋlɔme do amea ko . . . ko efo asi etua me. Ne ameyi be yeawɔ le ne Gbɔ nya trɔ viaɖe nya trɔ ŋlɔme do amea nya fo asi etuɔ me ko amea dzeŋe (AMEA KUNA!). Wo pɛtɛpɛtɛpɛtɛ Gbɔ le wó vɔ nene. Le wó vɔ, le dzo ya wó . . . ele dzo ya wó ko. (EGBƆ ZU ÐEKADZEA KEME . . . LE DƆWƆ ÐE ÐOÐONU.) Kaka koa, eh, ezi koe va tɔ. Wóbe yewoasi. Ameyi xe teŋ be yewomagate ŋu ado dzi atɔ te ɖe nu oa, yewosi. Alebe wóva kàkà.

Egbɔ ɖeka va tsi aƒeme. Evɔa ameyiwo sinu wòwu ƒo ɖe anyia, esugbɔ (ÐETSI!) kaƒi kpɔtɔewo kaka. Ne ele nenea, nɔvinye . . . ekpɔ ne wo ŋtɔ etsɔ tu yi gbeme xe va yi wu lā nenea vuu tsye meganya ɖuna o. (Ē!) Mhū. Koa elā va kpɔ̄ Gbɔ be magate ŋu aɖui o. Evɔ za va do. Eyi za do . . . za dze dodoa, Egbɔ, kpɔ ya ɖeka koe kpɔtɔ ga nye nugbagbe le nu gbógbó ma wo dome . . . vɔ gbògbó yiwo le fime ɖesiaɖe nye kukua. Egbɔ be kpao, fifia le xe wòlea, elebe yi tsye yeadzo ayi fi xe yeayi.

Egbɔ de afɔ dume le yiyi. Game tsi me dze dzadza o. Eza koe do alebe tsizi do. Etsi tsyɔ xexeme kplo! na be xe . . . viviti do gake tsia me dza o. . . . Medo o. Egbɔ le yiyi nene kakakakakaka. Sìgbè le xe ya ɖe ƒo nyitsɔ? Ehē! Eya ma va de asi ƒoƒo me. Elabe ebluawo gblɔ nya ɖe be kaƒi ne tsi ne dza, eyae doa ŋɔ. (Ē! EYAE NƆ ŊGƆGBE NA TSI.) Eya ma va de asi ƒoƒo me. Ebɔ de afɔ dume. Le du dzi kakakaka eya nu be yeatsɔ tɔ viaɖe koa, etsi gāa ɖe koe do. Tsia le Gbɔ ƒo, Gbɔ le yli do nene. BĒ! BĒ! (EGBƆ ME DZOA KU!) BĒ! BĒ! Le du dzi nene le tsi ma me kakaka koa, tòliò! Ðeko wòva ka ɖe dua ɖe me, sigbe Tove le gɛ le nene. Kpatakpata koa ye wò nya tso aŋɔmɔ me ko ya wòyi de ameɖe be xɔ xa. Vayi be ɖe xɔ gɔme le fimi. Vɔ etsia efoe ŋutɔ kaƒi wòva ɖo fima alebe avuvɔ lee. Megeɖe ame ɖeke dzi le aƒeme o, wòtsi fima, xɔ xa ɖo kaka ŋu ke. Eŋu ke kaƒi wòtó glia xa ɖɔɖɔɖɔ ge ɖe aƒea me. O!

Wónikpɔ ɖe . . . afetɔ ne kpɔ, elā ɖe. Wóyɔe biɛ se be ŋkɔ ɖe, wòbe yi ŋkɔe nye Gbɔ. Ya nye Gbɔ? Wòbe, "Ē." "Amania?" Egbɔ tsɔ amania bɔ ni keŋ, be le nyaa dzɔ ɖe yi dzi le gbeme. Ale wòdzɔ ɖe yiwo dzi enye yi, ya yi si, eza tsi gāa yi xe dza ɖe efo yi kaka va do glia xa. Game yi va ɖoa, wómlɔ anyi, yata yimeƒo vɔ na wo o, ya yitsɔ glia gɔme dɔ, ya ŋke ŋdi yi kaƒi yi le gegeɖe aƒeme loo.

Ya aƒetɔ be yoo. Ta ebe susu enye ka? Wòbe, O! Xe yi si le gbeame yi ɖeka pɛ kpɔtɔ. Xe yi si le fimie fifia ɖe ameyiwo xe kaka yimenya fika wógakaka yi o. Yata xe yiva ɖo fi fifiɛ ɖe, yeanɔ gbɔ. Enene ɖa? Wòbe, "Ē." Ya Gbɔ ge ɖe ame dome le aƒeme. Ya Gbɔ zu aƒemelā. Megale . . . eƒomevi ya megali gbeme o, xe woagayɔ be Gbɔ le gbemea, eya ya mega li o. Ya wòdzo va aƒeme. Tso gbemagbe dzi ya Gbɔ zu aƒemelā.

Yaa eh . . . etsi yi xi dza, nye tsi gāa ma xe foea, ya Gbɔ tukpe ke wówɔ nɛ gbemagbea, ye wòzu mí. Yata ne Gbɔ nye mia, mia nɔna sìgbè etukpe nene . . . "hangli." Egbɔmi nɔ si "haugli" nene. Tso gbemagbe na egbe ya Gbɔ zu aʃemelā . . . ya Gbɔ, tukpe megale be dɔme o, ya ebe tukpea zu emi.

Ya tɔgbuinyewo gblɔ mese kpɔ gbeðegbe. Gake nyemeŋlɔ nya be gbeðegbeðe o. Megale ŋku ðo edzi kaka na egbe. Ya mi ameyiwo xe ga ʃoʃu ðe fi ðe, miawo tsye miaga se. Ameyi xe naxle le agbalɛ me tsye ya tsye ne se be enene nya ðe dzɔ kpɔ gbeðegbeðe ðe ema loo.

Mese fi, midɔ agbe.

Yooooooooo. Woezɔ kakakakakakakaka.

Appendix

21.1.3. SPIDER IN THE VILLAGE OF ONE-ARMED MEN

Performer: Xoxoanu Klige, 65, farmer
Date: April 2, 1979, 4:30 P.M.
Place: Klige Kōdzi, Kpalime
Audience: 11 adults, 70 children

Listen to a folk tale. (LET THE TALE COME.)

The folk tale flew until it fell on Yi Gogoe. (OH! HIM AGAIN . . . THE BIG SNAKE . . . LEOPARD MAN. . . .) It also fell on his younger brother Nyanuwuyi, also known as Wawuie. (IT FELL ON HIM.)

In those days there was a great famine. Food was very scarce. (AH!) No one knew where to find food. Nonetheless, Wawuie tried to get some food for himself and all his children. During his search in the bush he came across a large tree in which many birds had made their nests. He contemplated how he could get up the tree. He had a thought. In those days there were no ladders so he had to devise a way to climb up.

He made pegs which he attached to the trunk of the tree. As he attached the pegs, he climbed up. That was how he got to the top of the tree. He caught some birds. (GOOD GOD!) He collected only the young birds in the nests. He did not catch any old ones. He caught just the newly hatched ones. (SO THAT THEY MIGHT BREED FOR HIM!)

After some time, Yi Gogoe learned about it and said, "Oh Wawuie, where did you find food for yourself and your children during this famine?" Wawuie replied it was God who had provided for him. Yi Gogoe said that he would go with him because he cannot hide food from him. Therefore they must go together.

Wawuie left by himself before dawn. Upon his return, he told his brother that he went to visit a friend in town. Yi Gogoe said, then how come his children were eating? Wawuie said they were eating yesterday's food. They continued to eat.

Yi Gogoe said he wanted to know the exact day they would go. Wawuie knew that his brother was a talker and could not keep a secret. That was why he didn't want to take him there. He said this to himself.

Yi Gogoe got up before midnight and lay down in back of Wawuie's house. As soon as Wawuie got up, they would go together. Wawuie got ready. At midnight, he was ready to set out. He opened the door and stretched out his feet when he shouted suddenly, "Oh, what in the . . . !" Yi Gogoe squealed, "It's me, it's me! Let's go. It is day!" Wawuie said, "What, in the dead of night?" Yi Gogoe said, "No, it's early. Look! Look!"

Yi Gogoe gathered the firewood he had collected, piled it up in the East, and set fire to it. (THE SUN HAD RISEN!) "Look at the sun. The sun has risen; day has broken," he exclaimed. (HE MADE THE SUN RISE. HE IS MORE THAN GOD!)

After a while, he went to the well, fetched some water, and poured it into pots making a great deal of noise and said, "Don't you see? It is day and the women are drawing water. Let us go."

They went to the big tree. When they got near it, Yi Gogoe told Wawuie that all the newly built nests in the tree were his. All of them! (HE SAID THAT ALL WERE FOR HIM?) The new ones—none of the old ones—belonged to Yi Gogoe. Wawuie must not touch a single one. Wawuie agreed. (HE WAS A FOOL!) Yi Gogoe then began to attach the pegs and climbed and climbed until he got to the top of the tree.

Up there a quarrel broke out between them. "If you touch any new nests," Yi Gogoe warned, "there will be a fight between us. Yours are the old ones; mine are the new ones." Wawuie agreed.

Hardly had Wawuie put his hand inside an old nest, when he found some young birds almost ready to fly, and he caught them. When Yi Gogoe put his hand in the new nests, he found they contained only eggs and some contained nothing at all. (HE KNEW TOO MUCH. HE WAS TOO CLEVER!) He was a fool—he knew nothing!

Wawuie went from nest to nest and collected many many birds. He filled his bag to the brim. Yi Gogoe became angry and groaned. Wawuie was still collecting the birds when Yi left him there and climbed down pulling up peg after peg as he went, until he pulled up the very last one. (SO THAT THE OTHER WOULD REMAIN THERE!) When Yi Gogoe had climbed down, he shouted, "Don't you want to eat birds? Stay up there and eat your birds!" Yi went away, he left.

Wawuie was stuck in the tree! How could he get down? (THERE WAS NO WAY!) He plucked the feathers off all the birds, flayed them, and dried them on the tree for three days.

On the third day, while Wawuie was there pondering his plight, a hunter fired in the distance. An animal ran until it fell. The hunter did not know where the animal had fallen. (THE BUFFALO HAD ESCAPED!) The hunter wandered around until he saw Wawuie and said to him, "Wawuie, is that you up there? I just shot Buffalo. Can you tell me where he fell?"

Wawuie said, "Oh Hunter, Buffalo is not lost. If you do me a favor, I will do one for you." He then asked the hunter to stack dry leaves under the tree until they reached the top of the tree so that he could jump down on them. Then he would show him where Buffalo fell. The hunter said he could do that. He took his cutlass and cut heaps and heaps of leaves and piled them high until they reached Wawuie. Wawuie jumped from the tree, fell onto the leaves and then—(THE LEAVES REALLY SAVED HIM!)—he reached the ground. He told the hunter, "Follow me and I will show you Buffalo. There he is; take him." The hunter said, "Wawuie, thank you. Don't go away just yet."

Together they skinned the buffalo—completely. The hunter gave Wawuie some meat but he refused, saying he preferred the entrails. (OH!) He did not want any meat. The hunter tried to persuade him but Wawuie refused. The hunter gave him the entrails but then said, no, he could not cheat him. He insisted that Wawuie take some meat in addition.

Wawuie left and came to a river. At the river he stopped and opened the bag of entrails, and emptied the contents into the river. The fish came and fed on the contents. Wawuie caught them, filling his sack. When the sack was full, he went home taking with him both the entrails and the rest of the meat. (HE WENT HOME.)

Upon his arrival, his children gathered around, each of them crying, "Papa, papa, papa, this is the third day. You are back. What happened to you?" He said, "*Hū, hū, hū*, things which happen when one goes hunting are never to be discussed."¹

He cooked the meat for his children and they had a huge feast. They tore at the meat, each of them trying to outdo the other. (THERE WAS GREAT JOY AT HOME!) Suddenly, Yi Gogoe came up, puffing heavily. "Wawuie, are you back?" He said, yes, of course he was back. "Where did you get those birds or are they the same old birds you've been eating all along?" Wawuie explained that a Buffalo was passing by. When it got close enough and started to urinate, he pushed his hand into the Buffalo's anus, pulled out its intestines, and emptied them into the river. (HE DECEIVED HIM! HE'S CLEVERER THAN YI GOGOE, ISN'T THAT SO?) He emptied Buffalo's entrails into the water. Then the fish came and ate in large numbers. That's how he caught them. That is what he was cooking, he told Yi Gogoe. He should look to see if there was any meat. It was all fish. Yi Gogoe was a big fool.

Early in the morning, Yi Gogoe got up and hid near the path where Buffalo walked. He did as Wawuie told him to do. The buffaloes came and started to urinate in torrents. Yi Gogoe got up, stretched out his hand, and thrust it deep into a buffalo's anus. (WHAT!) The buffalo dragged him along the ground. He pulled him here, he pulled him there . . . through the thorns. Yi Gogoe was shouting at him when suddenly his arm broke off! His arm was cut off! (THAT'S WHAT GREED DID TO HIM!)

Yi Gogoe went home. His wife asked, "Oh, Yi Gogoe, what happened to your arm?" He sighed, "*Hū, hū, hū*. . . ." He sighed and said that she should be quiet. Then he would tell her what happened. He was not, however, going to tell her the whole story. He said he had gone hunting, his rifle misfired and blew off his arm. "But the rifle, where is it?" asked his wife. He said he left it in the bush. (AHA! OH!) His wife got up, went indoors at once, collected her belongings, and left. She refused to be with a man with a cut-off arm. She left with all the children.

---

¹Taking the life of an animal is considered to be a sacred act and is accompanied by many different rituals. Hunting among the Ewe people is not considered a sport.

Appendix

As the woman went along one path, Yi Gogoe went along another one. He wrapped his arm in white linen and intercepted her on the path. He lifted his bandaged arm and said, "We are all people of cut-off arms here at Adā Kōdzi.[2]

The woman stopped, thought a bit, and decided to go back. Yi Gogoe also went back. Returning home, the woman took a different path. Yi Gogoe bandaged his arm in red cloth and crossed her path again. "We are all people with cut-off arms here at Adā Kōdzi," he said, waving his arm in his wife's face. (HE SAID THEY ARE ALL PEOPLE WITH CUT-OFF ARMS? IN THE TOWN NOBODY HAS COMPLETE ARMS?) Yes, they are all men with cut-off arms!

The woman stopped and thought and said, "Oh, this is very strange," and continued home. At daybreak, the woman picked up her bags and started walking again. This time Yi Gogoe bandaged his arm with indigo dye cloth and intercepted the woman again. The woman did not recognize him at all. "We are all people with cut-off arms here at Adā Kōdzi," he said, holding his arm up for her to see. The woman thought long and hard and said to herself that her husband's arm was also cut off. She said that she could not stay married to him, so she would go to another town and get a new husband. But it appeared that all the men there had cut-off arms as well! She might as well go back to her own husband with the cut-off arm! So the woman indeed went back to her husband.

From that day on, if a woman is married to a deformed man, she should not divorce him because of his infirmity. Until this very day, women will marry invalid men, and healthy men will marry invalid women. Had Yi Gogoe not done what he did, a woman would leave a man when he became an invalid and divorce him. Because of Yi Gogoe people marry invalids!

With this I was deceived and I come to deceive you in turn.

Yoooooooooooo.

---

[2] District of Adā.

21.2.2. MONSTERS EAT WITH THEIR ANUSES

Performer: Xoxoanu Klige, 65, farmer
Date: April 2, 1979, 4:30 P.M.
Place: Klige Kōdzi, Kpalime
Audience: 11 adults, 70 children

Listen to a tale. (LET THE TALE COME.)

The tale went around and fell on Yiyi Golotoe.[1] It fell on Wawuie.

In those days a great famine had fallen upon the whole country. (THERE WAS YET ANOTHER FAMINE!) There was always famine in that land. (WASN'T IT AT THE MARKET OF DZAMINAKOE?) Wawuie was going from place to place and arrived at the home of some monsters. Those monsters did not eat with their mouths. They ate with their bottoms. (THE SAME WAY THEY EASE THEMSELVES?) Yes, it was through their bottoms as well.

Wawuie was roaming and stopped under a palm tree. Underneath the palm tree was an extensive clearing. Wawuie said that he had never seen such a thing. He climbed up the tree and hid in the top to see what was going on. He was determined to see everything. He waited for some time. Porridge fell, then more food, then something else, and so on. Wawuie was amazed. Something was going to happen all right!

After some time, the monsters gathered. Monsters with seven, eight, nine heads—all came out one after another. Then came their chief. Before they started eating, they formed several groups of three. The one who was to eat cut a bit of porridge, threw it up, and opened his anus pointed upwards to receive the porridge which fell and landed in his belly. (YES, THAT IS XOXOANU FOR YOU—SURE ENOUGH!) I saw the thing with my own eyes. That is why I narrate it to you. Each of them did it as the one before until it was the chief's turn.

When they threw the chief's porridge up in the air, Wawuie took his knife and chopped off a bit. The rest fell into the chief's bottom. Wawuie put the cut-off piece into his sack. He continued doing this. By the time the long process of feeding the monsters had come to an end,

---

[1] There are many variations of Spider's name, such as Yiyi Golotoe, Yiyi Goe, Yi Gogoe, etc.

his sack was full. When all the monsters were gone, Wawuie also left, carrying porridge and soup with him.

Yiyi Goe[2] saw Wawuie's cache of food and said, "Where did that come from?" He wanted to go with him. Wawuie agreed to take him. Although it was far, he agreed to take him to the place. But if Yiyi gets killed, Wawuie should not be blamed.

They arrived at the palm tree. Yiyi was amazed. He shouted, "Oh! Oh! Why is the place so clean?" Wawuie said, "I told you so." Yi said he would be quiet. Wawuie started climbing up. Yiyi asked, "Where are you going? Why climb up a tree to get food?"

They got to the top of the tree and the monsters gathered again. They cut the porridge and let it fall. Soup fell after the porridge. Yiyi became restless and started prattling, "Oh, oh, Wawuie, I want to go and collect it." Wawuie silenced him. When the soup started to fall, Yiyi said, "Oh, oh, let me at it!" The food kept falling.

A monster arrived with just one leg. Yiyi cried, "Oh, Wawuie, what is . . . ?" Then another came along, one with five heads. Yiyi said, "Let's leave!"

Wawuie said, "Keep quiet." By then, all the monsters had arrived. They separated into groups. The one in charge of feeding them stirred the porridge, cut some off, and threw it up. Wawuie took his knife and cut off a bit. Yiyi was restless. "Oh, why don't you chop it all off? You chopped just a bit!" This went on until at last, Yi Golotoe said, "*Tsia, tsia*[3], I am not going to do this. I will fall into their midst and really chop some off."

Wawuie told him that is not the way it is done. Yiyi asked, "Whose lump is that?" Wawuie said that was for the chief. Spider said, "Well then, it's between me and the chief today." A monster threw a big lump into the air. The chief opened his anus and let the lump fall in. (WHY DOESN'T HE EAT WITH HIS MOUTH?) Instead of chopping off a portion of the porridge, Yiyi held on to all of it! They tried and tried to take it from him . . . but to no avail. He landed in the chief's belly.

They all went back to their places. Yi Golotoe took his knife and cut the chief's intestines into bits. The chief of the monsters died.

---

[2] This refers to the same character.
[3] Expression of disgust.

The monsters decided to open the belly of the chief to find the thing which had gone in. They cut open the belly of their chief and lo and behold . . . out came Yiyi Golotoe! They told him not to fear. They tied a string around him and allowed him to go back home.

The string, however, was enchanted. On the day of the chief's funeral, they would make incantations and pull the string. Yiyi would come back. They would give him food and allow him to go back home. (THE FOOL! HE DIDN'T KNOW THEY WERE GOING TO KILL HIM!)

Yiyi went home and met Goat on the road. He said, "Goat, where are you going?" Goat replied that he was going to his farm. Yiyi said, "Wait for me. Take this string. It was given to me by my grandfathers. One does not wear it when one attends to nature's call.[4] Hold it for me. I am going to attend to nature and will be right back. If you lose the string, you are finished. Is that clear?"

When Yiyi left to defecate, he never came back. The string was still around Goat's neck and Yi Golotoe never returned.

The time for the funeral came. They pulled the string. Goat came running, bleating all the way. "Oh Goat, what do you want here?" they asked. He said they had called him. That is why Goat is sacrificed for guests at funeral.

With this I was deceived and I want to deceive you with the same. Yoooooo.

---

[4] That is, when one relieves himself.

Appendix

21.2.4. MONKEY AND ANTELOPE

Performer: Xoxoanu Klige, 65, farmer
Date: April 2, 1979, 4:30 P.M.
Place: Klige Kōdzi, Kpalime
Audience: 11 adults, 70 children

Folk tale traveled and fell on Antelope; it fell on Monkey; it fell on Blacksmith.

Antelope and Monkey were cousins. They lived in the forest and were companions. While roaming in the woods, Monkey came across some palm nuts on a tree. Since Antelope was the younger of the two, Monkey asked him to climb up and pick some palm nuts for them to eat. Antelope said he was not a climber, so how could he climb up the palm tree?

Monkey told him to wait while he climbed up. As the palm nuts fell, Antelope took them, broke them in half, and swallowed them. Antelope did so until Monkey finally told him to stop. Monkey asked why couldn't he wait until he came down so they could eat together?

Antelope answered, why couldn't Monkey eat those that were on the tree? He should eat the ones on the tree. Monkey threw down the last palm nut and Antelope ate that one as well.

Monkey came down, he fell down—he was so very hungry. This is why Monkey does not climb down a tree, he jumps down. He does, however, climb up.

Monkey chased Antelope. Antelope ran to an old woman who was weeding grass on her farm. He cried out for help, "Save me, old woman!" The old woman told him to lie down so that she could put some grass over him. Antelope lay down and the old woman covered him up.

Monkey ran up to her and demanded to know if she had seen Antelope. She said, "No." Monkey said that if she would not tell him where Antelope was, he would show her what he intended to do to Antelope.

On hearing this, Antelope took to his heels. Monkey chased him furiously until they came to an old woman grinding maize on a stone. Antelope cried out, "Save me, old woman!" The old woman told him to hide under a stone. In ancient times they ground maize on that stone. In great haste, he dove into the cornmeal and the old woman covered him up. Monkey came and asked the old woman if she had seen Antelope. He said that if she did not hand over Antelope, she would be sorry.

When Antelope heard this, he rushed out, scattering cornmeal all over the place, leaving none on the stone. He ran fast until he came upon a hunter and shouted, "Hunter, please save me! Let me hide!" Hunter told him to hide behind him. He would watch to see where Monkey was going to pass by. In the meantime, he got his rifle ready to fire.

Monkey arrived and asked if he had seen Antelope. If he did not tell him . . . Antelope heard this and took to his heels and ran. Antelope continued running until he came to a blacksmith. He shouted, "Blacksmith, cover me up!" The blacksmith asked him what was the matter. Antelope told him the whole story. The blacksmith told him to stay and work the bellows for him . . . just let Monkey come.

Monkey came and asked if he had seen Antelope. The blacksmith said, no, he hadn't seen him. Monkey said that if he did not show him where Antelope was, he would be sorry. Antelope, in the meantime, was working the bellows, singing:

(Song): Akosomadze[1] is a fool,
Akosomadze is a fool.

The iron rod in the fire was red hot. Monkey said, "What did you say?" At once, Monkey pounced on Antelope. "Monkey, what do you want?" asked the blacksmith. Holding Monkey tight, the blacksmith placed Monkey's buttocks on the hot iron rod and said to him, "There is Antelope."

The buttocks of the Monkey were placed on the hot iron rod. That is why they are red. (THEY DID TO HIM WHAT HE WANTED TO DO TO ANTELOPE!)

That is what I was deceived with and it is what I deceive you with. Yoooooooooooo.

---

[1] "Akosomadze" is presumably another name for Monkey.

23.1.3.   SPIDER COMMITS INCEST

Performer: Kɔsi Klige, 41, tailor and farmer
Date: April 29, 1979, 3:30 P.M.
Place: Klige Kōdzi, Kpalime
Audience: 8 adults, 15 children

My people, listen to a tale. (LET THE TALE COME.)
The tale walked until it fell on Dagbo Dakli. (WHO AGAIN IS DAGBO DAKLI?) Yiyi-Gogoe, the Spider.[1] (uproarious laughter)

Yiyi had a child, a single child. The child was a girl. The girl stayed with him until she grew up. She cooked for him and he ate. If you saw the girl, you would see breasts bouncing on her chest hòlò hòlò hòlò hòlò hòlò! The Queen of Beauties! Yiyi was very jealous of her 0–0–0–0–OH! He wanted her never to talk with any man nor to be seen by any. (OH! LEOPARD MAN!)

Yiyi thought, Oh! what was he going to do with this child? He lusted for her. (WHAT DOES HE WANT TO DO WITH THIS CHILD?) He wants to make love to her! (OOOOOOOOOOO!) That's all he thought about.

One day Yiyi took an egg . . . took an egg and put it in his cheek. (OH OH!) He went to tell his child that he was ill. He was groaning hard, "Mmh, mmh, mmh, mmh, mmh. . . ." His child said to him, "Papa, papa, what's wrong?" He said, "Mmh, mmh, mmh, mmh, things aren't well with me." "Oh! What are we going to do?" she asked. He told her to go behind the house. A man lives there. He's a good diviner. She should take some money, run to the man, and ask him what exactly is killing him.[2]

The child ran. As soon as the child left the house, Yiyi went into the house, took out the egg, took some white powder and smeared it all over his face. He then took a sack and hung it around his neck, and

---

[1] Yiyi Gogoe is another name for Spider. Other variations of his name in this narrative are Eyi Gogoe, Ayi Gogoe, Yi Gogoe. For the sake of consistency, Spider will be called Yiyi.

[2] Literally: She should go get money and run and go to the person so that she would ask on his behalf what exactly . . . the thing . . . the thing will want to overcome him . . . he is going to die.

went to the back of the house. He did all this before the child arrived. (OH! LEOPARD MAN!)

The child said, "Agoo." The man answered, "Ame.[3] What's happened?" She said her father sent her on an errand. He said, "Is that so?" She nodded, yes. Yiyi sat down and started reciting lots of formulas and chants.[4] He said, "Dried excrement does not float on water. If excrement floated . . . one pole does not build a house . . . kerosene doesn't fry tarts . . . flour doesn't make *pin*."[5] (LORD!) He conjured . . . he conjured up objects. He prepared to give an oracle to the girl. He said the ancestors have come. She should go tell her father that his destiny is linked to hers . . . his fate is linked to hers . . . therefore he and the girl should make love seven times.[6] (MAKE LOVE?!)[7] Yes, they should make love seven times. (THE SICKNESS WILL SURELY BE OVER!)[8] They should make love seven times. (THE SICKNESS WILL BE OVER!) The sickness will all be over for him. (OH!)

Yiyi thought[9] . . . the child thought. . . . The diviner gave that oracle to the girl. The child thought a while and said, "Oh! But how?" Since he was her father, oh! . . . he has no other child she knows of. The child thought, went home, and told her father what the diviner had said. (BY THEN YIYI HAD RETURNED HOME!)

By the time the child arrived, her father was already there. There was a groan. It seemed as if he was dying. (AO!) "Mmh . . . mmh . . . mmh . . . mmh . . . mmh," he moaned. If you saw him you'd say Yiyi was already dead! (IS IT THAT HE WANTED TO MAKE LOVE TO HIS

---

[3] These are standard Ewe greetings.

[4] Diviners' chants are supposed to be unintelligible to the ordinary lay person, hence their abstruseness.

[5] *Pin* is a food made from *gari* (grated cassava) mixed with hot water. It cannot be made with flour. The colloquial equivalent is "You cannot fit a square peg into a round hole."

Diviners' chants are supposed to be unintelligible to the ordinary lay person, hence their abstruseness.

[6] Literally: go seven times.

[7] Literally: sleep. It is said by the audience with such gusto that the colloquial "screw" would be a more appropriate translation.

[8] In other words, he will be cured from what is ailing him.

[9] Narrator means "the diviner."

DAUGHTER THAT BADLY?) That's all he wanted! (laughter) (HIS OWN CHILD?) His own child. That's why he devised that trick.

Yiyi[10] ... the child told the story to her father, saying, well, this is what the diviner told her. (LORD!) Spider said, "What ... what ... what ... what ... who has ever heard of such a thing? A thing like that, who would do that? Well, okay, I've heard. Oh well, it's okay, I've heard."[11] Still he groaned as though he were dying. The child said, "Papa, will I be left alone in this village?[12] What are we going to do? This is not a public affair; it's a matter for the bedroom. But it's something we must do to stay alive. It's best that it be done now!" (YIYI MUST BE REJOICING!)[13]

When evening came he went to lie on her. (THE CHILD WENT TO MAKE THE BED.) The child made the bed for her father, then went to lie down. They both went to lie down. Yiyi went to lie on the child, saying, "Now you yourself know that I am not in good health ... you know I am not in good health, so you should count ... count well. I am not in good health ... so count."[14] He climbed on top of the child, then started:

(Song): Nana Zigolotuieee, Nana,[15]
One, one, one,
Nana Zigolotuie, Nana,
Two, two, two,
Nana Zigolotuie, Nana,
Three, three, three,
Nana Zigolotuie, Nana,

---

[10]The narrator corrects himself.
[11]Means, "I understand."
[12]The child is concerned that if her father dies, she will be left all alone.
[13]Literally: the heart will be smiling.
[14]The narrator makes his voice sound feeble and slightly nasal, a trait characteristic of Spider's speech.
[15]"Nana" refers to a woman; "Zigolotuie" suggests someone who is foolish or dumb.

> Four, four, four,
> Nana Zigolotuie, Nana.

Then he stopped and said, "Zigolotuie, Zigolotuie, how many have we done? How many have we done now?" The child said she had forgotten. She wasn't able.... He said, "O-o-o. I told you to keep count. (AH!) I told you to count. O-o-o, see now ... let's start again. This thing isn't easy to do." He started over again:

> (Song): One, one, one,
> Nana Zigolotuieee, Nana,
> Two, two, two,
> Nana Zigolotuie, Nana,
> Three, three, three,
> Nana Zigolotuie, Nana,
> Four, four, four,
> Nana Zigolotuie, Nana,
> Five, five, five,
> Nana Zigolotuie, Nana,
> Six, six, six,
> Nana Zigolotuie, Nana.

"Oh! Zigolotuie, how many did we do? How many did we do? How many did we do? How many ... how many did we get to?" The child said she forgot. (OOOH! SHE SHOULDN'T BE DOING THIS!) (peals of laughter) No, she shouldn't be doing this. Yiyi was on top ... on top of that child of his until he stood up. The child was dead, sprawled out beneath him. (AO!) Yiyi had screwed his child to death! He had to beg the villagers ... to come help him bury the child.

From that day they made a law that whoever has a child may not marry the child. If you do, the ancestors will be alɔkpli[16] between you and your child. You will kill your child. From that day on until today, child and father may not sleep together.

That's what was used to deceive me and I use to deceive you. You listeners of tales with good ears!

Yooooooo!

---

[16]This refers to a particular kind of taboo.

23.2.2. SPIDER THE TRADER

Performer: Xoxoanu Klige, 65, farmer
Date: April 10, 1979, 3:30 P.M.
Place: Klige Kɔdzi, Kpalime
Audience: 8 adults, 15 children

Listen to a folk tale. (LET THE FOLK TALE COME.)

Folk tale wandered and fell on Spider Round-belly.[1] (HEY! THE SAME SPIDER? THE SAME PERSON?) Yes!

Spider took his meal and went to the chief and told him to give him one *pfennig*.[2] With this he would buy seven slaves for the chief. The chief stared at him for a long while and said, "Oh. How can one pfennig buy seven human beings?" Spider told him to give him the pfennig and he would see. The chief thought this over and stared at Spider and agreed. The chief gave Spider the pfennig.

Spider took the pfennig and went to Dzaminakɔe market. (JUST ONE PFENNIG FOR DZAMINAKƆE MARKET?) It is the town where Death lives. Spider took the coin and bought pepper. Spider waited a long while at the market place. When it was dark, he went to the chief's house. He told the chief that he came from a very far away place. He wanted to spend the night and leave in the morning. The chief said he was welcome to stay.

When it was day, Spider bought fresh pepper. He wanted to dry it out in the sun; if not, it would rot. The sun was shining as Spider dried the pepper. The chief had a big rooster called Degbenuke.[3] It came and ate all the pepper. Spider saw it and said nothing, as though he were asleep.

When there was only one pepper left, Spider went and told the chief that he was ready to leave and asked to see the pepper he had dried. "Look, the rooster ate all my pepper!" cried Spider. The chief said, "Oh, what am I to do?" Spider said that he had been sent by his chief, a "brother chief," on this errand. What was he going to tell him

---

[1] Another name for Spider.

[2] The *pfennig* is a German coin introduced in Togo when Togo was a German Protectorate from 1884–94 and a German colony to 1919.

[3] Literally: It crows, day breaks.

now? The chief said he would pay for the pepper. Spider asked him where he was going to get peppers just like the ones eaten to take to his chief? (laughter) The rooster must be given to him in exchange for the pepper. (THE ROOSTER IN EXCHANGE FOR THE PEPPER?) Mhū. (THERE GOES DAGBO DAKLI AGAIN!)[4] The chief said he did not want any trouble and gave Spider the rooster. Spider left and went to another town.

When Spider was near the town, he went and hid under a tree. At night he entered the town and went to the chief. People welcomed him and addressed him, "Dagbo Dakli, where do you come from?" He replied, "I am from Dzaminakɔe market." As it was dark, he wanted to spend the night and leave for home in the morning. He was given a place to stay. They cooked for him and he ate. He asked where his rooster would stay. He was told the rooster could sleep with the chickens. "What! With the chickens? If my rooster kills your chickens, that will create trouble for me. No. My rooster is very large. He will stay with the rams. (AMONG THE RAMS?) They agreed and put the rooster in with the rams.

Around midnight Spider got out of bed, went and strangled the rooster, and hung it on the horns of the biggest ram. (OH!) When it was almost daybreak, he went and called, "Chief, Chief, Chief, I am leaving now. Could someone open the pen so I can take my rooster and leave?" (AFTER HE HAS KILLED IT?) When they opened the pen, there was the rooster on the horns of the ram. Spider said, "Oh Chief, look, this is what I feared. If I had kept my rooster among your chickens, it would be I who is in trouble. No rooster can replace this one. I will take the ram in exchange." The chief agreed and Spider left. (THEY GAVE HIM THE BIG RAM?) Yes. (THE BIG RAM TO TAKE AWAY. . . . THE PEPPER BECAME A ROOSTER AND THE ROOSTER BECAME A RAM!)

He arrived in another town and said, "Big Man, show me to the chief's compound." A child was told to take him there. The child led him to the door of the chief's compound. "Agoo,[5] agoo, Chief, good evening. It's me, Spider. My chief sent me to buy a ram. Night has

---

[4]Another name for Spider.
[5]Standard Ewe greeting.

descended upon me and the ram refuses to walk." (HAD DAGBO DAKLI BEEN CARRYING THE RAM?) God provides for him. "In the morning when it is day, I will leave," said Spider.

Quickly the chief ordered that water be brought for Spider to drink and that some water be heated for him to take a bath. They made dinner for him because he was a visitor. Spider said, "I am already sleepy. Where can my ram stay?" The chief told him to put it with the other rams. Spider said that the chief should look at his ram and see if it was equal to those of the chief. (THEY WERE NOT COMPARABLE!) "My ram, which is as big as an ox, won't it kill your rams?" asked Spider. The chief looked at the ram and ordered it to be kept among the oxen.

At two thirty in the morning, Spider got up and went and twisted the neck of the ram and put it on the horns of a big ox. Early in the morning, Spider told the chief, "Your oxen are very wild. My chief's ram has been killed by your oxen." (DOES HE WANT MONEY?) Even if you gave me money, where could I possibly get a ram to replace mine? (SPIDER IS GOING TO GET THE OX!) (laughter) The chief gave him the ox and Spider left.

While on the road, Spider suddenly heard people wailing *obobobobobi*. Spider tied the ox to a tree. He rushed to see what was happening. There among the people was a dead body being carried in a cloth hammock. Quickly Spider crossed the road, caught up with the people, and asked, "What happened?" They said that one of their relations had died. Spider said, "Well, then, give me the dead body. I will give you my ox. But don't tell anyone about this." (HE'S DEVISING ANOTHER PLAN!) The people wondered what kind of ox it was. The men put down the dead body and asked Spider where the ox was. Spider told them he would take care of it because they might run into trouble. "I am from the Chief's clan. I know what to do."

The people left the dead man with Spider, took the ox and left. Spider waited until night and continued on his way. (IT'S NIGHT AGAIN . . . DON'T YOU HAVE TO DO SOMETHING TO A DEAD BODY SO IT DOESN'T GET STIFF!) He arrived in the next village when it was very dark. "Hey there, little boy. Where's your chief? I've been traveling a long distance and am very tired. The man I'm traveling with isn't talking, he's so tired. We drank along the way and he got so drunk I had to help him walk. He tried to walk but couldn't. Spider rested the dead man in a standing position against the wall and said that if he laid him down, he would fall asleep, so he let him remain there.

The people cooked. Spider said, "If this drunken man eats, he will vomit." So Spider ate his companion's portion as well and said, "Chief, where will I sleep?" He was told to sleep with his companion. Spider said how could he, a grown man, sleep with a drunk? Spider said he had a woman waiting for him. If he slept with this drunk, where would the woman stay?[6]

Spider said, "Let the drunk sleep with his peers. Look at all these young men. Are they not his peers?" The chief said they were and ordered them all to bed. It was late. Spider said that since the drunk couldn't speak or understand their language, he would be bothered by the young men. Therefore Spider himself would put him to bed later.

The young men were asleep. Spider carried the dead body slowly and laid it at the feet of the young men. Spider himself did not sleep but stayed outside. At dawn he went and called the chief and said that since the man's stupor was over, they had better be on their way. They wanted to arrive before ten or twelve in the morning.

"Oh, Chief, didn't I tell you that I was traveling with a drunken man? Look, your children have stomped him to death! Look at him, not even on the bed but at the foot of the bed on the floor! What have they done to him? Is this the way your children behave? What am I going to do? What am I going to tell my chief? I know you don't want trouble. First, I need to urinate and then I'll be back."

Spider returned and said, "You see, Chief, now-a-days, one does not pay for a slave. I cannot take money from you. If you kill somebody, you must also be killed. Look! I will take all the boys who slept in the room in exchange for my man."

The chief and all his people went to consult each other on the matter. "Did you see the man who was brought to the house?" they asked. The chief said, "Yes." "Was it a dead man?" The chief said, "No."

---

[6]Spider invents this detail. There is no woman actually traveling with him.

"Did he (Spider) explain to you he was drunk?" the people asked. "Yes," answered the chief. "There you are! Your children killed him in his sleep!" said the elders. Then and there, they brought out seven of the chief's young maidens and handed them to Spider.

Spider went home and called on his chief. "Chief, I have come back." He then presented to him the seven women.

> (Song): Today we are going to do something,
> A dead frog does not argue.
> Hush, hush to digging an ant hill,
> Army ants are in the ant hill.

From that day on, when you enter a chief's house, you will find no chief with just one woman. Spider brought seven young women to the chief . . . that is why chiefs want to marry many women. They normally marry lots of women. (WHAT IF THE CHIEF MARRIES ONLY TWO OR THREE?) If he marries only two, that's no chief. (SO IT'S BECAUSE OF SPIDER?) Yes! And the dead person. All this because Spider was given a coin to buy women for the chief.

Yooooooooo.

23.2.3. SPIDER BRINGS DISHARMONY INTO THE WORLD

Performer: Kɔmi Klige, 22, chauffeur
Date: April 10, 1979, 3:30 P.M.
Place: Klige Kɔdzi, Kpalime
Audience: 8 adults, 15 children

Listen to a folk tale. (LET THE TALE COME.)

The tale flew and fell on a grain of corn. It flew with a rushing sound and fell on Rooster. From Rooster it fell on Hawk, then on Hunter, then on Snake. It also fell on Club, it fell on Fire, and then fell on Water. Spider is their leader.

One day Spider got up in the morning and said to himself, what could he do to bring a split between these people who are so close? Spider went to Grain and asked him to come work on his farm tomorrow morning. Corn asked, "Who else have you asked? If you asked Rooster, I will not come."

Spider rushed over to Rooster and asked him to come tomorrow morning to help him clear his farm. Spider said he needed his help badly. Rooster said, "Have you asked anyone else? If you have asked Hawk, I will not come." Spider said, "No. How could I ask Hawk? You are the only one I asked."

As soon as Spider got up, he went to Hawk and told him, when morning comes, he should come and work for him. Hawk said, "Have you asked anyone else?" Spider said, no. Hawk said, "If you ask Hunter to be there, I will not come."

Spider got up quickly, went to Hunter and told him, when day breaks, he should come and do some work for him. Hunter said, "Have you asked anyone else?" Spider replied, no. Hunter said, "If Snake comes, I will not be there."

Spider stood up and quickly went to find Snake. He told Snake, when day breaks, he should come and do some work for him on his farm. Snake agreed and asked if he had asked anyone else. Spider said, no. Snake replied that if he invited Club, he would certainly stay away.

Hardly had he stood up, that he was off to see Club. He told Club that at daybreak, he should come help him clear his farm. Club said he would not come if anyone else was there. He told Spider that if Fire was coming, he would not be there. Spider told him he had nothing to worry about, for Fire certainly would not be there.

When he left Club, he went to Fire and asked him to come help him the next day. "Will you come?" asked Spider. Fire accepted, but said he would come only if he had not invited Water. Spider said, no, he had not invited Water.

As soon as Spider stood up, he went to see Water. He told him, when day breaks, he should come to his farm—without fail. Water agreed and said nothing more. (THAT SHORT SPIDER SURE DOES TRY HARD!)

Night fell, followed by day. Spider arose early and climbed a tree to see how all these people were going to assemble on his farm. Grain of Corn arrived, there was Rooster! Rooster looked up and saw Hawk! Snake arrived, there was Club! Club looked up and saw . . . (FIRE!) Fire was shocked to see . . . (WATER! WHAT IS THIS? ALL THE ENEMIES HAVE COME TOGETHER!)

They were working on the farm . . . (HOW IS IT TO WORK IN THESE CIRCUMSTANCES?) Well, you see, Rooster became hungry. He tried to find an excuse to swallow Grain of Corn. With no hesitation, Rooster insulted Grain of Corn, "You lazy fool! Can't you do any work?" Grain of Corn lifted his head and told Rooster he was a useless creature. Rooster stood up, took hold of Grain of Corn, and swallowed him. (THERE WE GO!)

Hawk said, "What impertinence!" He then turned around, swooped down on Rooster and ate him. Hunter looked on with great indignation, then took his rifle and shot Hawk. Hawk fell to the ground with a thud! Then Snake twisted around and bit Hunter, who immediately fell down and died.

Club got up in confusion and said he would not tolerate this. With a hard whack, he killed Snake! Fire said, "How dare Club. . . ." He engulfed Club in flames and burned him up, *biðà, biðà, biðà, biðà.* Water poured on Fire and Fire was put out!

Spider managed to bring quarrel among these individuals and saw to it that if anybody wants to cook a chicken, Water is used. The

Hunter uses Water. Look at the Snake and other living things. Water is in all their food.

With this I was deceived by the elders and I use it to deceive you. Yooooooooo.

28.2.6. THE CHIEF AND HIS TWO DAUGHTERS

Performer: Kɔmlā Tonyo Agbadzi, 30, farmer
Date: May 9, 1979, 6:30 P.M.
Place: Noefe Kōdzi, Kpalime
Audience: 23 adults, 25 children

Friends, listen to a tale. (LET THE TALE COME.)

The tale went . . . went . . . went until it fell on a man who was very very jealous . . . he was very jealous. (CAN A MAN ALSO BE JEALOUS?) It fell on him.

He said his daughter's vagina . . . nobody will see it. (OH!) That's right. This man had two children but only he knew their names. He never mentioned them to anybody. (EXACTLY.) Only the daughters knew their names. (THAT'S IT! OH!) Some man! Oh! These daughters finally blossomed in beauty . . . these two girls blossomed into uncommon beauties. (YEAH!) If you saw them, my brothers, you who are with me here . . . my penis is already getting erect . . . *egalī galī*![1] (uproarious laughter)

These beauties were so attractive, it wasn't easy. Every kind of animal came to court these beauties. Their father offered lots of money saying that whoever correctly names the girls, will inherit the chief's money, the chiefdom, and both beauties. (HOW ABOUT THAT!) Oh! Spider thought a while . . . thought it over and over and said, "This man is no fool."

There was a farm road with a log that had to be straddled to get to the other side. Spider went and set a trap in the tree trunk. When Spider set the trap in the trunk . . . when Spider set the trap in the trunk . . . the trap was there and Spider hid. One of the girls was in front. . . . She walked until she reached the tree trunk and the trap caught her.[2] The one behind her said, "Akpalagbon, move on, let's go." The one in front said, "Agbedesɔkɔ, I've been trapped!" (laughter) Thus, Spider heard their names, Akpalagbon and Agbedesɔkɔ. (HMMMMM . . . HAS SPIDER EVER BEEN TO SCHOOL?)

---

[1] Describes the erect penis.
[2] It is not clear how this trap works.

Spider went into the crack of a wall and made a flute. He played the flute *toto filo filo filo fĩ*, and sang, "The women whom we are not supposed to marry, one is named Akpalagboŋ, the other is Agbedesɔkɔ . . . Akpalagboŋ, Agbedesɔkɔ. . . ." (uproarious laughter) Oh! Not long after, Spider started to play the flute. Spider's mind slipped and he forgot both names in a flash rrrrrrrm! (AO! HE IS SUCH A MEATHEAD!) Spider said the world has beaten him.[3]

Spider started to run again . . . run again . . . run again until he hid again in the trunk of the tree. This time he did not merely hide there, he made a hole and inserted his penis . . . eh . . . Yiyi neatly placed his penis in the hole. When the girl wanted to straddle the log, Yiyi inserted his penis deeply into her and captured her there. The thing felt so very good to the girl. Agbedesɔkɔ said, "Akpalagboŋ, move on, let's go." Akpalagboŋ said she was "coming" and said she should be patient with her. (uproarious laughter) Oh! He was giving it to her and the girl was spinning r-r-r-r-r-r-r (AI!)

Spider tried to remember . . . he carefully wrote down their names, Akpalagboŋ and Agbedesɔkɔ. Then Spider went home. The day for guessing the names was still off. He called his children together and made flutes for them. "Now all of you listen!" he said, "*toto filo filo filo filo filo toto filo filo filo filo fiifi.*" Oh! (giggles from the children) "It goes, "*Toto filo filo filo fifi li fifi vavo fif li vili vovovi.*" (DOOODOOO-DOOODOOODOOODOOODOOO)[4] Oh! "One is called Agbedesɔkɔ, Akpalagboŋ, Agbedesɔkɔ. . . ." He said all his children should play their flutes that way. (JUST SO HE WOULDN'T FORGET!)

In the meantime, while the children were playing, he said to his wife, "Big flat-headed Funɔ, tomorrow I am going to divorce you and marry two different women, then bring them to the village." Oh! Funɔ just stood there and said nothing.

During that time, Lizard and Spider were close friends. Spider practiced the song for some time. He thought it over and said, no, as for his friend, he could not give him one of the women. Since both women were Spider's, he would not teach the song to his friend, Lizard. Spider

---

[3] Literally: the world has gotten the best of him.
[4] Means "slowly" or "take it easy."

practiced the song until the two names, Akpalagboŋ and Agbedesɔkɔ, came to him just like blinking or drinking water.

Finally the day arrived, just like today. Spider put on a tie . . . put it on again . . . put it on again . . . put it on again.[5] (MAN! LORD! OH! BECAUSE HE WAS GOING TO GET A WOMAN!) He wore *oheneba*[6] . . . he put them on . . . put them on again . . . and even put on a second pair of shoes! (AI!) He wore a pair of pants . . . put them on . . . put them on again. (AI!) He wore a pair of pants . . . put them on . . . put them on again. (AI!) Then he tied on a loin cloth in addition. (LORD! A GENTLEMAN INDEED!)[7] He made his body look *kpoyo kpoyo*.[8] (IS HE A VOODOO PRIEST?) Oh!

Spider walked along the road alone . . . the road was not wide enough for him. It started to rain . . . it rained like crazy, making the ground slippery. Before one entered the chief's compound, there was a big pit one had to leap across. (AO!) Oh! Spider, where are you going? the people asked. Well, just as Spider prepared to leap over the pit, my friends, misfortune befell him *ha aδi*![9] (MM-M-M-M-MMMMMMM MMMMMMMMMOOO . . . IS IT A BALL OF EXCREMENT?)[10] Spider fell into the pit. It would be six months before the ground dried up enough for him to come out of the hole. "Oh! I am doomed!" Spider lamented. He said that his friend Lizard needed to be called.

Lizard came and put his head to the ground. "What do you have to say?" he asked. Spider said he was going to play a tune. He should listen to it carefully, then go to the chief's house and climb the tree that is there . . . he should climb to the very top. It's a very serious matter that he was going to tell Lizard about. "Listen," he said, "the first girl's name is Akpalagboŋ, the second is Agbedesɔkɔ." Lizard asked him to repeat what he had said. Once again, Lizard put his ear to the ground while Spider played the flute close to his ear. Then Spider threw the

---

[5]The performer emphasizes Spider's vanity.
[6]This is a type of sandal.
[7]Literally: Making like a *klake*. *Klake* is a vulgarized version of "clerk."
[8]The sound made by a grass skirt, traditionally worn by fetish priests.
[9]Sound of Spider falling into the pit
[10]Reference to the sound of excrement as it falls into the latrine or outhouse.

flute to Lizard. Lizard caught the flute, played it . . . played it . . . played it . . . exactly!

Spider said he should go and when he marries the girls, the first one will belong to Spider. He will give Lizard the second one. Also, the chiefdom will be Lizard's, but after six months when Spider comes out of the pit, the chiefdom will belong to Spider. Lizard thanked him.

Lizard went . . . went to the top of the tree. Oh! (HE TOOK HIS PLACE.) He took his place exactly *goŋ goŋ goŋ goŋ goŋ goŋ*. The girls and the treasures were displayed. A man got up, "Her name is Abra, Adzo, Afi, Masa . . . Akuvi. . . ." Every name was mentioned. They went on calling for a long time. The chief said he was going to take the girls back to their room. He told the suitors to wait. People went on calling names. Whatever name they could think of, they called out.

All of a sudden, Lizard blasted away with his flute from the top of the tree, *tofilo filo toto filo lo fitoto tofilio lio lio lio*. (laughter) "Oh! Who is up there playing the flute like that?" asked the chief. It was Lizard playing thus, "*Toto filio tofi toto filio lio lio*. . . . One is called Akpalagboŋ, the second is called Agbedesɔkɔ." Oh! The chief just held his head thinking, "What is this?" He ordered the one playing to come down from the top of the tree. Lizard with his big flat head climbed down *xladza xladza* (laughter) and with his arm *kunya kunya kunya*.[11] Oh! Lizard climbed down the tree and blasted away at his flute, calling "Akpalagboŋ . . . Agbedesɔkɔ . . . Akpalagboŋ . . . Agbedesɔkɔ . . . Akpalagboŋ . . . Agbedesɔkɔ . . . Akpalagboŋ . . . Agbedesɔkɔ." It was no joke!

Oh! The chief said he was finished . . . he was finished . . . he was finished.[12] Where had Lizard learned the names? The two girls, the chiefdom, and the treasures were given to Lizard. As Lizard left, Spider said, "Don't forget, mine is the first one!" Lizard collected some sand and threw it in Spider's face in the pit. (laughter) Spider said, "I shit on you! Was it you who suffered with me in the pit? Ê! We'll see!" (OH!)

Lizard insulted Spider every way possible and even threw sand on him again. Spider kept talking as though nothing had happened. He

---

[11]Sound of Lizard's body coming down the tree.
[12]The matter of finding a suitor was resolved.

just kept on yelling that she was his wife.[13] Spider said, "No matter. You see? You see, the villain has forgotten. The victim still remembers."[14] (THAT'S ALWAYS THE CASE!)

Lizard went to the village with all the treasures. When he got to Spider's village ... (HOLY COW! WHAT A LEOPARD MAN!) ... it was no joke! Spider's children were there starving. Funɔ's head had become even flatter. All the children had grown lean. Spider's house had collapsed ... it was made of thatch ... and had completely collapsed. (AO!) The walls had collapsed. Spider's children were overcome with misery. Oh! Lizard paid no attention to his friend's children and their plight.

Just then the dry season came and Spider ... the pit became dry. Spider climbed out very slowly ... he arrived! Oh! (IF HE PROCEEDED TOO HASTILY HE WOULD NOT BE ABLE TO GET OUT.)

Briefly speaking,[15] the women were spoiled, so they liked sweet things. Spoiled women like only sweet things. Spider went to collect some honey and stored it *gò egò egò egò egò*.[16] If he kept it there, the women, by chance, might come to drink it and he would get even with Lizard.

Spider went to collect the honey, put it in the gourd, and set it on the roadside. Meanwhile, both of Lizard's new wives went to the river to fetch water and came across the honey. They drank until they were full. They liked the honey very very very very much, unbelievably much.[17] Oh! They went to find Lizard and said they had tasted some honey in Spider's village. If Lizard didn't agree to gather some honey, they would divorce him and marry ... this one ... (SPIDER?) Yes, Spider. (OH!)

---

[13] Spider is claiming the first woman for himself.

[14] This refers to an Ewe proverb which says that the person who did the wounding has forgotten, while the person with the sore still remembers.

[15] This is an abrupt transition but shows Spider's main concern, i.e., the two women Lizard has taken from him.

[16] Meaning "gourd by gourd."

[17] This performer uses the Ewe *kakakakakaka* very often for emphasis meaning "very much."

Well, Spider . . . as for Lizard,[18] he assumed Spider had forgotten everything because it had been a long time. Lizard went to Spider and said, "My friend, I beg you. My wives, all they drink is honey." He did not know how to collect honey. (LIZARD IS DEAD!) Spider said, "No problem, that's no problem." He will teach him everything he needs to know in order to do for his wives.[19] (HIS WIVES, HA!) Yes! (A TRAP . . . HE HAS SET A TRAP FOR HIM. IT SERVES LIZARD RIGHT!)

"Lizard, my brother, where are you going?" asked Spider. (LIZARD IS IN TROUBLE.) My friends, Spider has finished him! He told him he should go make a torch and get himself a gourd. They will then go and gather honey. When they get there, Spider will stir the beehive with his hands. The bees will be disturbed and hum *bzzzzzzz*. Lizard should stick out his tongue. While the bees sting his tongue he should spit into the gourd and say, "Grandfather . . . grandfather's water . grandmother . . . grandmother's water." If he continues to do this, the gourd will fill up. However, while he is being stung he will need courage, Spider told him. You see, Spider had smeared medicine all over himself, and only then went into the midst of the bees to stir them up. The bees swarmed but he was not stung. Lizard said, "My brother, thank you." (laughter)

Lizard carried a large gourd and tied a rope around himself. Spider said he should tie himself to the tree because if he's stung and he isn't tied to the tree, he will fall to the ground. Therefore, he should tie himself very well. He should not make a "woman's knot" but a "man's knot" . . . very tight. (TO BE VERY STRONG.) He should tie himself so hard that he cannot fall through the rope. (LIZARD WAS ANXIOUS!) Lizard . . . my friends, some people have big heads but they are very dumb.

Lizard with his big head went to tie himself up so that only his head was showing. He was roped in. Oh! Lizard took his time. He went to stir the beehive and stuck out his tongue. "My brother, I beg you!" he moaned. (laughter) The bees were stinging him and he begged and begged. The bees were stinging him, he was begging. (WAS HE

---

[18]The performer corrects himself.

[19]He will teach him everything he needs to know in order to gather honey for his wives.

BEGGING THE BEES OR SPIDER?) Lizard was being stung and he was screaming in the rope. (AO!)[20] Lizard's face and body were very swollen before the bees finally settled down. By the time Lizard finished untying himself, he couldn't . . . he did it monkey's way; it's easier to fall than climb down *a-a-ti*! Lizard fell to the ground.

Lizard's tongue was swollen . . . filling his entire mouth. Before, Lizard was talkative. Now, Lizard's mouth was totally swollen *gbeŋ gbeŋ gbeŋ*. He went to Spider, who was on the wall, and said, "My friend, why have you done me so?"

That is why, whenever you see a big old ugly lizard, he will be on the wall knocking his head against the wall saying, "Why have you done me so . . . done me so . . . done me so . . . ? See, the culprit forgets but the victim remembers. If you hurt somebody, you should be *kleva*[21] until you die. That's the only way you will be free from him. (SHOWMAN!)

Woezɔ kakakakakakaka.

---

[20] The audience expresses pity for Lizard.
[21] The performer interjects the English word "clever."

29.1.5.   MONSTER FLOGS SPIDER

Performer: Kɔmi Nofegali, 22, bricklayer
Date: May 9, 1979, 6:30 P.M.
Place: Noefe Kɔdzi, Kpalime
Audience: 23 adults, 23 children

Listen to a spider tale. (LET THE TALE COME.)

Spider tale walked and fell on Spider. (IT FELL ON HIM.) It fell on Monster. (IT FELL ON HIM.) It fell on Monkey. (IT FELL ON HIM.) That's right!

In those days a severe famine came over the land. (I SWEAR TO GOD!) In the whole country it was only Monster who had a farm. Everyone had cultivated and planted, but their farms were scorched. Monster was the only one who had any food to sell in the market. Monster went and employed some youth from Ablogome to carry food from his farm and sell it at the market for people to buy.

Yiyi was the only one who never bought food from the young people. Anytime that Monster left his farm, Spider would go to the farm, take what crops remained, and bring them back for his wife Funɔ to prepare. Monster watched him the whole time.

One day Monster went and hid on the farm. Spider went to the farm and shouted, "Hey! Is the owner here?" When nobody answered, Spider quickly gathered the crops, aided by Funɔ, who followed him.

Monster again went and hid on the farm. Spider came again. Monster remained quiet without even winking an eye. Spider collected the crops.

Monster said, "Yiyi, I've caught you today!" Spider said, "Uncle, you've caught me indeed." Monster asked Spider how he wanted to be punished. Spider told monster that he would clear his whole farm for him so that he might be forgiven. Monster said, no. He should take home with him instead the cassava he had just dug up. When he got home he should get some shea butter and rub it all over himself. The next morning Monster would come and flog him.

Spider thought this was a joke. He collected the necessary items and carried them home. Very early in the morning Spider heard a rushing noise in the distance. He wondered what it could be, rrrrrrrrrr! Monster arrived. He took hold of Spider and flogged him well. Then he gave him a penny to buy more shea butter to rub all over himself in order to get himself ready for the following morning when Monster would come again.

Early the next morning, Spider was sitting in the yard of his house when rrrrrrrrrrr! Monster arrived, took hold of Spider, and thrashed him well. Then Monster gave Spider another penny to buy more shea butter with which to rub himself in order to get his skin supple for the following morning.

The next morning Funɔ got up early, while Spider went to hide in an enamel bowl. Cassava was grated and used to cover him up. Monster came and asked Funɔ where Spider was. She said she did not know. Monster had a diviner's bag. He threw down the cowrie shells. *Afã*[1] revealed that Spider was hiding in the grated cassava.

Spider was caught and flogged soundly. He was told to apply more shea butter. The flogging would be repeated the next morning when Monster would come again. (AHA! HE WAS IN TROUBLE!)

The next morning Spider got up very early. He asked his wife to take off her undercloth.[2] Spider hid between her legs as she put the cloth over him. Monster came and threw the cowrie shells.[3] He asked Spider's wife to loosen her cloth immediately. Spider was pulled out and given a good thrashing. He was then told to apply more shea butter to make his skin even more supple.

Spider got up and saw Grain of Corn. He commanded Corn to break in two for him to hide in. Grain opened and Spider jumped in. Rooster was passing by. (THE ROOSTER SWALLOWED THE GRAIN.) He swallowed Grain of Corn. If only Rooster would stay in the house. But no, he went to the dung hill. Fox caught Rooster and ate it. After Fox had swallowed Rooster, would he not remain quiet? No, he went roaming about. A Python swallowed Fox, found an anthill and coiled up inside it.

---

[1] *Afã* is the oracle common to the Ewe and Yoruba people.

[2] Traditional clothing for Ewe women, as for women in all of West Africa, consists of a sewn top and one or two pieces of cloth wrapped around as a skirt.

[3] Cowrie shells are what diviners use to "see" the future.

All of a sudden, Monster came, but did not see Spider. He threw down the cowries, and Afã told him to go to the dunghill. There, as he cast the cowries again, Afã said he must go to the anthill, for there was something in there. The thing must come out. Python came out and was asked if he had something in his belly. He said he had just swallowed a fox. He commanded Fox to come out at once. Monster asked him, "What do you have in your belly?" Fox said he swallowed a rooster. Monster said Rooster must come out at once.

He asked Rooster what he had in his belly. Rooster said he had swallowed Grain of Corn. That was what had gotten him into this trouble. He told Grain of Corn to come out at once. Grain of Corn came out and said, yes, he was hiding Spider. Spider came out and was flogged as never before. He was told to use more shea butter, for Monster would be back again.

The next day Spider got up early and sat down on a stool. All of a sudden he heard the sound of Monster's footsteps coming toward him. Spider got up and fled. He took to his heels, while Monster chased him. Spider ran and came upon some men who were working very hard hoeing. Spider begged them, for Monster was chasing him.

The men asked whether there was anyone stronger than themselves. They covered him up with weeds and wondered whether the heavy steps *gbì! gbì! gbì!* belonged to Spider's assailant. How could such a small fellow be chased by something so big?

Monster went to the farmer but the farmer did not want the monster to stop. He pointed to Spider who was running as fast as he could. He ran until he came upon Lion sitting in the sun.

Lion asked Spider what the trouble was. But Spider said he could not tell him. Lion told him to sit down and wait. Lion heard the heavy steps approaching in the distance. He told the intruder not to bring any trouble, for he had learned about suffering long ago. He must not bring him any trouble because Lion had all he could handle. Hearing this, Spider fled and came upon Monkey.

Monkey was a blacksmith. Lord! What a blacksmith! Monkey was in his workshop forging iron with great energy. He asked Spider what was the matter. Spider said, "Uncle, if you do not save me from the danger I face, I am dead." Monkey sat down, put an iron rod into the

Appendix

fire and asked Spider to work the bellows. When the time came, he would tell him what to do.

Monkey heard the heavy steps approaching and asked Monster, "What do you want?" Monster said he was after Spider. Monkey said Spider was sitting over there, but he could not take him away. (WHAT A MAN!) Whatever Monster wants to do, he must do it quickly and be gone.

Monster took hold of Monkey and swallowed him! Monkey came out through his anus! (OOOOOOOOOOO! THAT MAN! THE SON OF MAN!) Monkey said, "You must be joking!" He turned around and swallowed Monster, who in turn came out through Monkey's anus!

Monkey told Spider that he should watch the iron rod in the fire. When he and Monster struggle, Monkey will swallow Monster. Monkey will turn his bottom to Spider and Spider must then thrust the iron rod into Monkey's anus. (THAT WAY MONSTER COULD NOT COME OUT!)

The struggle took a long time. Finally, Monkey caught Monster and swallowed him. Monster wanted to come out but Monkey turned his bottom to Spider. At once, Spider thrust the hot rod into Monkey's bottom. And so, Monster remained in Monkey's bottom. That is why Monkey's bottom is like it is. It is the red hot iron that made his bottom so red.

That is what I was deceived with and I use it to deceive you.

Yooooooooo.

30.1.2. SPIDER DECORATES EGGS

Performer: Kɔsi Gavo, 10, school boy
Date: May 13, 1979; 3:30 P.M.
Place: Vɔlɔve
Audience: 18 adults, 30 children

Listen to a tale. (LET THE TALE COME.)

The tale went until it fell on Spider. It went and fell on Crocodile.

They were there . . . they were there. Crocodile laid eggs and he asked Spider to come and decorate them for him. Spider agreed. Spider went . . . he came . . . he said . . . Crocodile laid enough eggs to fill six rooms. He said Spider should draw on the eggs for him in all six rooms and Spider agreed. Spider drew on an egg, then showed Crocodile the egg he had just decorated. He ate one of the eggs, then showed Crocodile the egg he had decorated. He ate the rest of the eggs . . . a whole roomful! He defecated in the room so that the room was full. He closed the door, took the one egg he had decorated and placed it on top of his excrement. He did this in all six rooms.

He told Crocodile he was leaving, so Crocodile should transport him across the river. Crocodile agreed. Spider said when he is gone, he should not open the door. He should wait five days before opening the door. Crocodile agreed. Just as Crocodile was carrying Spider across the river, Crocodile's wife opened the door to look into the room. There was excrement . . . a whole roomful! The room was full. She called to Crocodile to bring back the spider. "He has filled the room with excrement! Bring him back!" she shouted.

Spider told Crocodile that his wife is trying to tell him that rain is threatening, so he should move more quickly to cross the river. Crocodile nodded. Spider said that rain was threatening. In fact, Crocodile's wife was telling him to bring back the spider because he had defecated in all the rooms . . . he should bring him back. But Spider said it was going to rain, so he should move quickly and transport him across the river. Crocodile ferried him across the river to the other side.

Crocodile left and went home . . . he went to see. . . . There was excrement piled high in all the rooms. Crocodile said he would go . . . he would follow Spider.

Spider shaved his head clean and carried a hoeing stick. As Crocodile went and saw Spider, he asked if he wasn't the one who had decorated Crocodile's eggs. Spider said he doesn't remember the last time he decorated an egg . . . he hasn't decorated eggs in a long time. He told him to see a brother of his, a miller who lived a little further down the road. He should go see him. Crocodile agreed.

Spider ran ahead, painted his head with charcoal, and started grinding. He said it had been more than ten years since he last decorated eggs. A brother of his, however, was down the road gathering stones. He should go see him. He ran ahead again and put on a long robe, a Hausa robe, painted his head with charcoal, and started gathering stones. Crocodile asked him whether he had not decorated Crocodile's eggs. Spider said, no, it's been a long time since he's decorated eggs.

Then Spider asked Crocodile where his fatal spot was. Crocodile said, as for him, his fatal spot is his nose. Spider asked Crocodile to help him lift a heavy load to Spider's head. As Crocodile helped him, Spider let the load fall on Crocodile's nose, killing Crocodile.

Spider took Crocodile, put him in a bag, and left. Large animals . . . large animals came across Spider, asking him what was in the bag. He said his father had died and he was carrying him home. They said they wanted to look inside the bag. He said, no, it was his dead father he was taking home. They grabbed him and seized the sack. Lo and behold! . . . there was Crocodile in the bag. They took Crocodile from him and prepared it for cooking.

Spider said he was going to show them.[1] He went and decorated his child's teeth. He said to his child that he should go bare his teeth to the big animals hī hī hī hī[2] . . . (laughter) . . . so that the decoration is visible. Spider's child agreed. The child went to the fireplace.[3] They

---

[1] He was going to teach them a lesson.
[2] He should bare his teeth to the animals and make this noise while doing so.
[3] Presumably, the animals were seated around a fire.

said, "Who has painted your teeth so beautifully hī hī hī hī. . . ?" The child had done as he had been told. "Oh, who has painted your teeth so beautifully?" they asked again.

As the child returned home, the fire went out. Spider said the child should go again. The child went again, did it again . . . he was doing it. The large animals questioned him. He was doing it hī hī hī hī . . . showing the decoration on his teeth. Spider told his child he should tell the animals to carve pegs. They should carve them with very sharp points. One animal should carve four pegs, the others should make four also. They should bring them so that Spider could nail the animals to the wall and decorate their teeth. The child nodded.

The child went and gave the animals instructions. They ran and prepared the pegs. Spider nailed the pegs to the wall. Then he said, "I'll show you today." He went and took . . .[4] he said the children should go and bring the cooked meat. He took the meat and ate it, throwing the soup in the animals' faces. He fetched the soup and poured it in their faces. Oh! He finished eating the meat and left. Spider went to another village.

Ant was passing by. The large animals asked him to chew the pegs for them so they could get down. Ant said whenever they were in the forest, they stepped on him. He would not chew the pegs for them. Ant refused and left.

Snail was passing by. They asked the snail to put slime on the pegs to loosen them so they could get down. Snail said whenever they met in the bush, they stepped on him. Snail left.

Termite was passing by. They asked the termite to chew the pegs. He chewed the pegs and the animals were freed from the wall. The large animals went and informed Spider that they were coming to see him. Spider agreed.

Spider told his children that when the animals come, they should empty all the water pots, then go to the river bank. At the well there is a gourd hanging on the side. When they go to the river bank, they should leave their buckets and run into the gourd. The children agreed.

---

[4] The narrator corrects himself.

The large animals . . . the large animals came. Spider said, "I don't have any water. Go fetch some." The children took the bucket, went to fetch the water, left the bucket by the well, and jumped into the gourd. They all hid in the gourd. "Oh why have my children not brought back the bucket quickly?" Spider mused. Spider said he would go look for them. He followed them and also hid in the gourd.

The large animals began to get thirsty. They said they would go to the well. Just as they got there, a child said, "Father has farted, father has farted!" (laughter) "Why are you saying that I have farted? You yourself farted!" Spider retorted.

Lion pawed the gourd and the gourd fell. Spider's children dashed out and ran into a hole. Spider sharpened a knife . . . the knife was sharp. Spider made a fire in the hole. The large animals were there and Monkey was passing by. They told Monkey to dig a hole for them. Monkey wanted to do with his hand like this,[5] when Spider tried to plunge the knife into his face. Monkey ran . . . Monkey did like this . . . he said he wouldn't do it. Monkey left.

Pig was passing by. They said Pig should dig a hole for them. Pig said, whenever he says, "*Huihui huihui*," they should push him farther into the hole. The large animals agreed. As you know, the large animals were strong. Pig stuck his snout in the hole . . . thrust his snout in the hole while the animals pushed. Spider was chopping off Pig's snout, giving pieces to his children who were roasting and eating . . . roasting and eating it until only a little piece of snout kept Spider from Pig's teeth.

Just then, Pig excreted in the faces of the animals. The animals took off. Pig also fled . . . he left.

Pig had a child and the child asked Pig what had happened to his snout. Pig replied that he was young yet and would know when he grew up.[6]

---

[5]The performer makes a gesture showing how the monkey was going to dig the hole.

[6]This refers to a proverb which says that when a little pig asks an elder pig what made its mouth so ugly, the elder pig answers that when the little one grows up, he will understand.

That's what I want to deceive you with, you and the white person here.

Yoooooo. Woezɔ kakakakaka.

30.2.2. SPIDER REFUSES THE CHIEF'S DAUGHTER

Performer: Volovetɔ, 25, farmer
Date: May 13, 1979; 3:30 P.M.
Place: Gbalave, Vɔlɔve
Audience: 11 adults, 30 children

Listen to a tale. (LET THE TALE COME.)

The tale wandered and fell on an old man. (IT FELL ON HIM.) It fell on a chief. (IT FELL ON HIM.) It fell on a woman. (IT FELL ON HER.)

A man[1] married and had a very beautiful daughter. In fact, if you saw this girl, you would lust for her. Because of her extreme beauty she lived in an upstairs room. As this girl grew up, many young men came to ask the chief for the girl's hand in marriage. The chief acknowledged their desire but told the suitors he would first set a task. The one who could complete the task would be the groom. The suitors agreed.

The chief said he had a forest and anyone who could clear the forest could marry his daughter. After the forest was cleared, he would give a large ram as a token of appreciation. The task was set. Everyone complained how difficult the task was and gave up. Beasts, flies, birds, venomous creatures—all who lived in the forest—each one mocked the one who came before and failed in turn.

There was one stipulation. If, while clearing the forest, the suitors felt irritations on any part of their body, they may not scratch. This was why so many had failed in the past.

Yiyi[2] thought for a long while about this and finally went to the chief, offering to make an attempt. He too wanted to try.[3] He asked the chief to allow one of his sons to accompany him. The chief told his son to go and watch Yiyi. If, while clearing the forest, Yiyi felt any irritations on any part of his body, he was not permitted to scratch. During his work Yiyi stopped periodically and asked the boy, "Does the chief's ram

---

[1] The narrator uses the word *tɔgbui* meaning "an older man." It is a term of respect for an elder.

[2] "Avatrɔafenyi" is another name for Spider but "Yiyi" is the most common.

[3] Literally: Spider also wanted to dip his hand into this bloodbath to see whether he would be able.

have spots here? . . . spots there?"[4] The boy replied, "No." Spider continued the same way until the forest was completely cleared. Both Spider and the boy left.

The boy reported to his father that Spider had cleared the entire forest. "Is that true?" asked the chief. "Yes," the boy replied. The chief wanted to know whether Spider had scratched any part of his body while working. "No," answered the boy.

After hesitating a bit, Spider refused to marry the girl and took only the ram! The chief pleaded with him but Spider insisted on taking only the ram. The chief said, well, if he refuses to marry the girl, what's to be done? The chief gave him the ram.

Spider thought a while and said to himself, "That ram for which I have endured so much, must I share it?" No! Spider took the ram with him and farted into a gourd. After traveling some distance, he opened the gourd. If flies gathered, that meant people were near. He did this several times. He went very far until he came to a solitary place. He opened the gourd but no flies came. He was content and said this is what he wanted.

He built a house there, prepared the ram, and placed it on the fire. He seasoned the meat and said it was a great day for him. He saw a palm tree in the distance. While he was cooking, the agɔ fell ti! He went to pick up the nut . . . ē ē, it was no easy job.

Spider turned to run away when a monster, Ndo, appeared and said to him that he must not run away, he must come back. If he does not come back, he will swell up and die at once. Spider thought it was a joke. He turned to run away but the monster commanded him to swell up and die . . . Spider was stone dead. The monster commanded him to revive and he revived. The monster said he had warned him. He commanded Spider to carry him on his back. They were going to eat the mutton together.

Spider complained, "What is this that has befallen me?" Oh! Spider's heart could not bear it. He lamented having to share the ram with the monster. Let's see what happens. Spider carried the monster and placed him by the mutton. The mutton was cooked. He lifted the

---

[4]Obviously, while pointing to these places on his body, Yiyi scratches himself.

Appendix *261*

meat off the fire. The monster warned Spider that if by mistake he put a piece of meat into his mouth, he would swell up and die. What could he do? Spider fed the monster until the last morsel was eaten. The monster consumed all the meat. The monster looked up and saw tears dropping from Spider's eyes. He asked Spider why he wept. Spider said he was feeling sorry for the monster because he was eating so slowly. (laughter) It was pitiful . . . Spider was actually feeling very sorry for himself!

Spider thought about the trouble he had gone to, to get the ram in the first place . . . then this terrible treatment from Ndo. Spider decided to pay him back . . . now! Spider told the monster he was going to build a house to shelter him from the rain. Spider built the house, raising the posts. To these he tied the monster's hairs and then took some kerosene. He poured the kerosene on the monster and set him on fire. The monster was well roasted! Spider said he was going to eat the monster in exchange for the mutton the monster had eaten. Spider had several baskets of corn bread baked for him. He ate the monster with all the bread. Spider wanted to get up but could not. He was crippled! Every animal passing by questioned him. He said he was crippled. When they tried to lift him, they could not. He was stuck fast where he was. That is why Spider lives on the ground and no longer flies.

While I was passing by, an old woman deceived me with this and I use it to deceive this white person.

Yooooooooo.

51.1.3. SPIDER AND THE KENTE CLOTH

Performer: Nugbemado, 47, teacher
Date: August 16, 1979, 7 P.M.
Place: Ho, Ghana
Audience: 8 adults, 4 children

Listen to a tale. (LET THE TALE COME.) The tale fell on a great chief. (IT FELL ON HIM.) It fell on his wife. (IT FELL ON HER.) It fell also on the whole nation. (IT FELL ON THEM.) Then it fell on Yiyi. (IT FELL ON HIM.)

After a long while, the chief had three daughters. They were very beautiful. (LIKE SQUIRRELS!) One's face was smooth, the other's face was oval. Their beauty made you salivate! They needed to marry, but that was difficult because they never left the house. They were always indoors and everything was done for them. Marriage became a very difficult thing. Their father wanted them to marry by all means, but the suitors first had to learn the girls' names. No one knew their names. That's why marriage was so difficult.

The chief made an announcement. Anyone who learned the girls' names would marry them. But since the girls never went out, nobody knew their names. When Yiyi heard this, he said, "How shall I marry the girls?"

The girls usually went to the stream to fetch water for their bath. There was a mango tree near there. Yiyi knew that the girls went there at dawn. He climbed the mango tree and took with him three pebbles.

The girls arrived and were fetching water. Yiyi dropped a pebble into the stream. One of the girls said, "Gatete, someone threw a pebble into the stream." Yiyi remembered that. A while later he threw another pebble into the stream. "Adegble, someone just threw a pebble into the stream." Yiyi kept that in mind as well. Some time later, he threw another pebble into the stream. "Bunubu, someone just threw a pebble into the stream." Yiyi memorized all three names: Gatete, Bunubu, Adegble . . . Gatete, Bunubu, Adegble. (GATETE, BUNUBU, ADEGBLE!) He chanted the three names to himself to remember them. Nobody knew what he was doing.

One day he sent a message to the chief saying he was ready to attempt to guess the names of the chief's daughters. The one whose name he calls correctly will be the one he will marry. The chief said more important people had tried to guess his daughters' names and failed. How could someone as insignificant as Yiyi succeed? He was wasting his time! (I WAS THERE THAT DAY!)[1] Let the song come:

(Song):   Mary, Mary, come here,
          Mary, Mary, come here,
          Mary Victoria, come here,
          Abladzodidi, sit down. (laughter)
          (THAT DAY YOU SURELY WERE YIYI)! (laughter)

The chief had to keep his word. An order was given for all the people to assemble. Yiyi claimed to know the girls' names. Poor Yiyi![2] He had his drum in his armpit. He put on a big splendid *kente* cloth.[3] The chief and the people took their seats. The girls, looking ravishingly beautiful, also took their seats. Yiyi, wearing his *kente* cloth, stayed at a distance beating his drum and singing a song. The people could not hear what he was singing until he came to the center of the crowd.

The linguist[4] was called and was asked to inform the chief that the names of the three daughters were known. Was the chief ready to hear the names? The chief said he was ready. The drum was beaten. "Gatete, Bunubu, Adegble . . . Gatete, Bunbubu, Adegble." Yiyi was beating his drum and calling the names but people still did not hear what he was saying.

---

[1] Conventional formula for introducing a song.

[2] Said out of playful affection for Spider, not sympathy.

[3] *Kente* cloth is traditional ceremonial cloth worn on special occasions. It is very heavy and often woven in beautiful bright hues of black, red, yellow, and blue.

[4] The linguist in Ewe culture is the spokesman who mediates between the chief and the people. In Ewe culture, out of respect for the chief, people never address him directly, nor does the chief address his people directly. This tradition emphasizes the importance of the chief and focuses attention on the importance of the spoken word.

He did this for some time, then stopped. Yiyi said that the chief should know that the name of the eldest girl was Gatete! The chief should know this. The chief nodded but said nothing. He asked for the second name. Yiyi answered that the name of the second girl was Adegble. The chief shook his head in disbelief. "And the third one?" asked the chief. "The third one, her name is Bunubu!" exclaimed Yiyi. Yiyi called the names and said to the chief, "What do you have to say?"

The chief said, indeed, those were the names of his daughters! There was shouting and great commotion. Yiyi adjusted his cloth with great ceremony and beat his drum: "Gatete, Bunubu, Adegble . . . Gatete, Bunubu, Adegble . . . (GATETE, BUNUBU, ADEGBLE.)

The chief said, "Those are indeed their names!" Yiyi was to select one of the girls to marry. Who was it to be? Yiyi thought for some time but he didn't know what to do. Truly, the girls were so beautiful, he didn't know which one to select. He pondered, "Who shall I select? Who shall I leave? Who shall I select? Who shall I leave?"

He looked at them standing there, their faces radiant. One had a round face with sparkling eyes. (WHEW!) The other had a broad face. (THAT'S RIGHT!) Finally, he decided on the middle one. (THAT'S RIGHT!) She was the one he was going to marry. The girl didn't like Yiyi but the chief said she had to marry him.

The chief gave them a large house with many stories to live in.[5] The girl wept for a long time at the thought of marrying Spider. "What shall I do?" she moaned. "There is nothing to be done. The chief's word has to be obeyed."

They climbed up.[6] The cloth Yiyi wore was borrowed. (laughter) Just then there was a knock on the door. Spider had told the owner of the cloth that he needed to go somewhere and promised to return the cloth as soon as he returned. The man had to attend a celebration and needed his cloth back. That was why he was at Yiyi's house. Yiyi's new wife was also there. She told Yiyi that the owner of the cloth wanted his cloth back.

---

[5]Traditional houses in Eweland are usually one-story dwellings. The author has embellished his tale to create the image of great wealth and prestige.

[6]They climbed up the stairs of the house.

Spider didn't know what to do. What was he to do? He had to give the cloth back to the man. He screwed up his courage and took off the cloth. There Yiyi stood in his nasty-looking skin![7] (AO!) The girl jumped up screaming, "What has my father done to me?" (laughter) Yiyi answered that he had married her fair and square. He said in a nasal voice, "I am the one who tricked you into telling me your name."

The girl thought she was going to die! (laughter) "What am I going to do?" she wailed. There was nothing that could be done. The cloth had been taken away, exposing Yiyi's nasty skin. Quickly, the girl ran home to tell her father the whole story . . . how the one who married her had tricked her into revealing her name. She wanted to retain her royal family name and said she would never stay married to Yiyi.

The chief thought about what he should do. He had given his word and could not break it. (THAT'S RIGHT!) Otherwise, he would be destooled.[8]

It was very difficult for the chief to tell Yiyi that his daughter did not want him. For many weeks, no one knew what to do. A decision was finally made to kill Spider. He would be ambushed and killed. This would solve everything. The woman would become a widow and be free at last. The chief's conscience bothered him but he had to do something because he knew Spider was not fit for his daughter. Only royalty could marry royalty, but no chief's son could be found who knew the names of his daughters.

At dawn they knocked on Yiyi's door. Thinking it was his wife, Yiyi opened the door. The king's men pounced on him and killed him!

That is why Spider is spread all over the world. You hear about him here, there, everywhere. That is why when you split firewood, you hear an echo in the distance.[9]

On the way here, I met Tɔgbui Adiko who told me to come and do something for him. On my way here an old lady called me, told me this story, and asked that I narrate it to you.[10]

---

[7] Yiyi's skin was apparently very rough and ugly-looking.
[8] Equivalent of being dethroned.
[9] It is Spider's echo you hear.
[10] This ending is characteristic of story tellers in the Volta Region in Ghana where the narrator attributes the story to a third person. This is another

This is my story. Yooooooooooo. (YOUR MOUTH IS FIT FOR STORYTELLING.)

---

example of the narrator's attempt to make more believable the artful "lie" that has just been told.

Tɔgbui can mean either grandfather, father, or uncle. It is a term of respect for an elder.

51.1.5.   SPIDER POUNDS FUFU

Performer: Alice Tse, early 30's, rice hawker
Date: August 16, 1979; 7 P.M.
Place: Ho, Ghana
Audience: 8 adults, 4 children

Listen to a tale. (LET THE TALE COME.)

The tale went until it fell on Adjaye.[1] (IT FELL ON HIM.) It fell on his relatives. (IT FELL ON THEM.)

One day Spider planted yams. When they were ready, he saw they were going to be very big. Every time he went to the farm, the farm looked beautiful. So one day Spider came and said he was ill. He was ill for a long time and then "died." He lay very still and very flat. They went and made a coffin for him. Spider said if he died, they should take a mortar and pestle and bury them with him. (I WAS THERE THAT DAY.)

>   (Song):   Big man, kind yet cruel,
>   Big man, kind yet cruel.

They said, "Okay." The day Spider died, they went to bury him. They took a mortar and pestle, salt, pepper—everything, and put them in the coffin with Spider. They took Spider out and buried him.

After he was buried, when it was night, Spider got up and stealthily pounded *fufu*[2] on the farm. When Funɔ and the children went to the farm, they didn't know who was stealing the yams. This continued. They went to the farm . . . again the same thing. Spider continued to pound *fufu*. (I WAS THERE THAT DAY WHEN HE WAS POUNDING *FUFU*.) While pounding he sang:

>   (Song):   *Protoko, protoko*,[3] Funɔ and the children are such
>   fools,

---

[1] Another name for the spider.

[2] *Fufu* is made of pounded yam, cassava, coco-yams, or plantains and eaten with soup.

[3] The sound of *fufu* being pounded.

> *Protoko, protoko*, Funɔ and the children are such fools.
> Are mortar and pestle buried with the dead?
> Are pot, salt, and yams buried with the dead?
> *Protoko, protoko*, does a living person get buried for no reason?

Spider kept pounding *fufu* until everything was gone on the farm. While he pounded *fufu*, he sang:

(Song:) Funɔ and her children are such fools,
Funɔ and her children are such fools.
Are mortar and pestle buried with the dead?
It's pounded, it's mashed, it's taken out.

Spider took the *fufu* and ate it . . . until all the yams were gone on the farm.

So one day the villagers took . . . covered a tree with tar and left it on the farm. Spider came again. He saw the tree but didn't know exactly what it was or what it was doing there. Spider walked toward it and all of a sudden he got stuck! He wanted to touch the tree but saw that he was glued to the tree! By the time people arrived, there was Spider stuck to the tree, the cooked *fufu* by his side.

From that day on, Spider was ashamed and went away . . . away . . . to the corner of the house. It was because of what happened that day that if you see Spider, he'll be in the corner of the house.

As I was coming, I hit my foot, which caused me such pain I didn't know what to do. When I reached the place, Mr. Nugbemado came out to meet me and asked me where I was going. I told him I was going to the house. He deceived me with this tale and I, in turn, deceive you with it.

You have a tongue for storytelling! Yooooooo.

51.2.5. SPIDER AND THE BEANS

Performer: Mary Alomo, early 30's, teacher
Date: August 16, 1979; 7 P.M.
Place: Ho, Ghana
Audience: 8 adults, 4 children

Listen to a tale. (LET THE TALE COME.)

The tale left *tiŋdi tiŋdi tiŋdi tiŋdi*, it went and fell on the same spider. (IT FELL ON HIM.) It fell on Funɔ. (IT FELL ON HER.) It fell on Spider's mother-in-law. (IT FELL ON HER.)

They were there . . . they were there. They were there when Funɔ . . . Funɔ is Yiyi's wife. They were at home. (FINE!)[1] Anything that pleased Funɔ he did for her . . . for his wife Funɔ. One day the news came that Funɔ's mother had died . . . Yiyi's mother-in-law. Yiyi lay down and pondered a long time what exactly he would do to let the whole population know that he was grieved by his mother-in-law's death. Spider decided he would not eat. When they went to the funeral, he would not eat so that the people would know that the death truly grieved him.

They left and traveled until they arrived in the village. Everybody was there. Funɔ's sisters' husbands . . . all came. They all met at the funeral. Food was prepared and they called Yiyi, but Yiyi said he would not eat. Yiyi just wept and wept. Usually at daybreak it was customary that everyone leave quietly and get something to eat before returning.[2] (laughter) They called Yiyi but Yiyi said his mother-in-law . . . his mother-in-law's death pained him too much. He said he would never ever eat again. They called him, they dragged him, but he refused. (I WAS THERE THAT DAY WHEN HE WEPT!)[3]

---

[1] Ghana is English-speaking and therefore, English words are interspersed among the Ewe text. The meaning of "fine" in this instance is "hey," "right," "peacefully."

[2] Literally: Usually at daybreak everyone will go and hide somewhere and put something in their stomachs before returning.

[3] "I was there that day" is a conventional formula for introducing a song.

(Song:)   My child, oh my child,
My child, oh my child,
This is my beloved one
Of whom I am so very fond.
This is my beloved one
Of whom I am so very fond.

Things continued like that. Funɔ thought to herself, "Spider cannot stay even one hour without eating. What's happened to him? Is it the death which has touched him so deeply? What kind of love is this? Does Yiyi really love me so much?" Imagine! It takes her mother's death for her to learn this! They tried everything possible but they could not convince Yiyi to eat.

The first day passed and Yiyi did not eat. The second day passed and still Yiyi did not eat. Funɔ was puzzled because normally Yiyi is a heavy eater. (laughter) How could he go for two days and still not eat? This puzzled her greatly. He just kept on weeping. Oh! It appeared to the people that the death truly pained him.

By the end of the second day, mmmmmmm, Yiyi went to bed but still he did not eat. Hunger was killing his stomach so much . . . hunger was killing Yiyi . . . hunger was killing Yiyi that even tears no longer came. He wept with dry eyes. The sounds came but no tears fell. Hunger gripped him. Yiyi thought about it . . . what exactly was he going to do?

Meanwhile, during the funeral, beans were being cooked, pots and pots of beans . . . large pots of beans were on the fire to feed the mourners. There was *akplẽ*[4] and other things, but Yiyi relished beans. He watched the people eat, but he had sworn an oath that he would not eat. He was determined. He pondered what exactly he was going to do.

It was day again. Everyone was bustling back and forth. Yiyi's oath, however, didn't allow him to go and eat . . . at least not until the funeral was over. They called Yiyi again but Yiyi refused, saying he would not go.

---

[4] A cooked dough made of ground cornmeal.

Meanwhile, there was a large kitchen. . . . The pots of beans were . . . the pots of beans were cooking on the fire . . . in heaps! Yiyi disappeared from the people.[5] He had a hat . . . he liked wearing hats. Yiyi went into the kitchen to one of the pots of beans, the pot which was well-done. It was also well salted. He opened the beans, took a ladle, put the beans into his hat, and started to eat.

Every now and then while eating, he would look outside to see if anyone was coming. He scooped and ate, scooped and ate the hot beans.

Suddenly the mourners asked, "Where has Yiyi gone?" They no longer heard his weeping because . . . the whole time his cries were louder than everybody else's. So when they did not hear his weeping, they knew Yiyi no longer . . . maybe he went someplace or something had happened to him . . . not knowing Yiyi was eating beans in the kitchen.[6]

By the time people noticed,[7] Yiyi was already in the kitchen eating beans! (laughter) However, they did not see him clearly because the big pot blocked him from view. As soon as he saw the people, he took the hot beans and the hat—everything—and put them on his head! (laughter) The beans were smoking *li li li li li*! The beans . . . the beans were burning Yiyi's head! Yiyi was spinning underneath! He danced to the drums as though he were still weeping (WEEPING!) . . . he was really weeping! (laughter) The beans were burning his head!

He was vigorously shaking his head while the people asked, "Oh! What's happened to Yiyi? He's behaving strangely!" The people said, "Is hunger no longer killing him?" But those who saw him were suspicious.[8] They started whispering among themselves and Yiyi knew . . . he knew that he was going to be found out.

Someone asked him why he was shaking his head like that. He said there was a head-shaking festival at his father's village (laughter)

---

[5]Yiyi left the group of mourners to go to the kitchen.

[6]The narrator does not complete her thought.

[7]Means, "By the time people noticed his absence . . ."

[8]Literally: People wondered whether it was the hunger that was pressing him so. But the person who saw him in the room . . . when he saw him, he saw something he did not like.

and he was rehearsing so he could do the head-shaking dance . . . the head-shaking dance. The people were not convinced so they started to chase him, when lo and behold! Yiyi took off the hat with all the hot beans and dropped it. All the hair was burned off Spider's head!

He ran and hid in the crack of the wall. From that day on, Spider no longer has any hair on his head. (laughter) (YOU HAVE A TONGUE FOR STORYTELLING.)

You good listeners, you!

51.2.7. SHEEP AND GOAT

Performer: Comfort Kuna, 22, trader
Date: August 16, 1979, 7 P.M.
Place: Ho, Ghana
Audience: 8 adults, 4 children

Listen to a story. (LET IT COME.) The story fell on Sheep and Goat. (IT FELL ON THEM.) It landed on Leopard. (IT FELL ON HIM.) It landed on Hyena. (IT FELL ON HIM.)

One day there was a great famine in the land. There were no clothes or shelters. So one day Sheep and Goat decided to build a house. They looked for a place to build a house. They looked for a place to build where nobody would know where their house was. This secret site would be the ideal place for their house. They searched and searched and came to a vast forest. They looked around and did not see anyone. They weeded the place and left.

The following day when they went to the site, someone had already cut the stakes! They said it was probably their grandfather's ghost who had cut them. They planted the stakes and planned to put up the walls the following day. The next day, again the work was done for them! They said this was probably the work of their grandmother's ghost. For this they were grateful.

They did not know that it was Hyena and Leopard who were responsible, for they too were looking for a building site. When they found the site they liked, they started to build the walls. They did not know about Goat and Sheep.

The roof was put on and the day was set for moving into the house. When Goat and Sheep arrived, they discovered Hyena and Leopard already in the house!

Goat told Sheep to look at the people in the house! Goat said they would play a trick on Hyena, who was their bitter enemy. There was no way that Goat and Hyena could live together in peace under the same roof.

Goat called, "Friend." Hyena answered, "Yes." Goat said, "Is this your house?" Hyena said it was. Goat said they would like to stay there for a while and Hyena agreed. Goat and Sheep were given a room, while Hyena and Leopard stayed in another room.

Together, Hyena and Leopard plotted against Goat and Sheep. They wanted to eat their house guests but did not know how to trap them. So one day Hyena and Leopard made plans to tap some palm wine. After tapping, they would get Goat and Sheep drunk and then eat them.

Goat told Sheep that Hyena and Leopard wanted to eat them. That was why they went to tap palm wine. Goat explained that when Hyena and Leopard gave them wine to drink, they should drink only a little and pour the rest out. Sheep should not drink the wine because as soon as they were drunk and asleep, Hyena and Leopard would try to eat them. Sheep nodded.

Hyena and Leopard tapped the palm wine. When they returned, they called their guests. When Sheep was served, he drank all the wine. When Goat was served, he drank only a little and threw the rest away. They went to lie down. It was now Hyena and Leopard's turn to get drunk.

Deep in the night when Hyena and Leopard called, "Goat, Goat . . . ," there was no response. They called again, "Friend, friend . . ." and this time Goat responded. Hyena and Leopard asked, "Aren't you asleep yet?" Goat said his skin itched so he could not sleep. Hyena and Leopard left. Goat said to Sheep, "See, wasn't I right about Hyena and Leopard?" Sheep nodded. So, when Hyena and Leopard went out again, Sheep should drink only a little.

The next evening Hyena and Leopard returned. Sheep was given his share and he drank it all. When they served Goat, he tasted the wine and threw the rest away. In the night Sheep was fast asleep while Goat remained awake. When Hyena and Leopard called, Goat was awake. Only Goat responded. Goat said to Sheep that since Hyena and Leopard wanted to get them drunk, the next night they should pretend they are drunk and sing like drunkards.

Once again, they were given palm wine and they started to sing:

(Song): Big man, Hyena,
Big and hard-hearted,

> Big man, Hyena,
> Big and hard-hearted.

Goat and Sheep sang like drunkards and went to bed.

Hyena and Leopard decided that Goat and Sheep were finally drunk. They would eat them that night.

Goat told Sheep that they should run away. They would put stones and other things in their bed and cover them up. Sheep agreed. They did this and ran away.

After they were gone, Hyena and Leopard opened the door and called, "Friend, friend . . ." but there was no response. They called again but still no response. They jumped on the bed and started to tear their guests into pieces but quickly realized there was nobody in the bed! When they removed the sheets, they found stones and other things! Hyena and Leopard ran outside and saw Goat and Sheep on a hill far off in the distance. They immediately gave chase.

Sheep and Goat came to a stream but did not know how to cross the stream. Sheep knew how to swim but Goat did not. Sheep jumped into the stream and swam to the other side, but Goat remained. Sheep decided to throw a stone to Goat so that the stone could carry Goat to the other side of the stream. Goat agreed. Sheep threw the stone which indeed carried Goat to the opposite bank of the stream.

Hyena and Leopard came to the stream but did not know how to cross it. They stood there not knowing what to do.

Sheep and Goat ran away. That is why they became domestic animals.

When I was coming here, an old lady deceived me with this tale and I, in turn, deceive you with it.

Yoooooooooo.

54.1.4.   NYANUWUFIA

Performer: Agbemenyo Abalu, 68, farmer
Date: September 5, 1979, 8 P.M.
Place: Ŋotse-Adzigo
Audience: 21 adults, 10 children

Listen to a tale. (LET THE TALE COME.)

The tale went around and fell on Yiyi. (THAT'S GOOD.) He was there . . . he was there . . . he's never missing in a tale.[1]

There we were until . . . the olden days . . . when a man was married to a woman and she was three months pregnant. In the olden days of our grandfathers, he would name the child . . . he would name the child. If you had a child, only the grandfather could name him. You yourself didn't have the right to name it. (THE CHIEFS WERE THE ONES WHO NAMED THE CHILD.) This was in the olden days.

At that time a woman became pregnant. When a woman was pregnant, it was customary that her family should go let the chief know that the woman was pregnant. A woman was three months pregnant. Yes, it was time for her husband to go tell the chief. The fetus in the womb, however, asked his mother what his father was saying . . . the fetus did not agree with him. (MŨ!) The woman was frightened. The child asked whether they were going to ask . . . whether they were going to tell the chief that she was pregnant. She said, "Yes."[2] When they go, the parents should tell the chief that the fetus' name is Nyanuwufia.[3] They should say that to the chief. (THE FETUS IN THE WOMB?) Yes, the fetus in the womb. The father said he could not go say it. The child said, in that case, he himself would go tell the chief that his name is Nyanuwufia. The father said, "Is that so?" The child said, if the father could not tell the chief, the child himself would go.

---

[1] This tale is not about Spider, although he does appear briefly, but not as a major character.

[2] There is a certain amount of confusion in this opening portion. In particular, the time sequences are disjointed and it is not clear just when the visit to the chief takes place and who actually goes. Note also that the performer has a number of "false starts" whereby he corrects himself and begins again.

[3] Means "Know More than the Chief."

The father should stay put . . . he should not go anywhere. (IT HASN'T BEEN BORN YET?) It hasn't been . . . it's in the womb. (laughter) (THE FETUS WAS IN THE WOMB!)

Eventually, the child was born. He said the parents should go tell the chief that he had been born and that his name is Nyanuwufia. They went and told the chief, who said, "His name is Nyanuwufia? Okay. I've heard."[4]

Three months passed. The child asked his father whether he had told the chief.[5] Hadn't the chief asked about him yet? The child would go see him. If the chief wouldn't come to him, he would go to the chief. (IS THE CHILD A PHANTOM OR A REAL CHILD?) He is a child who was actually born. (IS THAT A FACT? BORN IN THE WOMB?) Yes!

One day the child got up and went to the chief and asked if he was at home. He was there. He told the chief he had sent a messenger to him. Had he received the message? The chief said a person had come. The child said he is Nyanuwufia. "Is that right?" asked the chief. "Okay," he said. He's heard. (DIDN'T THE CHIEF SLAP HIM IN THE FACE?)[6] No, he didn't say anything. (DID HE WALK THERE HIMSELF?) Yes, indeed! (HE WALKED THERE HIMSELF!)

The chief said the child should leave, and in three days he would send for him. On the third day a chief sent a messenger to greet Nyanuwufia. In three more days Nyanuwufia should come to the chief.

Three days passed and he went to the chief. The chief asked if his name was Nyanuwufia. He replied yes, his name was Nyanuwufia. The chief told him he should leave and return another time when he would send him on an errand. He should come back again.

The child left and came back three days later. The chief gave him money to go buy him a surprise. (A SURPRISE?) Yes, to buy him a magical object. A magical object, eh? Yes. Well okay, he's heard. The chief gave him the money and the child put it in his pocket. (HE DIDN'T MENTION ANYTHING IN PARTICULAR TO HIM?) No, he

---

[4] This is a convention which acknowledges what the other person has said. The equivalent in English is "Okay, I understand."

[5] Because the chief has been told the child's name is "Know More than the Chief," the expectation is that the chief would inquire about this child.

[6] For being so insolent!

mentioned nothing. (laughter) Spider was with the chief when he gave the money to the child. The chief told Spider that the child said he is wiser than the chief. Therefore he gave him money to buy the sun and moon. "Let's see if he can buy them," said the chief. (HE SAID THAT? WELL! THE SUN AND THE MOON, EH?) If he goes . . . ah well, yes . . . the sun and moon.

Three days passed. The child grew feathers, covered himself with many things and flew over the chief's house *xafo xafo xafo xafo*.[7] Someone said, "Oh . . . oh . . . a bird? A bird? What a bird!" The bird flew around like that for a while and left. The chief said, "See, he said he is wiser than the chief. He's been given money to buy the sun and moon. Let's see if he can do so." The child left and came back with the sun and moon for the chief! Hadn't he asked for a magical object? The child said that's what he ordered.[8]

Spider was with the chief when the child came. The chief called Nyanuwufia, who responded. A bird flew by. They tried to find out its name but to no avail. They didn't know its name. The child said, "Oh, the bird's name is Sesegbemava."[9] (I HAVE COME FOR WHAT?) Spider asked, "Is that so?" Didn't he tell the chief that if Nyanuwufia were around, he'd know the bird's name?[10]

Four or five days passed. The chief summoned the child to send him on an errand. Obediently, the child came on the third day. The chief asked him whether he had seen his son. Nyanuwufia answered that he had. Nyanuwufia was told that the chief's friend lives in Atakpame with whom the chief has left something. Nyanuwufia should take the chief's son and go there to pick up the parcel. Nyanuwufia agreed. As soon as the chief spoke with his son, they could go.

The chief went into the house. He posted people along the road . . . troops, in fact. (*JUJU* MEN?) *Juju* men. (SO THEY PUT A CHARM ON HIM?) No, so they shoot him! (TO KILL HIM WITHOUT DELAY?)

---

[7] This is the sound of a bird flapping its wings.

[8] It is not clear what in particular the chief ordered, since he did not specify. But since Nyanuwufia "knows more than the chief," it is assumed that he knows even that which the chief does not articulate.

[9] Means "I have come to listen."

[10] This is proof of Nyanuwufia's infinite wisdom.

Yes! They were told to shoot to kill. They were told that when two people pass ... one would be wearing a *kente* cloth.[11] The person wearing the *kente* should be killed. One person will be wearing tattered street clothes. He must not be shot. The juju men agreed.

In a room Nyanuwufia was given the *kente* cloth which he put on. They gave the tattered cloth to the chief's child. As they went along, Nyanuwufia said to the child, "Is this how clever your father is? You, who are the chief's child, to be seen wearing a tattered cloth, while I, a stranger, wear *kente*? Take the *kente* and I will wear the rags." (laughter) The child agreed, took the *kente* from Nyanuwufia, and put it on. Nyanuwufia said the chief's child should lead the way and he will follow ... because the child knows the way.

They went until they were surrounded by the ambushers. (JUJU MEN?) *Gbao!*[12] Yes, *gbao!* They shot the chief's child! The chief's child fell down dead. Nyanuwufia took the *kente* off the child and left. (HE RETURNED?) Yes, he returned. (laughter) Finally, he arrived at the chief's house, gave him the *kente* saying, "Oh ... your child has been killed." "What! He's been killed?" asked the chief. "Yes," said Nyanuwufia. (laughter) "How was he killed?" (I WITNESSED IT ... I SAW IT HAPPEN!) You did *not* witness it. (YES, WE DID!)[13]

(Song:)   We have been ambushed,
          We have been ambushed,
          We were going and we were ambushed,
          We were going and we were ambushed.

Nyanuwufia told the chief that while they were traveling along, they hadn't gotten very far when the child started crying. (BECAUSE HE WANTED THE CLOTH?) Yes, because he wanted the cloth. Nyanuwufia couldn't refuse because it was the chief's cloth. He gave it

---

[11] An elaborate traditional cloth worn on special occasions.

[12] This is the sound of a gun firing.

[13] This is a very comical ripost between the performer and the audience. Normally, when a song is introduced, an audience member swears that he or she was there when it all happened and then starts the song. Here, the performer playfully questions the audience's claim of veracity.

to him and as they walked, he was shot. (IS THAT SO?) Yes. Okay, he's heard. He got the cloth.

Four or five more days passed and the chief again summoned Nyanuwufia to come so he could tell him something else. The third day Nyanuwufia went to the chief's, who asked whether Nyanuwufia had seen the male goat. Yes, he had, he said. Well, he should take and breed it. When it has given birth to kids, Nyanuwufia should give the chief some of them. (SAY WHAT!) Nyanuwufia agreed . . . when the male goat bears kids.

Nyanuwufia brought the goat to stay with him for about three months. One night in the third month, a dried axe . . . there was a dead tree in front of the chief's house. Nyanuwufia sharpened his axe and when everyone was asleep, he started cutting the tree *gbòo gbòo gbòo!* The chief roared from his room, "Who is making that racket?" Nyanuwufia said it was he. The chief asked what was the matter. Nyanuwufia said his father has been in labor for three days. (laughter) (A MAN?) Yes, his father has been in labor for three days.

They tried to "cure" him.[14] They consulted the oracle and learned that they needed a piece of the tree root which is in front of the house in order to help his father . . . before he can deliver. That's why he was cutting the tree. "What! A man can give birth?" exclaimed the chief. Nyanuwufia told him, yes, since he was wiser than the chief . . . since the chief had told him to rear a billy goat until it bore kids. (laughter) (A MALE GOAT WILL DELIVER KIDS . . . AND A MAN?) How come a male goat can bear kids while a man cannot? The chief simply stared into space.[15] Nyanuwufia said he was going home. He told the chief, "Tomorrow send someone . . . better yet, you yourself come and get your goat!"

Nyanuwufia left to go home. The chief stared into space and wondered what exactly he should do with Nyanuwufia. The chief summoned his people and said, yes, he knows what he will do to Nyanuwufia. He's had it with him. The chief ordered people to go make a big pit. Anyone who falls in it will never be seen again. He said

---

[14] By delivering the baby.
[15] The chief was dumbfounded.

this is where he will ... he'll bring him ... he'll fall into the pit ... he'll finally kill Nyanuwufia now.

The chief waited for Lūmɔ.[16] Lūmɔ was hungry. From morning to night. . . . (HE'S NOT EATEN?) No, he had not eaten. Lūmɔ left and went to see Nyanuwufia. When Nyanuwufia saw him, he said, "Lūmɔ, where are you coming from looking so filthy?" Nyanuwufia's wives got water for him to bathe. There was a chicken sitting on some eggs. "Go get it, kill it, and make some soup," said Nyanuwufia to his wives. (laughter) (OH! HE'S GOING TO GOSSIP NOW!)[17]

The chicken was killed. But why was Lūmɔ so filthy? Lūmɔ said he could not lie to Nyanuwufia. He said he's been digging Nyanuwufia's grave because Nyanuwufia was going to be killed. He, Nyanuwufia? Yes! "What should I do?" asked Lūmɔ. Nyanuwufia told him he should dig a hole from Nyanuwufia's house to the one already dug.

Lūmɔ dug the hole until it joined the hole already dug. (MHŪ!) Nyanuwufia was ready. Had Lūmɔ finished digging? He said he was finished. Okay. On the third day, the chief announced that everyone should gather. He had something to tell them. Everyone came. The firewood gatherers collected firewood. (ARE THEY GOING TO MAKE A FIRE?) Yes! They are going to make a fire in the pit. As soon as Nyanuwufia falls into the pit, then ... (THEN HE'LL BE BURNED!) Yes!

They gathered a big pile of firewood and laid a mat over the pit. One person sat on one corner of the mat, another sat on another corner, a third person sat on the far corner, until all around ... leaving the center open.[18] Nyanuwufia arrived. People were sprawled all over. Well! "What's the matter?" asked Nyanuwufia. "It's only you they are waiting for," the people answered. He said he was there. They said he should come and sit down, which he did.

"Nyanuwufia, wouldn't you like to move to the center of the mat so you can stretch your legs out on the ground?" asked the townspeople. "Me?" asked Nyanuwufia. "Yes, you!" "Me?" "Yes, you!" Well, just as

---

[16] *Lūmɔ* is a type of anteater.

[17] This means that the mole is now going to reveal some secrets.

[18] At this point, the audience makes some remarks about the place reserved for Nyanuwufia, but the comments cannot be clearly heard on the tape.

"Nyanuwufia, wouldn't you like to move to the center of the mat so you can stretch your legs out on the ground?" asked the townspeople. "Me?" asked Nyanuwufia. "Yes, you!" "Me?" "Yes, you!" Well, just as Nyanuwufia moved to the center of the mat, one person got up, another got up . . . *vluivò!* Nyanuwufia fell into the pit! The chief said he had taught him a lesson today! He who thinks he is wiser than the chief, he showed him! They closed the pit . . . closed it *kpí kpí kpí kpí*[19] and dispersed.

Nyanuwufia was already in his house weaving cloth![20] (laughter) Yes, he went home. (THE FIREWOOD . . . WHAT HAPPENED TO THE FIREWOOD?) They put it in the pit thinking Nyanuwufia would be burned in the pit. (HE WOULD BECOME FIREWOOD?)[21] Yes!

On the third day, the chief's children were bird-hunting. Nyanuwufia was weaving cloth at the loom, *tegeðe tegeðe tegeðe tegeðe*. The children asked, isn't that Nyanuwufia over there? No, that can't be Nyanuwufia. They approached him . . . lo and behold! It was Nyanuwufia, for sure! The kids left and went to tell the chief that . . . their father, that by the time they got to Nyanuwufia's house, there he was weaving! The chief said, "It's a lie!" He'll send Spider to see if it was indeed Nyanuwufia.

Spider knocked. Nyanuwufia exclaimed, "You saw me die and didn't bother to help me? I've been here all day weaving!" (laughter)

Spider went to tell the chief that Nyanuwufia was indeed at home. The chief said that he had heard. Tomorrow he will make . . . (AH! HE'S STILL MAKING PLANS FOR NYANUWUFIA?) Yes, he'll set a time for him. Everybody should come to his house. He has something he wants to say to them.

The people got there. He said, "Let it be known . . . that if anybody's wife has a child, the family should name the child." He, the chief, will not give the name. That's all.

If the chief had not done that, when anybody's wife got pregnant, it would be the chief who gave the name. It was Nyanuwufia who did

---

[19]This ideophone emphasizes how tightly they closed the pit, that is, how solidly they packed in the dirt.

[20]Weaving is largely a male activity in Togo.

[21]Literally: he would turn to ashes.

If the chief had not done that, when anybody's wife got pregnant, it would be the chief who gave the name. It was Nyanuwufia who did that. That's why if you have a child, give the child the name that pleases you.

Yoooooo! Woezɔ kakakakaka!

54.1.8.   SPIDER AND RAT

Performer: Afatsao Keke, 65
Date: September 5, 1979, 8 P.M.
Place: Ŋotse
Audience: 21 adults, 10 children

Listen to this tale. (THE TALE MAY COME.) The tale rose and fell on Rat. (THAT'S RIGHT!) Do you know the animal which is called *kotoe*? He is also called *kisi* or *zātɔ*.[1] The tale also fell on Spider.

A big famine came. A single grain of corn cost one hundred thousand francs.[2] (OH! THINGS ARE HARD!) Rat made a farm along a path and made seven yam mounds there. He made *juju*.[3] If anyone counted the mounds and uttered the number "seven," he would die! (AH!)

When Spider heard this, he too made *juju*. When the animals passed by on their way to the fields, Spider lay in wait for them. He would say, "Hey! Where are you going? To the fields when it's dry like this? If you would, please count these yam mounds for me. I've made them, but now the earth is hard and I don't know how many I have."

The animals did not know he had set a trap for them. They would say, "I don't know how to count very well, but I'll give it a try. 'One, two, three, four, five, six, seven!'" (THE ANIMAL IS DEAD!)

Spider had found food.[4] He and his children ate well. Spider repeated this every day. Finally, he came upon Rat. Rat had his own *juju*. (THAT'S RIGHT!) They had an argument. Spider told Rat to count the yams for him. Rat told Spider to count them himself. Spider would count, "One, two, three, four, five, six. . . ." He said he did not know the rest. Rat said he too did not know. He told Spider to say it.

They went on like that until Spider finally said, "Is that man going to be more clever than me?" He told Rat to count again. Rat counted to

---

[1] *Zātɔ* is a type of ant.
[2] The currency in Togo is the CFA franc, whose value is approximately 300–350 CFA to the U.S. dollar. 100,000 CFA is roughly the equivalent of US $300.
[3] Literally: he cast a spell.
[4] Spider's ruse was successful.

six. Spider said, "Say it . . . just simply say 'seven.'" (laughter) As soon as Spider said it, he fell to the ground . . . dead. Rat took him, prepared him, and ate him. (laughter)

Spider's children were ashamed and went to hide in the clefts of the walls. So when you build a house, take care of it as best you can. However, no matter how careful you are, you will always see Spider hiding in the cracks. (EXACTLY!)

The ancestors deceived me with this in the morning. I deceive you with it at night.

Yooooooooo.

Bibliography

Abrams, David, and Brian Sutton-Smith. "The Development of the Trickster in Children's Narratives." In *Journal of American Folklore*, 90 (October–December 1977), pp. 29–47.

Agblemagnon, N'Sougan. *Sociologie des Sociétés Orales d'Afrique Noire: les Ewe du Sud-Togo.* Paris: Mouton, 1969.

Agudze-Vioka, Ozafri Bernard. "L'Homme et le Monde à Travers les Proverbes Togolais de Langue Ewe." Doctoral thesis, Paris, 1976.

Allerton, D.J. *Essentials of Grammatical Theory.* Boston: Routledge and Kegan Paul, 1979.

Ansre, Gilbert. "The Tonal Structure of Ewe." Thesis, Hartford Seminary Foundation, 1961.

Babcock, Barbara, ed. *The Reversible World.* Ithaca: Cornell University Press, 1978.

———. "A Tolerated Margin of Mess: The Trickster and His Tales Reconsidered." In *Journal of the Folklore Institute*, XI (1974), pp. 147–86.

Barthes, Roland. *S/Z.* New York: Hill and Wang, 1974.

Bascom, William. "The Forms of Folklore: Prose Narratives." In *Journal of American Folklore*, 78 (1965), pp. 2–20.

Beidelman, T. O. "Ambiguous Animals: Two Theriomorphic Metaphors in Kaguru Folklore." In *Africa* (1975), pp. 183–200.

———. "Further Adventures of Hyena and Rabbit: The Folktale as a Sociological Model." In *Africa* (1963), pp. 54–69.

———. "Hyena and Rabbit: A Kaguru Representation of Matrilineal Relations." In *Africa* (1961), pp. 61–74.

Benthall, Jonathan, and Ted Polhemus, eds. *The Body as a Medium of Expression*. New York: Dutton, 1975.

Bergson, Henri. *Laughter: An Essay on the Meaning of the Comic.* Trans. Brereton and Rothwell. New York: Macmillan, 1911.

Berry, Jack. *The Pronunciation of Ewe*. Cambridge: Heffer, 1951.

Birdwhistell, Ray L. *Introduction to Kinesics*. Louisville, Ky.: University of Louisville Press, 1952.

———. *Kinesics and Context*. Philadelphia: University of Pennsylvania Press, 1970.

Bjornson, Richard. *The Picaresque Hero in European Fiction*. Madison: University of Wisconsin Press, 1977.

Black, Max. *Models and Metaphors: Studies in Language and Philosophy*. Ithaca: Cornell University Press, 1962.

Broderick, Modupe. "The Tori: Structure, Aesthetics and Time in Krio Oral Narrative-Performance." Diss., University of Wisconsin–Madison, 1977.

Brown, Norman O. *Hermes the Thief.* Madison: University of Wisconsin Press, 1947.

Chapman, Raymond. *Linguistics and Literature.* Lanham, Md.: Littlefield, Adams, 1973.

Cirlot, J. E. *A Dictionary of Symbols*. Trans. Jack Sage. London: Routledge and Kegan Paul, 1967.

Colardelle-Diarrassouba, Marcelle. *Le Lièvre et l'Araignée dans les Contes de l'Ouest Africain*. Paris: Union Générale d'Editions, 1975.

Cornevin, Robert. *Le Togo Nation-Pilote*. Paris: Nouvelles Editions Latines, 1963.

Crowley, Daniel J. *I Could Talk Old Story Good: Creativity in Bahamian Folklore*. Berkeley: University of California Press, 1966.

Culler, Jonathan. *Structuralist Poetics*. Ithaca: Cornell University Press, 1975.

Davidson, H. R. Ellis. *Gods and Myths of Northern Europe*. Baltimore: Penguin Books, 1968.

de Saussure, Ferdinand. *Course in General Linguistics*. Eds. Charles Bally and Albert Sechehaye. New York: McGraw-Hill, 1966.

de Vries, Jan. "The Problem of Loki." In *FF Communications*, no. 110. Helsinki: Suomalainen Tiedeakatemia Societas Scientiarium Fennica, 1933.

Dorson, Richard M. *The British Folklorists*. London: Routledge and Kegan Paul, 1968.

Douglas, Mary. *Purity and Danger*. London: Routledge and Kegan Paul, 1966.

———. "Social Control of Cognition." In *Man*, 3, no. 3 (1968), pp. 361–76.

Dundes, Alan, ed. *Essays in Folkloristics*. New Delhi: Folklore Institute, 1978.

———. "The Making and Breaking of Friendship as a Structural Frame in African Folk Tales." In *Structural Analysis of Oral Tradition*. Eds. Pierre and Elli Kongas Maranda, pp. 171–85. Philadelphia: University of Pennsylvania Press, 1977.

———. *The Study of Folklore*. Englewood Cliffs, N.J.: Prentice-Hall, 1975.

Durkheim, Emile, and Marcel Mauss. *Primitive Classification*. Trans. and ed. Rodney Needham. Chicago: University of Chicago Press, 1963.

Edmonson, Monro S. *Lore*. New York: Holt, Rinehart & Winston, 1971.

Ekman, Paul, and Wallace V. Friesen. "The Repertoire of Nonverbal Behavior: Categories, Origins, Usage, and Coding." In *Semiotica*, 1. The Hague: Mouton, 1969.

Eliot, T.S. *The Complete Poems and Plays 1909–1950*. New York: Harcourt, Brace and World, 1971.

Empson, William. *Seven Types of Ambiguity*. London: Chatto and Windus, 1931.

Evans-Pritchard, E.E. *The Zande Trickster*. Oxford: Clarendon Press, 1967.

Feinberg, Leonard. *The Secret of Humor*. Amsterdam: Rodopi, 1978.

Freud, Sigmund. *Wit and Its Relation to the Unconscious*. New York: Moffat, Yard, and Co., 1917.

Gebauer, Paul. *Spider Divination in the Cameroons*. Milwaukee: Public Museum Publications in Anthropology, 10, 1964.

Gluckman, Max. *Rituals of Rebellion in South East Africa*. Manchester, U.K.: Manchester University Press, 1954.

Gossen, Gary. *Chamulas in the World of the Sun; Time and Space in a Maya Oral Tradition*. Cambridge: Harvard University Press, 1974.

Greenway, John. *Literature Among the Primitives*. Hatboro, Pa.: Folklore Association, 1964.

Grindal, Bruce T. "The Sisala Trickster Tale." In *Journal of the Folklore Institute*, 9 (1972), pp. 173–75.

Guillen, Claudio. *Literature as System*. Princeton: Princeton University Press, 1971.

Haring, Lee. "A Characteristic African Folktale Pattern." In *African Folklore*. Ed. Richard D. Dorson, pp. 165–79. New York: Doubleday, 1972.

Herskovits, Melville J., and Frances S. *Dahomean Narrative*. Evanston, Ill.: Northwestern University Press, 1958.

Jacobson, Roman. "Linguistics and Poetics." In *Style in Language*. Ed. Thomas A. Sebeok. Cambridge: M.I.T. Press, 1960.

Jordan, A.C., trans. *Tales From Southern Africa*. Los Angeles: University of California Press, 1973.

Jung, Carl C. "On the Psychology of the Trickster Figure." Trans. R. F. C. Hull. In Paul Radin, *The Trickster*. New York: Schocken Books, 1972.

Kozelka, Paul R. *Ewe (for Togo)*. Brattleboro, Vt.: Experiment in International Living for ACTION/PEACE CORPS, 1980.

Kris, Ernst. *Psychoanalytic Explorations in Art*. New York: International Universities Press, 1962.

Kunene, Daniel P. *The Ideophone in Southern Sotho*. Berlin: Verlag von Dietrich Reimer, 1978.

Kwakume, Henri. "Précis d'Histoire du Peuple Ewe." In *Grammaire Simple et Complète*. 2nd Edition. Lyon: Missions Africaines de Lyon, 1951.

Laffont, Robert. *Dictionnaire des Symboles*. Paris: Editions R. Laffont et Editions Jupiter, 1969.

Langer, Susanne. *Feeling and Form*. New York: Scribner's, 1953.

LaPin, Deirdre A. "Story, Medium and Masque: The Idea and Art of Yoruba Storytelling." Diss., University of Wisconsin–Madison, 1977.
Leach, Edmund. *Culture and Communication.* New York: Cambridge University Press, 1976.
Lemon, Lee T., and Marion J. Reis, trans. *Russian Formalist Criticism, Four Essays.* Lincoln: University of Nebraska Press, 1965.
Lévi-Strauss, Claude. *The Raw and the Cooked.* Trans. John and Doreen Weightman. New York: Harper and Row, 1969.
Lyons, John. *Semantics.* Vol. 1. New York: Cambridge University Press, 1977.
Magel, Emil. "Caste Identification of the Hare in Wolof Oral Narratives." In *Research in African Literatures*, 12, no. 2 (Summer 1981), pp. 185–201.
Makarius, Laura. "Ritual Clowns and Symbolic Behavior." In *Diogenes*, 69 (Spring 1970), pp. 44–73.
Mehrabian, Albert. *Nonverbal Communication.* Chicago: Aldine, Atherton, 1972.
Morgan, Charles, "The Nature of Dramatic Illusion." In *Reflections on Art.* Ed. Susanne Langer, pp. 99–102. New York: Oxford University Press, 1961.
Noss, Philip A. "The Performance of the Gbaya Tale." In *Forms of Folklore in Africa.* Ed. Bernth Lindfors. Austin: University of Texas Press, 1977.
Ogden, C.K., and I.A. Richards. *The Meaning of Meaning.* New York: Harcourt, Brace & Co., 1938.
Ong, Walter J. *The Presence of the Word: Some Prolegomena and Religious History.* New Haven: Yale University Press, 1967.
Paulme, Denise. "The Impossible Imitation in African Trickster Tales." In *Forms of Folklore in Africa.* Ed. Bernth Lindfors. Austin: University of Texas Press, 1977.
Paz, Octavio. *Claude Lévi-Strauss, An Introduction.* Trans. J.S. Bernstein and Maxine Bernstein. New York: Dell, 1970.
Pelton, Robert D. *The Trickster in West Africa: Study of Mythic Irony and Sacred Delight.* Berkeley: University of California Press, 1980.

Pope, Alexander. *Essay on Man*. Oxford: Clarendon Press, 1884.
Pratt, Mary Louise. "The Short Story: The Long and Short of It." In *Poetics*, 10 (1981), pp. 175–94.
Propp, Vladimir. *Morphology of the Folktale*. 2nd Edition. Austin: University of Texas Press, 1968.
Radin, Paul. *The Trickster: A Study in North American Indian Mythology*. New York: Schocken Books, 1972.
Raglan, Lord. *The Hero*. New York: Oxford University Press, 1937.
Rapp, Albert. *The Origins of Wit and Humor*. New York: Dutton, 1951.
Rattray, R.S. *Akan-Ashanti Folk-tales*. Oxford: Clarendon Press, 1930.
Richards, I.A. *The Philosophy of Rhetoric*. New York: Oxford University Press, 1965.
Read, Hubert. "Psycho-Analysis and the Problem of Aesthetic Value." In *The International Journal of Psycho-Analysis*, XXXII (1951), pp. 73–82.
Rollin, E. "Nature, Convention and Genre Theory." In *Poetics*, 10 (1981), pp. 127–43.
Ryan, Marie-Laure. "On the Why, What and How of Generic Taxonomy." In *Poetics*, 10 (1981), pp. 109–26.
Samarin, Willliam J. "Perspective on African Ideophones." In *African Studies*, 24, no. 2 (1965), pp. 117–21.
Scheub, Harold. "Body and Image in Oral Narrative Performance." In *New Literary History*, VIII, no. 3 (Spring 1977), pp. 345–67.
———. "Narrative Patterning in Oral Performances." In *Ba Shiru* 7, no. 2 (1976), pp. 10–30.
———. "Oral Narrative Process and the Use of Models." In *New Literary History*, VI, no. 2 (Winter 1975), pp. 353–78.
———. "Parallel-Image Sets in African Oral Narrative-Performance." In *Review of National Literatures*, 2, no. 2 (Fall 1971), p. 222.
———. *The Xhosa Ntsomi*. New York: Oxford University Press, 1975.
Schneider, Daniel E. *The Psychoanalyst and the Artist*. New York: Farrar, Straus, 1950.
Sebeok, Thomas A., ed. *Sight, Sound, and Sense*. Bloomington: Indiana University Press, 1978.
———, ed. *The Tell-Tale Sign*. Netherlands: The Peter de Ridder Press, 1975.

Singer, Andre, and Brian V. Street, eds. *Zande Themes*. Oxford: Basil Blackwell, 1972.
Skinner, Neil, ed. and trans. *Hausa Tales and Traditions*, Vol. 1. New York: Africana Publishing Corp., 1969.
Steiner, George. *After Babel*. New York: Oxford University Press, 1975.
Stephens, Connie. "The Relationship of Social Symbol and Narrative Metaphor." Diss., University of Wisconsin–Madison, 1981.
Stevens, Anthony. *Archetypes*. New York: William Morrow, 1982.
Stonequist, Everett. *The Marginal Man*. New York: Scribner's, 1937.
von Sydow, C.W. *Selected Papers on Folklore*. Copenhagen: Rosenhilde and Bagger, 1969.
Tanna, Laura. "The Art of Jamaican Oral Narrative Performance." Diss., University of Wisconsin–Madison, 1980.
Toelken, Barre. "'The Pretty Languages' of Yellowman: Genre, Mode, and Texture in Navaho Coyote Narratives." In *Folklore Genres*. Ed. Dan Ban-Amos. Austin: University of Texas Press, 1976.
Turner, Victor. *The Forest of Symbols*. Ithaca: Cornell University Press, 1976.
———. "Myth and Symbol." In *International Encyclopedia of Social Sciences*, 10 (1968), pp. 576–82.
U. S. Department of State. *Background Notes: Togo*. Washington, D.C.: Government Printing Office, 1976.
Van Gennep, Arnold. *The Rites of Passage*. Trans. Monika B. Vizedom and Gabrielle L. Caffee. Chicago: University of Chicago Press, 1960.
Verdier, Paul. "Structure et Imaginaire dans le Conte Togolais." Doctoral thesis, Université de Grenoble, 1971.
Warburton, Irene, et al. *Ewe Basic Course*. Bloomington: Indiana University Press, 1969.
Westcott, Joan. "The Sculpture and Myths of Eshu-Elegba, the Yoruba Trickster." In *Africa*, 32 (1962), pp. 336–53.
Westermann, Diedrich. *Gbesela Yeye (English Ewe Dictionary)*. Berlin: Dietrich Reimer, 1930.
———. *A Study of the Ewe Language*. Trans. A.L. Bickford-Smith. London: Oxford University Press, 1930.

Wheelwright, Philip. *Metaphor and Reality*. Bloomington: Indiana University Press, 1975.

Whitman, Daniel. "The Picaresque in African Fiction." In *Ba Shiru*, 7, no. 2 (1976), pp. 44–53.